Model Railroad
RESOURCES
A Where-To-Find-It Guide for the Hobbyist

Model Railroad
RESOURCES
A Where-To-Find-It Guide for the Hobbyist

krause publications

700 E. State Street • Iola, WI 54990-0001
Telephone: 715/445-2214

ISBN: 0-87341-887-5

Library of Congress Catalog Card Number: 99-68138

Compiled and edited by Allan W. Miller

Book design by Heather Ealey

Cover photograph by Ken Patterson. A Camelback locomotive handles warehouse switching duties in a typical Eastern U.S. city scene from around the midpoint of the twentieth century.

Back cover photograph courtesy of Marx Trains

Published by Krause Publications
700 E. State Street
Iola, WI 54990-0001
Phone: 715-445-2214

To place an order or to obtain a free catalog , please call toll-free: 800-258-0929
Or, use our regular business phone number, 715-445-2214, for editorial comment and to obtain further information about our book publishing program.

Printed in the United States of America

CONTENTS

Introduction

Model railroading scales
and gauges

How to use this guide

1. Z scale (1:220) resources
- Manufacturers
- After-market manufacturers/suppliers
- Major Z scale retailers
- Associations and clubs
- Magazines and periodicals
- Web sites

2. N scale (1:160) resources
- Manufacturers
- After-market manufacturers/suppliers
- Major N scale retailers
- Associations and clubs
- Magazines and periodicals
- Web sites

3. HO scale (1:87) resources
- Manufacturers
- After-market manufacturers/suppliers
- Associations and clubs
- Magazines and periodicals
- Web sites

4. HO scale & N scale dealer listings

5. S scale/S gauge (1:64) resources
- Manufacturers
- After-market manufacturers/suppliers
- Major S scale/S gauge retailers
- Associations and clubs
- Magazines/periodicals/guides/videos
- Web sites

6. O scale/O gauge (1:48) resources
- Manufacturers
- After-market manufacturers/suppliers
- Major O scale/O gauge dealers
- Associations and clubs
- Magazines/periodicals/guides/videos
- Web sites

7. Large Scale (on #1 gauge track) resources
- Manufacturers
- After-market manufacturers/suppliers
- Major Large Scale retailers
- Associations and clubs
- Magazines and periodicals
- Web sites

8. Standard/Wide Gauge (2-1/8" three-rail track) resources
- Manufacturers
- After-market manufacturers/suppliers
- Major Standard Gauge retailers
- Associations and clubs
- Magazines and periodicals
- Web sites

9. Small Scale Live Steam resources
- Manufacturers
- After-market manufacturers/suppliers
- Major Small Scale Live Steam retailers
- Associations and clubs
- Magazines and periodicals
- Web sites

10. Model Railroading in Cyberspace

11. Model Railroading References

12. Glossary of Model Railroading Terms

ACKNOWLEDGMENTS

Special thanks to Wendy Chia-Klesch and Jim Bunte for their invaluable assistance in researching and compiling the extensive manufacturer, after-market manufacturer, and dealer listings for select sections of this book. Thanks, also, to Heather Ealey, who took the raw text and made it into a book that is attractive, legible, and easy-to-read.

The following accomplished model railroaders also contributed in significant ways:

Robert Kluz wrote the introduction for the Z scale section, and Bill Kronen also assisted with Z scale.

Bob Russell provided valuable assistance with the N scale section.

Rob Adelman helped with the O scale/gauge section.

Joe Mania assisted with the Standard Gauge section.

Steve Galovics contributed to, and reviewed, the Small Scale Live Steam section.

Photographs for the book were provided by the following individuals:

Ken Patterson—front cover photo, HO scale, and HO/N dealers section photos

Paul Brooke—Z scale section photo (courtesy *Ztrack* Magazine)

Bob Russell—N scale section photo

Don Thompson, of S-Helper Service—S scale/gauge section photo

Rob Adelman—O gauge section photo

Peter Riddle—Standard Gauge section photo

Valerie Myers—Large Scale section photo

Steve Galovics—Live Steam section photo

Debby, Sandi, and Jim, at Marx Trains—back cover photo

INTRODUCTION

Over the course of many years of participation in model railroading—both as a hobbyist and through direct involvement in the hobby industry—I've found that the most often-asked question in model railroading, or just about any other hobby for that matter, is generally prefaced by the words: "Where (or how) can I find out about. . . ?"

This book has been developed to help answer that question. Its goal is to assist model railroaders—regardless of preferred scale, and irrespective of whether they consider themselves to be operators or collectors, or both—in quickly identifying sources of information related to their particular (and sometimes very specialized) interests. In these pages, you'll find sources and resources equipped to expertly address just about any question you might have about this fascinating hobby, and, in turn, lead you to greater enjoyment of a pastime that is diverse, creative, challenging, fulfilling, and rewarding.

A key word in the preceding sentence is "diverse." Model railroading is undoubtedly a very diverse hobby, made up of a variety of popular modeling scales, each of which enjoys its own passionate and dedicated following. If you are already an active model railroader, you're probably aware of this great diversity. You may even feel that you are fairly well informed about sources of information pertaining to your modeling scale. But suppose you want to explore the possibility of diversifying and expanding your interests into another scale. This book will tell you where to seek the information you need in a quick, easy, and straightforward manner.

If, on the other hand, you're brand new to the hobby, or simply interested in exploring its great potential, this book is just the ticket to get you started on the right track (pardon the pun). Browsing through these pages, you'll learn something about the special features that distinguish one scale from another. And, you'll learn something about each scale's respective advantages and limitations. In short, you'll gain the information you need in order to determine what's available and where it's available, and to then make reasonable decisions based on your personal preferences in regard to interests, ability, available time, and financial resources.

Although the presence of real railroads in our day-to-day lives has been somewhat diminished in recent years, there's no arguing the fact that railroading in general, and trains in particular, still hold great fascination and appeal for countless millions of children and adults alike. And, there's no disputing the fact that the fascinating hobby of model railroading continues to grow and attract new followers—many of whom will quickly discover that involvement with toy and model trains can lead to a lifetime of relaxation, personal enrichment, and wonderful friendships. Come aboard, and enjoy the ride!

Allan W. Miller
Editor

MODEL RAILROADING SCALES & GAUGES

"Gee, I really like these trains, and I sure would like to be involved in model railroading, but I just don't have any space in my home for a train layout."

Ah! The excuses! The above comment— perhaps the most common excuse of all, by the way— really doesn't hold water! If you carry a briefcase to work, and have room to park that briefcase in your house when you arrive home in the evening, you do have enough space for a model railroad. Z scale trains, for example, are small enough to permit an entire operating layout, complete with scenery and structures, to fit snugly inside a conventional attaché case or small suitcase.

"Yes, but I'm totally confused by all of this talk I've heard about 'scales' and 'gauges.' I can't begin to sort out all the differences!"

OK, fair enough! The variety in sizes of equipment available to model railroaders can appear a bit intimidating and confusing to the uninitiated. Perhaps the most difficult concept for folks to grasp (and this even includes some seasoned modelers, at times) is the one relating to the distinction made between "gauge" and "scale" in model railroading.

It's perhaps best to start by defining "gauge," since that is the easier concept to understand. In railroading—both real railroading and model railroading—"gauge" refers strictly to the actual distance between the two outside running rails of the track. This is a precise measurement, in feet and inches (or in meters, in the case of European and some other overseas rail lines), and it is determined by measuring the distance between each running rail. In the United States, this measure starts and ends at a point 5/8-inch below the inside top edge of each railhead, to allow for the rail's slight curvature. In the most general sense, there are two track gauges in real-life railroading in the United States: Standard gauge and narrow gauge; with standard gauge being, by far, the more common.

Standard gauge American railroads—the trains you may see blocking your way as you drive to work each day—measure exactly four feet, eight-and-one-half inches between the running rails. Don't try this experiment at home—just take our word for it—but if you were to take a tape measure down to your local rail line, and have someone hold one end at the inside top of one running rail, then extend the tape until it touches the inside top of the other running rail 5/8-inches from the top, you would confirm a rail-to-rail measure of exactly four feet, eight-and-one-half inches! All major railroads in the United States operate with this track gauge.

Narrow gauge is a bit more complicated, but the term is generally applied to any U.S. railroad (and many overseas lines) that operates on rails that are spaced *less* than four feet, eight-and-a-half inches apart. You won't find many such railroads operating in the United States these days, but in the nineteenth century, and even into the early years of the twentieth century, narrow gauge rail lines—normally associated with logging and mining operations—were quite prevalent. A number of overseas rail lines still operate on narrow gauge track. And, in real-life early American railroading, there were even a few systems that operated on wide gauge track, which applies to anything wider than standard gauge.

Popular model railroading gauges:

In model railroading, as in real-life railroading, gauge refers exclusively to the distance between the running rails of the track. There are seven popular model railroad track gauges, each of which, depending on what scale is being modeled, can represent either standard gauge track or narrow gauge track for the model trains that operate on them. Keep in mind that these model railroad track gauges are fixed, meaning that they remain the same regardless of how big or how small a locomotive or car is placed on them (as long as the wheels of the car rest properly on the railheads).In terms of the actual, measurable distance between the two outside running rails, the popular, commercially available model railroad track gauges in the U.S. are:

Z GAUGE TRACK= 6.5 mm between the running rails	O GAUGE TRACK= 1-1/4 inches between the running rails
N GAUGE TRACK= 9.0 mm between the running rails	STANDARD GAUGE TRACK= 2-1/8 inches between the running rails (note: "Standard" has a unique meaning here—see below)
HO GAUGE TRACK= 16.5 mm between the running rails	
S GAUGE TRACK= 7/8 inch between the running rails	#1 (G GAUGE) TRACK= 45 mm (approx. 1-3/4 inches) between the running rails

Popular model railroading scales:

"Scale" refers solely to the proportional size of the model itself, when it is compared with a real-life example of the identical object. Scale may be expressed as a proportion, or as a fraction. For example, O scale may appear in print as a proportion of 1:48, or as the fraction 1/48, meaning that the model itself is one forty-eighth the size of its prototype. An O scale locomotive operating on O gauge track is, for all intents and purposes, a correct 1/48-size modeled representation of what would, in the real world, be a full-size locomotive operating on standard gauge track.

Following are the popular, commercially available, model train scales that conform to the track gauges listed above:

Z SCALE= 1:220 (or 1/220)

N SCALE= 1:160 (or 1/160)

HO SCALE= 1:87 (or 1/87)

S SCALE= 1:64 (or 1/64)

O SCALE= 1:48 (or 1/48)

STANDARD GAUGE= There is no precisely defined scale for Standard Gauge trains, which were the creation of Joshua Lionel Cowen, founder of Lionel Trains. In the early years of the twentieth century, Cowen produced a line of electric toy trains and track that he wanted to be accepted as the "standard"—hence, the name. Many of these tinplate toy trains (originally made by Lionel and later offered by others as "Wide gauge") are roughly 1:24 or so in scale, although almost none were manufactured to any strict scale proportions.

LARGE SCALES= 1:32 is the correct proportion for representing American standard gauge trains on a 45mm track gauge; 1:20.3 is the correct scale for representing American narrow gauge trains operating on 45mm track gauge; 1:22.5 is the correct scale for representing European narrow gauge trains operating on 45mm track gauge.

Note that the "Standard Gauge," listing above is in no way related to "standard gauge" as the term is applied to prototype railroading track gauge. It would be nice if this entry could be designated as "Standard scale," but that's not possible because, as noted above, the toy train models themselves—developed in the early years of the twentieth century—don't really conform to any precise scale. Their track gauge remains consistent at 2-1/8 inches between the running rails, but the models themselves range from "pretty big" (about twice the size of O scale) to "humungous."

You'll find that some non-conformance of this sort applies to a couple of other track/scale combinations as well: most notably, S and O. Hence, you'll sometimes hear hobbyists talking about a particular model being "S gauge" or "O gauge," instead of "S scale" and "O scale." When doing so, they are correctly referring to a model that is not-quite-to-scale, but which operates on the referred-to track gauge. In essence, this is what separates "toy trains"

from "scale models." Most toy trains are built somewhat out-of-scale to permit them to operate reliably on the tight curves associated with traditional toy train track. So, for example, the combination of not-quite-to-scale O trains running on O gauge track is referred to somewhat generically as "O gauge."

However, when it comes to really confusing the issue about gauge and scale in model railroading, nothing can quite compare to the can of worms opened when we discuss the classification collectively and commonly referred to as Large Scale. Suffice it to say that the generic term "Large Scale," as it will be used in this book, applies to model trains of several scales that all operate on 45mm gauge track. For a more detailed explanation of that "can of worms" referred to above, consult the introduction to the Large Scale section of this book.

It's important to note that all of the major model railroad scales and their related model railroad track gauges, as listed above, conform to what, in real life, are standard gauge railroading operations. For example, an O scale locomotive is 1/48th the size of a locomotive that you might see running through your own town, pulling a train along standard gauge track. That said, it's also worth noting that some model railroaders prefer to model narrow gauge trains on these same commercially-available model track gauges, even though the track itself was intended to be a scaled-down representation of standard gauge track.

The designation applied to narrow gauge railroad models is not too terribly difficult to understand. You start with the correct scale designation; follow that with a lower-case "n" to indicate a "narrow gauge" model; and then follow that combination with a number that designates the prototype's track gauge in inches, feet, or meters. A modeled narrow gauge scale of, for example, On30 (ready-to-run sets in this scale are currently being offered by Bachmann Industries) means that these are O scale models of narrow gauge equipment that operated on track with railheads spaced 30-inches apart.

Relative popularity of the various scales:

On the popularity chart, **HO scale** leads the pack in terms of product availability and widespread acceptance. HO has the most of just about everything: the most manufacturers, suppliers, and after-market manufacturers; the largest range of products; the greatest number of dealers nation wide; the most local clubs; and even the greatest number of books and periodicals devoted primarily to modeling in this scale. HO gained its dominant position shortly after World War II, as homes became somewhat smaller, and as advances in plastics and other manufacturing materials and methods made smaller products not only possible, but also more affordable. Over the years, increasing numbers of large and small manufacturers have contributed to the growth of HO scale, to the point where, today, a modeler can expect to find just about anything he or she desires in this scale—either built-up, or in kit form.

Hobby industry surveys rank **N scale** as the second most popular model railroading scale. Boasting models half the size of HO but with equally fine detailing, N scale provides an opportunity for packing more railroading action into a limited amount of space. And, in recent years, not only has the number of products available to N-scalers increased significantly, so too has the overall quality of these items. N scale also inspired an innovative new form of model railroading: Modular model railroads. Ntrak, the leading modular group in any scale, developed a simple but detailed set of standards for N scale modules. As a result, it's now possible for large numbers of model railroaders from around the nation or the world to gather at one location with their individual modules, and link them together to form very extensive operating model railroads.

In the years leading up to World War II, **O scale/gauge** ranked as king in model railroading. Shortly after the war, as noted earlier, HO took over, and it has held a commanding lead ever since. Nevertheless, in the last half-dozen years or so, O has made something of a remarkable comeback (see the O scale/gauge section of this book for more details). Long the favored scale for collectors of Lionel's renowned electric toy trains, the O scale/gauge market really took off when, in recent years, several aggressive new competitors began challenging the century-old Lionel for market share. In large part, they did this by introducing high-quality, affordable products designed primarily for operation, not necessarily collecting. Outfitted with sophisticated sound systems and other advanced technological features, and constructed to near-scale proportions, these more recent O gauge offerings have helped convert thousands of one-time collectors into layout-building model railroad operators, and they have also lured many newcomers to this long-dormant scale.

It's probably safe to say that **Large Scale** trains, as a group, hold fourth place in terms of overall popularity. This rather unique segment of the market really didn't catch on until the 1970s—after the German manufacturer, Lehmann, introduced its line of LGB trains to the U.S. market—so it's a relative newcomer when compared with the three more popular scales noted above. To some extent, growth in Large Scale model railroading—a term which actually covers several loosely related scales—has been somewhat hampered by a lack of industry standards relating to the various scales of the trains, all of which run on 45mm gauge track (see the Large Scale section of this book for further information). Nevertheless, Large Scale is, indeed, unique in the respect that these large, rugged, and very durable trains can operate with equal reliability outdoors as well as indoors. This scale, like N scale, has spawned a whole special sub-group of model railroaders known as "garden railroaders." Practiced individually, in homes that combine a railroad with a landscaped outdoor garden, and in clubs, wherein members construct extensive layouts for public displays, garden railroaders discover a family and social bond often missing in the other scales. In fact, many model railroaders practice their hobby in two scales: One layout indoors in N, HO, or O scale, and a Large Scale setup outdoors designed for family fun and participation.

Holding firmly to a small but highly dedicated following is **S scale/gauge**. Primarily the bastion of collectors and operators of the former A.C. Gilbert Company's American Flyer line of S gauge electric toy trains, these devotees believe that S scale and S gauge—with trains that are larger than HO, but smaller than O—constitutes something of an "ideal" model train size. S gauge—the term generally applied to the not-quite-to-scale segment of the scale—was actually developed on a mass production basis by Albert Carlton Gilbert in the years following World War II as part of his effort to effectively compete with Lionel's O gauge electric trains. The plan worked in the short term, but eventually Lionel bought the American Flyer trademark and tooling, and the trains are today being produced in limited numbers by Lionel LLC. In recent years, several other manufacturers have started to offer a growing assortment of new locomotives, cars, and accessories for the S gauge community, and this has led to a resurgence of interest in S as an eminently viable modeling scale.

Z scale, the smallest of the commercially available, electrically powered model railroading scales, was the creation of the German firm, Märklin—the world's oldest and largest producer of electric model trains. Initially regarded as something of a novelty in the realm of model railroading, Z scale, with its precision locomotives that comfortably fit in the palm of your hand, has grown to the point where it now enjoys a worldwide following of fans who are genuinely interested in packing the greatest amount of model railroad into the least amount of space. Z scale layouts range in size from those which comfortably fit inside a small briefcase, to room-size empires that come as close as possible to duplicating the vast amounts of territory covered by full-size railroads. Hobbyists interested in constructing towering mountains, raging rivers, expansive forests, and deep gorges on their model train layouts will find Z scale ideal for placing the trains in a more proper and realistic relationship with their surroundings.

Appealing primarily to those wanting to preserve and perpetuate the true heritage of toy trains in America, **Standard Gauge** commands the attention of a small but dedicated band of supporters who enjoy operating and displaying these big, colorful, all-metal trains and accessories. Standard Gauge trains conform to no particular scale, but are roughly equal in size to many of the Large Scale products. Created by Lionel's founder (see the Standard Gauge section of this book for details), Standard Gauge ruled the toy train world in the early years of the twentieth century. However, by the start of World War II, Standard Gauge had been replaced by O gauge, which required less space in the average home, and was less expensive to both manufacture and acquire. But in the late 1980s, Standard Gauge received a new shot at life when Lionel Trains, Inc. reintroduced a number of these items in their "Lionel Classics" series. Although Lionel's renewed involvement in Standard Gauge last only a few years, the banner was picked up by M.T.H. Electric

Trains, and that firm continues to manufacture a full line of reproduction Standard Gauge trains and accessories. If you're anything of a nostalgia buff, you're certain to love Standard Gauge!

Last, but certainly not least, is **small scale live steam**—a viable and growing model railroading pastime. Due to the technical/ mechanical nature of live steam operations, the expense of the locomotives themselves, and the amount of effort needed to operate and maintain these trains, this type of railroading appeals most to a small group of devotees who are interested in learning all they can about operating and fine-tuning locomotives that operate just like their full-size sisters. Because the group of live steam enthusiasts nationwide is a small one, they share a common bond and sense of fellowship that transcends distance. On many occasions throughout the year, live steam operators gather at local, regional, or national events known as a "steamups," where they happily exchange information and ideas while operating their live steam locomotives. At other times, these live steamers can be operated on the same 45mm track used in most garden railways. For the mechanically-inclined railroad enthusiast, live steam comes as close to real-life railroading action as you can possibly get!

Which scale is best for you?

Let's clarify one thing before proceeding: There is no "best" scale or "right" scale in all of model railroading, although devotees of one scale or another may try to convince you otherwise.

What you elect to pursue in this hobby should be entirely your own choosing, based on your individual interests, the type of railroad you wish to model, your financial resources, your space limitations, and the availability of products that meet your needs and desires, among other factors. The best advice is to explore a bit—this book will certainly help you in that regard—and take a look at what is actually available in the hobby, and how it is being used.

Of all the factors that should be considered before you select a particular model railroading scale, especially if you plan to have an operating layout, the one that does merit some realistic thought is the one relating to space requirements.

Generally speaking, the smaller the scale, the less amount of space needed for an operating layout. As was already noted, a complete Z scale layout can actually be constructed in a briefcase or small suitcase. Some beautiful N scale layouts have been built into glass-topped coffee tables. In the larger scales, creative modelers have erected point-to-point layouts atop bookcases, or circling the entire room on wall- or ceiling-mounted shelves so none of the actual living space is sacrificed. The possibilities are really limited only by your imagination!

Still, from a practical point of view, a model railroad is very likely going to have curves, especially if trains are expected to run continuously in a closed loop, and those curves will need to be of a certain minimum radius if equipment is going to operate properly. The minimum radius required for a complete a circle of track in a scale you may be considering will give you a good starting point for determining just what your ultimate space requirements might be. Following are the minimum radii for the popular model railroading scales:

Z SCALE= min. radius of 5-3/4 inches

N SCALE= min. radius of 7-1/2 inches

HO SCALE= min. radius of 15 inches

S SCALE= min. radius of 22-1/2 inches (does not apply to non-scale S gauge trains, which can operate on tighter curves)

O SCALE= min. radius of 24 inches (does not apply to non-scale O gauge trains, some of which operate on curves slightly less than 30 inches in diameter)

STD. GAUGE= min. radius of 21 inches

LARGE SCALE= min. radius of 24 inches (45 mm track gauge; includes small scale live steam)

Of course, you really don't need any space inside your home to actively participate in model railroading. You could build a garden railway out in the back yard, for example. Or, you might just acquire locomotives and rolling stock that represent your favorite railroad and/or era of railroading, and then join a model railroad club in your area so you'll have a place to run your trains.

How do you find these clubs? Well, start with a visit the local hobby shops in your hometown—all of them, if possible—and, while you're there checking out the merchandise they stock, you can also ask the dealer about any local clubs. You may even run into a club member while you are there, and he or she might extend an invitation to attend the next meeting or operating session. Accept the offer, if you can, because it will give you a chance to experience firsthand the social aspects of the hobby, and to see what can be accomplished when a group of creative and talented individuals direct their efforts toward a common goal.

Whatever you do, if you are just starting out in the hobby, start in a modest way. Model Railroading can be a very affordable hobby, or it can rather quickly become a very expensive hobby. Get your feet wet with a modest investment in quality items offered in the scale that initially interests you. Work with that scale for a while, and see if it truly provides what you are looking for. If it doesn't fulfill your expectations, it's fairly easy to switch scales before you have a whole lot invested in locomotives, rolling stock, track, and accessories.

Always keep in mind that model railroading is a leisure time activity. It is supposed to help relieve the stresses of your work-a-day life, and provide you with a relaxing, rewarding, and personally satisfying way to spend the little leisure time that most of us have. Don't ever let this hobby, or any other hobby, be anything more than a source of lots of fun!

HOW TO USE THIS GUIDE

The extensive listings in this book were compiled to help scale model railroaders, and toy train collectors and operators, to quickly and easily identify sources of products and information relevant to their specific modeling interests. Regardless of whether you consider yourself a novice or an expert in the hobby, you'll find valuable leads here that will help you locate just about any information you may be seeking.

Each section of the book is devoted to a popular model railroading scale, ranging from Z scale—representing the smallest commercially-available electrically powered model trains—to Large Scale, which includes trains large and rugged enough for outdoor operation in all types of weather conditions. Small scale live steam, a unique subset of the Large Scale category, is also represented by its own section, as is the tinplate toy train category known as Standard Gauge.

Each of these scale-specific sections include a number of listings categories, which are arranged as follows:

• **Manufacturer** listings in this book are arranged alphabetically by the firm's name.

Major manufacturers in this category are considered to be those who produce, at minimum, powered locomotive units. Nearly all major manufacturers also complement their locomotive offerings with appropriate rolling stock items—passenger, freight, or both. Major manufacturers in many of the more popular scales provide full product lines, including sets, track, turnouts, control units, and a wealth of accessories.

• **After-market manufacturer and supplier** listings are arranged alphabetically by manufacturer or product name.

After-market manufacturers/suppliers are those who supply any of a wide variety of items or services in support of product lines developed by the major manufacturers. The range of possible after-market products is both extensive and all-inclusive, encompassing everything from structure kits, scenery materials, and display cases, to modeling tools, layout design software, and digital control systems.

• **Retail dealer** listings are arranged alphabetically by state, and then alphabetically by city within that state.

If a retail dealer has advertised exclusivity or specialization in a particular scale or scales, that dealer is listed in the appropriate dealer section for those scales. In the case of HO and N scale dealers, the lists are combined into one comprehensive section, except for those dealers identified as dealing in N scale exclusively or as a specialization—those N scale dealers are listed in the N scale section. The HO/N dealer list was combined simply because, with some exceptions, the vast majority of dealers who stock one of these two-most-popular scales also stock some assortment of the other.

• **Magazine/periodical/video** listings are generally presented in that described order, except in select cases where entries considered most relevant to the subject scale may be listed first.

• **Association and club** listings are generally arranged alphabetically by the organization's name, except in select cases where entries most relevant to the subject scale are listed first.

In all cases, these are national or international organizations open to anyone wishing to join, subject, in some cases, to certain membership criteria, including annual dues. Some of these organizations are sponsored by, or affiliated with, major manufacturers, while others are independent and self-sustaining in every respect. Nearly all of these organizations regularly publish newsletters or magazines for their membership.

• **Web sites** are listed in order of their perceived relevance to the scale and/or gauge covered in that section. Other sites of more general interest to all model railroaders may also be listed.

These World Wide Web listings are, admittedly, somewhat selective and subjective. The total number of railroad-related (including model railroad) sites on the web is tremendous, and grows almost daily. At the same time, many web sites change their web address or disappear altogether at nearly the same rate.

Listed in this book are what might best be considered "primary" or "key" web sites related to a specific model railroading scale—those deemed to provide the best point-of-entry access, or "key," to the vast wealth of hobby information available on the Internet. Individuals visiting these key sites will find significant amounts of useful information there, and, just as importantly, will usually find "links" to a number of other related sites that focus on the same topic. It's perhaps easiest to visualize each of these key sites as the trunk of a tree, linked to a number of "branch" web sites, which may themselves, in turn, be linked to many more "secondary branch" sites, and so on.

A few additional words about the dealer listings. . .

This book lists more than 1,500 model railroad hobby retailers—far more than are available in any other single published source. These lists have been compiled from a variety of sources, including books, magazines, club periodicals, manufacturer authorized dealer lists, a national network of hobbyists, individual research, and various resources on the Internet and World Wide Web.

Wherever possible, dealer listings are related to the scale or scales in which they reportedly specialize. Thus, there's no need for the reader to review a lengthy list of 1,000-plus hobby shops to locate dealers who specialize in, for example, Z scale products. Those specialized dealers are all conveniently listed in the Z scale section of this book (although they may also be listed elsewhere if they stock and advertise multiple scales).

An exception to the above relates to the HO and N scale dealer listings. Following the HO scale section, you'll find an extensive listing of more than 1,000 known hobby shops that stock model railroad equipment and supplies. In the vast majority of cases, these shops will likely offer a fair to excellent selection of HO items, and, generally, a somewhat smaller selection of N scale items. Because HO scale ranks as the most popular model railroading scale, and boasts the largest number of available items, nearly every hobby shop not specializing in some other scale stocks HO equipment. And, because N scale ranks second in overall popularity, the majority of these hobby shops also stock some assortment of N scale items.

Each retail dealer listing contains as much information as could be located and verified. At minimum, each entry contains the name of the establishment; the street address and/or P.O. box; city, state, and ZIP information; and an information/contact phone number. The firm's toll-free telephone number for orders only, if there is one, is not provided, since a call to determine item availability is generally necessary in any event. In some cases, other information is also presented with the listing, including fax number, e-mail address, and web site address.

Keep in mind that regardless of how comprehensive these listings may be, they should not be considered as complete. There are many more hobby supply retailers who, for various reasons, do not promote their establishments or advertise in media outside their local areas. Perhaps they simply cannot afford the expense of print or on-line advertising. In any event, these retailers—found in communities large and small throughout the United States—nevertheless deserve consumer support, and especially the support of consumers residing in their local area. Retailers like these can usually be found in the Yellow Page listings of the local phone directory. It's always a good idea to see what's available in your own area before shopping elsewhere, since local merchants depend on your support for their continued existence. And, in most cases, these local dealers will service what they sell; answer any questions you may have; and stand behind the products they stock. This level of after-sale support is generally not seen in mail order purchases, or purchases made via the Internet.

Yet another way to find a hobby dealer who may not be listed in this book is to check with the manufacturer of the specific product you are seeking. Most major manufacturers have a number of authorized sales and service outlets, and they will provide a list of these facilities upon request. Perhaps the easiest way to access this information is through the manufacturer's web site—most major manufacturers do have such sites.

And, always keep in mind that the vast majority of hobby shops are small entrepreneurial operations. Like most small business enterprises, they appear and disappear on a regular basis. A shop that existed when these listings were compiled may no longer be in business by the time this book is printed. And, of course, a few new ones may have appeared on the scene within the same period.

Finally, a request for assistance. . .

This initial effort at compiling a comprehensive directory of important resources available to the model railroading community will undoubtedly fall somewhat short of its lofty goal. Somewhere in these pages, an after-market manufacturer will have been overlooked; a dealer's area code will have changed; or the name and address of a significant organization or web site will have been omitted. This was not our intention, of course, and we ask for your help in making subsequent editions even more comprehensive and accurate.

If you believe that an error has been made in a listing in this edition, please write and tell us exactly what the error was. If you have access to e-mail, that is perhaps the fastest and easiest way to reach us.

Also, if you aware of something that was not included in the book, but really should be included in the next edition, please send as much detailed information as you can provide.

And, if you feel that there are other ways we can enhance the value of this book, please feel free to pass along your comments.

In order to encourage feedback, we have provided several "notes" pages at the end of this book so you can, in the course of your travels and shopping, record corrections, changes, and/or possible additions to the listings. After you have compiled a few of them, please make a photocopy of that note page (or copy the information onto a separate sheet) and send them in. As an alternative, you can send your comments to the editor via e-mail. Your input is both needed and appreciated.

Address all comments to:

Allan W. Miller
Editor—MRRD
P.O. Box 2686
Chesapeake, VA 23327-2686
e-mail: traderbooks@home.com

This roundhouse scene comprises just a small portion of a beautifully detailed two-foot by four-foot (yes, that's 2 x 4 *feet*) Z scale layout constructed by Paul Brooke for fellow Z scale enthusiast Bert Freeman. This photo provides a striking example of a true advantage of Z scale: The ability to pack a whole lot of model railroading into a very small space.

Photo courtesy of Paul Brooke and Ztrack Magazine

Z SCALE
(1 : 2 2 0)

At 1/220 the size of the real thing, Z scale trains are the smallest commercially produced electric model trains on the market. But don't let their diminutive size deceive you—the Z scale equipment offered today often features a superb level of detail that rivals what is seen in many of the much larger scales. You may need a magnifying glass to read the extremely fine print on the side of a Z scale boxcar, but it can, indeed, be read!

In 1972, the model railroad industry was shocked by Märklin, the world's oldest and largest manufacturer of toys and scale model trains. During the 1972 Nurnberg Toy and Train Fair in Germany, Märklin introduced a new scale, which was even smaller than the still-infant N scale. Märklin called their line "Mini-Club." The model railroad world would soon come to know it as Z scale.

At a scale of 1:220, Z scale trains were, and still remain, the smallest commercially produced electric model trains in the world. The diminutive size of the cars and rolling stock quickly sparked the imagination of railway buffs everywhere. Ads were released that featured a steam locomotive nestled in half of a life-size walnut shell. Though small, the detailing and lettering was incredible. Much of the lettering on the cars required magnification to be read. The Märklin track system allowed for easy assembly and prototypical operations. Märklin even provided a working catenary to furnish electrical power to pantographs mounted on the roofs of electric-style locomotives.

Treated as something of a novelty at first, Z train layouts were displayed in briefcases, on hat brims, on record players, in guitar cases, and even in a cigar box. However, it was not long before the true potential of Z scale would emerge.

The first Z models were heavily weighed in favor of European prototypes. Within a few years, enterprising individuals began to expand the Z line on their own. By the end of the 1970s, basic U.S. prototypes began to emerge as Z scale gained strength in the U.S. market. During this time, Märklin continued to expand their line, and they increased their market share.

The 1980s marked a transition period for Z scale. Z was no longer isolated to the briefcase. Larger, more permanent Z scale layouts began to appear. At twenty four feet, a Z layout equates to one full prototypical mile. Before long, large layouts appeared that depicted realistic scenes in which every tree, bush, and building were modeled without any selective compression. In no other scale could such accurate and precise modeling be achieved, while still maintaining a relatively small overall layout space.

In the mid-1980s, Micro-Trains Line offered a comprehensive line of U.S.-style rolling stock. It was based around their staple F7 diesel locomotive shell and chassis. The reaction was immediate.

More and more Z scalers entered the hobby in the United States during the 1990s, and more manufacturers joined the Z market. Lines of accessories were produced to complement the fine rolling stock already available. Though selection remained limited compared to the other popular scales, what was available was made to the highest quality. New prototypical pieces from Micro-Trains Line and Märklin added to the interest and respect that Z scale was gaining.

Today, as we enter a new millennium, Z scale continues to expand in interest and availability. Throughout the years, many of Märklin's releases have become very collectible. Z scale collectors have been a major force in this segment of the hobby, often driving up prices of discontinued and limited edition items. Nevertheless, the operators are still the backbone of Z scale. Modular layouts are appearing around the world. Small, high-quality manufacturers of brass Z scale rolling stock and accessories have also entered the market. Märklin and Micro-Trains Line are continually adding to their product lines to meet the demand. As technology improves, the effects of miniaturization have been especially beneficial to Z scale. Digital command control is now a reality. Improved manufacturing techniques have only increased the level of detail. For those with limited space, the size is ideal; but for those with big dreams, Z scale offers the fulfillment of the fantasy.

—by Robert J. Kluz, Publisher, *Ztrack* Magazine

Z SCALE (1:220) RESOURCES

manufacturers of Z scale locomotives, rolling stock, and accessories

FREUDENREICH FEINWERKTECHNIK
Rostocker StraBe 16
D-18209
Parkentin/Mecklenburg, Germany
FR.models@T-Online.de
(locomotives and rolling stock—American and European)

MÄRKLIN, INC.
P.O. Box 510559
16988 W. Victor Rd.
New Berlin, WI 53151
www.marklin.com/z
(locomotives and rolling stock—American and European)

MICRO-TRAINS LINE CO.
P.O. Box 1200
351 Rogue River Parkway
Talent, OR 97540-1200
541-535-1755
www.micro-trains.com
(locomotives and rolling stock—American)

after-market manufacturers and suppliers
of Z scale equipment

AZTEC MFG. COMPANY
2701 Conestoga Dr., #113
Carson City, NV 89706
775-883-3327
fax: 775-883-3357
e-mail: aztecmfg@usa.net
www.aztectrains.com
(track cleaning cars in all scales)

DOUGLAS BROOKS CREATIVE MODELS
307 MacKay Ave.
Ventura, CA 93004
http://swiftsite.com/
   dbcreativemodels
(model palm trees—all scales)

E-Z STRUCTURES
P.O. Box 832901
Richardson, TX 75083-2901
972-783-1314
(structures)

ITTY BITTY LINES (IBL)
5452 Cascade Dr.
West Bend, WI 53095
262-675-6220
(various accessories and pre-formed layouts)

MANCHESTER HOBBY PRODUCTS
449 Wild Wood Parkway
Ballwin, MO 63011
636-391-9361
(various accessories)

MICRO-STRUCTURES (MILLER ENGINEERING)
P.O. Box 282
New Canaan, CT 06840-0281
512-292-7065
www.microstru.com
(structures)

MICRON-ART
8400 Washita Dr.
Austin, TX 78749-3908
512-292-7065
www.micronart.com/
(photo-etched brass and steel structure kits)

PENZEE
1333 Crums Mill Rd.
Harrisburg, PA 17112
717-540-8853
fax: 717-540-0761
e-mail: pennzee@aol.com
www.z-world.com/htdocs/
   manufacturers/pennzee.html
(rolling stock)

RAILROADS UNDER GLASS
East Meredith, New York
607-278-5201/203-877-7086
(call for appointment)
(Z and N scale layouts custom-built into tables)

RELCO ELECTRONIC TRACK CLEANER
c/o Glenn & Sandy Stiska
1045 Porter Dr.
Largo, FL 33771
727-535-3819
e-mail: stiska@idnsi.net
(rail cleaning devices)

SCENE CLEAN, INC.
P.O. Box 205
Fairview Village, PA 19409-0205
877-4-SCENERY
fax: 610-935-5995
(layout scenery cleaners)

SIEVERS BENCHWORK
Jackson Harbor Rd.
Washington Island, WI 54246
(ready-to-assemble custom benchwork)

WOODLAND SCENICS
P.O. Box 98
Linn Creek, MO 65052
573-346-5555
e-mail: webmaster@
  woodlandscenics.com
www.woodlandscenics.com
*(variety of scenery materials for
all scales)*

Z TRAIN STRUCTURES
6937 Lakeview Drive
Central Point, OR 97502
541-826-3163
www.ztrainstructures.com
(structures)

ZTRACK
8648 Seabright Dr.
Powell, OH 43065
614-764-0965
e-mail: ztrack@aol.com
(Z scale automobile models)

leading retailers of Z scale trains and accessories

Note: The following list includes hobby dealers who support Z scale through regular paid advertising in the hobby press or in club periodicals. This list does not necessarily include all dealers who may be listed as "authorized dealers" or "authorized service centers" by the major Z scale equipment manufacturers. Current lists of authorized retailers and service centers are provided at each major manufacturer's respective web site. In Z scale, these sites are:

Märklin: **www.marklin.com**   Micro-Trains: **www.microtrains.com**

CA **CASA ROYALE**
3177 Futura Point
Thousand Oaks, CA 91362
805-492-8777
e-mail: casaroyale@vcnet.com

FL **DISCOUNT TRAIN
& HOBBY**
312 E. Oakland Park Blvd.
Ft. Lauderdale, FL 33334
954-561-0403
fax: 954-564-5367
e-mail: dtl@ix.netcom.com
www.discount-train.com

**MICRO MACRO MUNDO,
INC.**
2604 N.W. 72nd Ave.,
Miami, FL 33122
305-594-6950
fax: 305-594-3795
www.rocousa.com

TEXNRAILS
16115 SW 117th Ave.,
Suite A-9
Miami, FL 33177-1614
305-255-1434
fax: 305-255-9458
e-mail: sales@texnrails.com
www.texnrails.com

IL **REYNAULD'S
EURO-IMPORTS**
113 S. 3rd Street
Geneva, IL 60134
630-262-0771
fax: 630-262-0778
e-mail: eurotrains@inil.com
www.eurotrains.com/
  index2.htm

MCMASTER'S INC.
584 Western Ave.
Lake Forest, IL 60045
847-234-1900

KA **BOB'S MODEL
RAILROAD SUPPLIES**
16665 K16 Highway
Oskaloosa, KA 66066
913-863-3090
e-mail: bmrrs@ruralnet1.com
http://members,xoom.com/
  bmrrs/Bmrrs.htm

MA **JIM'S HOBBY**
P.O. Box 323
Boxford, MA 01921-0323
508-887-7406
e-mail: jg@shore.net
www.jjhobby.com

MD **M.B. KLEIN**
162 N. Gay St.
Baltimore, MD 21202
410-539-6207
fax: 410-539-6207
e-mail: mbkleininc@
  starpower.net

**STONELEIGH CYCLE
& HOBBY, INC.**
6717 York Rd.
Baltimore, MD 21212
410-377-4447

NJ **DK&B RAILWAY SUPPLIES**
114 Main St.
Hightstown, NJ 08520
609-448-5070
www.dkbmodels.com

NY **THE CABOOSE**
8 West Shore Dr.
Huntington, NY 11743
800-327-3088
fax: 516-423-7432

THE RED CABOOSE
23 West 45th St., downstairs
New York, NY 10036
212-575-0155
fax: 212-575-0272

NORWOOD HOBBY SHOP
2-4 South Main St.
Norwood, NY 13668
315-353-6621
www.norwoodhobby.com

OH **BUKI'S**
1093 W. 1st Ave.
Columbus, OH 43212
614-424-9901
www.bukis.com/

ORMANDY'S
10 Public Square
Medina, OH 44256
330-722-1019
fax: 440-647-3903

TED'S TOYS & TRAINS
614 Wooster Pike
Terrace Park, OH 45174
513-248-1999
e-mail: ted@tedstrains.com
www.tedstrains.com

OR **MODELLBAHN G.**
FORTKORD
P.O. Box 20552
Portland, OR 97294
fax: 503-254-4416

PA **MODELLBAHN OTT**
HOBBIES, INC.
1145 E. Philadelphia Ave.
Gilbertsville, PA 19525
610-367-5925
fax: 610-367-5925
e-mail:
mdlbahn@ptdprolog.net
www.modellbahnott.com/

TX **COLLECTIBLE TRAINS**
AND TOYS
109 Medallion Center
Dallas, TX 75214
214-373-9469
www.trainsandtoys.com

VA **HELMUTS HOBBY**
SPECIALTIES
83 Brookshire Dr.
Warrenton, VA 21086
540-349-4910
fax: 540-349-4910
e-mail: hhsweb@aol.com

CAN **WESTEND TORONTO**
TRAINS
17 Arnold St.
Toronto, Ontario
Canada M8Z 5A5
416-251-6124
fax: 416-251-8980
e-mail:
msorg@westentrains.com
www.westendtrains.com

associations and clubs of interest to Z scale model railroaders

MÄRKLIN CLUB—
NORTH AMERICA
P.O. Box 510851
New Berlin, WI 53151-0851
414-784-0717
www.marklin.com

MÄRKLIN ENTHUSIASTS
OF AMERICA
c/o Tim Eckert, Sec.
P.O. Box 21753
Charlotte, NC 28221-0153

NATIONAL MODEL RAILROAD
ASSOCIATION (NMRA)
4121 Cromwell Rd.
Chattanooga, TN 37421
423-892-2846
fax: 423-899-4869
www.nmra.org

Z CLUB 92 (INTERNATIONAL)
Publishes Club-Revue Magazine
and Z-News bulletins)
e-mail: service@zclub92.com
www.zclub92.com

EUROPEAN TRAIN
ENTHUSIASTS
P.O. Box 22392
Sacramento, CA 95822
http://www.ete.org

Z CLUB—INTERNATIONAL
Falkerstrasse 73
D-70176 Stuttgart
Germany
x49-711-22 62 666
fax: x49-711-22 38 282

Z CLUB —GREAT BRITAIN
36 Floribunda Drive
Briar Hill
Northampton NN4 8RZ England
e-mail:
graham@ford.demon.co.uk
www.ford.demon.co.uk

magazines and periodicals of interest to Z scale model railroaders

MÄRKLIN INSIDER MAGAZINE
(Official publication of the Märklin Club)
Märklin Club
North America
P.O. Box 510851
New Berlin, WI 53151-0851
414-784-0717
www.marklin.com

ZTRACK MAGAZINE
8648 Seabright Drive
Powell, OH 43065
614-764-0965
e-mail: ztrack@aol.com
www.ztrack.com

MODEL RAILROADER MAGAZINE
21027 Crossroads Circle
P.O. Box 1612
Waukesha, WI 53187-1612
800-446-5489
fax: 414-796-1615
e-mail:
customerservice@kalmbach.com
www.modelrailroader.com

web sites and on-line discussion forums for Z scale hobbyists

www.ztrack.com
(Ztrack Magazine site)

www.z-world.com
(Self-described "place for Zed heads." Provides links to a variety of sites of interest to Z scale modelers)

http://members.aol.com/ HVMarklin/index.html
(Hudson Valley Märklin Club home page)

www.scintilla.utwente.nl/ marklin
(Märklin Mailing List home page)
http://members.aol.com/HVMarkli
n/index.html
(Hudson Valley Märklin Club site)

www.ete.org
(European Train Enthusiasts site)

www.railnet.net
(prototype information for modelers in all scales)

www.zclub92.com
(Z-Club 92 multi-language list group)

www.onelist.com/ viewarchive.cgi?listname= z%5Fscale
(Z Scale List at OneList—English language only—direct line to the subscribe page, and list description)

aol.com
(Available to America Online members only. Z scale forum. From AOL home page, click on Hobby Central; then click on Scale Models; then select Railroad Model/Railfanning.)

http://titan.glo.be/~pr002441
("The Z Collection." Depicts every Märklin Z scale catalog item produced since the inception of the product line in 1972. Compiled by Joris Ilegems. Ideal reference souce for item identification.)

www.trainfinder.com
(On-line directory to model train related web sites)

www.railserve.com
RailServe Home Page
(On-line directory to rail-related content on the Internet.)

www.ehobbies.com
(model railroad discussion groups and general interest train topics)

www.eppraisals.com
(On-line appraisal services, including toy and model trains.)

www.amazon.com
(Internet auction site)

www.boxlot.com
(Internet auction site)

www.collect.com
(Internet auction site)

www.ebay.com
(Internet auction site)

www.train-station.com
(Internet auction site)

A panoramic view of Bob Russell's Sun Belt Lines, created in N scale, provides ample evidence of the extensive modeling capabilities of this second-most-popular model railroading scale.

Photo courtesy of Bob Russell

N SCALE
(1:160)

For a period of time, N scale was the most diminutive of scales, both desired and derided for its jewel-like nature. Indeed, the story of N scale is one that provides an interesting study into the machinations of both the hobby industry in general and model railroaders in particular.

This small scale (1:160 in proportion, and with models that are approximately one-half the size of HO) began largely as the product of Arnold of Germany, an old-line toy manufacturer who had competed for nearly 100 years with fellow German toy manufacturer and HO proponent, Märklin. Seeking a competitive advantage, Arnold rolled out their new "N scale" product line in the 1960s as their answer to space requirement concerns normally raised as an issue with larger scales and gauges. In America, Aurora Plastics Company, the model kit and slot car giant, marketed Arnold's products as "Postage Stamp Trains," largely as a toy item designed for the slot car-crazed teen set. The marketing effort would last only a few years, but its impact is felt to this day, with some scale model railroaders feeling that N scale is too "toy-like" to be taken seriously.

Standing in stark contrast to this opinion are the thousands of incredibly detailed and accurate model railroads created during the past thirty years by avid N scale enthusiasts. Indeed, many N scalers today rank among the most accomplished model railroaders in any scale, and manufacturers have responded to their growing numbers with detailed and high-performance motive power offerings, an amazing array of rolling stock and structure kit offerings, and even digital command control.

Ranking second in popularity among the various model railroading scales, N scale has a whole lot to offer the individual who has limited space for a home layout, or the person who simply may want to make better use of the space that is available.

In fact, there are thousands of active N scale model railroaders who don't even have a home layout, in the conventional sense of the term. Instead, these modelers construct individual modules of about two-feet by four-feet in size—all of which conform to established specifications relating to track placement, electrical components, and the like. They then connect their module (or modules) with those similarly constructed by other N scale operators—erected in a meeting hall, or at a mall or train show, for example—thereby creating a wide variety of extensive layouts that afford ample opportunities for operating realistically long freight and passenger trains over extensive distances limited only by the number of modules available for the event.

It's probably safe to assert that the first and still most popular modular railroading group in any scale, known as Ntrak, was truly something of an inspirational force in cultivating N scale's steady growth in the United States. Initially formed in the early 1970s as a way of displaying the potential of N scale at model railroading conventions and various public events, the idea of small, portable modules—most of which will easily fit into the back seat or trunk of the family car—quickly caught on. Today, there are local N scale clubs in just about every region of the country (as well as in Canada, and overseas), and the acceptance of N as a viable modeling scale has been resoundingly validated.

Even if you only have space for a small shelf-type layout in your living room, N scale will allow you to develop a complete operating railroad in far less space than is required for the four-foot by eight-foot sheet of plywood normally needed for a small HO scale layout, or a very simple O gauge pike.

It's fair to say that the only limits to what can be achieved in N scale are those imposed by the modeler's imagination. Check out N scale, and see for yourself that good things do, indeed, often come in small packages!

N SCALE RESOURCES

manufacturers of N scale locomotives and rolling stock

ARNOLD
c/oWm. K. Walthers, Inc.
5601 W. Florist Avenue
Milwaukee, WI 53218
e-mail: custserv@walthers.com
www.walthers.com
(locomotives, rolling stock, sets, accessories)

ATLAS MODEL RAILROAD, INC.
603 Sweetland Ave.
Hillside, NJ 07205
908-687-0880
fax: 908-851-2550
e-mail: atlasrr@atlasrr.com
www.atlasrr.com
(N scale locomotives, rolling stock, track, and accessories)

BACHMANN INDUSTRIES, INC.
1400 East Erie Avenue
Philadelphia, PA 19124
215-533-1600
fax: 215-744-4699
e-mail: bachtrains@aol.com
www.bachmanntrains.com
(locomotives, rolling stock, track systems, accessories, structures, sets)

BROOKLYN LOCOMOTIVE WORKS
168 Pine Brook Road
Manalapan, NJ 07726-8451
732-446-2179
fax: 732-446-2639
e-mail: blworder@aol.com
www.blwnscale.com
(N scale custom-painted locomotives and rolling stock)

CON-COR
8101 E. Research Court
Tucson, AZ 85710
888-255-7826
e-mail: concor@azstarnet.com
www.all-railroads.com/concor
(N scale locomotives and rolling stock)

FLEISCHMANN
c/o Daylight Distributors
4411 Sepulveda Blvd.
Culver City, CA 90230
310-313-9370
(European-prototype locomotives and rolling stock)

HALLMARK MODELS, INC.
4822 Bryan Street
Dallas, TX 75204
214-821-2558
fax: 214-824-2101
e-mail: hmmcrown@aol.com
www.hallmarkmodels.com
(N scale brass locomotives)

INTERMOUNTAIN RAILWAY COMPANY
30 E. Ninth Ave.
P.O. Box 839
Longmont, CO 80502-0839
303-772-1901
fax: 303-772-8534
e-mail: intermountain@sni.net
www.intermountain-railway.com
(locomotives and rolling stock)

KATO USA, INC.
100 Remington Road
Schaumburg, IL 60173
847-781-9500
fax: 847-781-9570
e-mail: kato@katousa.com
www.katousa.com
(N scale locomotives, rolling stock, track, and accessories)

KEY IMPORTS, INC.
P.O. Box 1848
Rogue River, OR 97537
(N scale brass locomotives)

LIFE-LIKE PRODUCTS, INC.
1600 Union Ave.
Baltimore, MD 21211
800-638-1470
e-mail:
feedback@lifelikeproducts.com
www.lifelikeproducts.com
(N scale locomotives, rolling stock, sets, and accessories)

MICRO-TRAINS LINE
351 Rogue River Parkway
P.O. Box 1200
Talent, OR 97540-1200
541-535-1755
fax: 541-535-1932
e-mail: mtl@micro-trains.com
www.micro-trains.com
(N scale and Nn3 scale locomotives and rolling stock)

MODEL POWER
180 Smith Street
Farmingdale, NY 11735
516-694-7022
fax: 516-694-7133
e-mail: mdlpowr@aol.com
www.modelpower.com
(locomotives, rolling stock, set, structure kits, accessories)

OVERLAND MODELS, INC.
3808 W. Kilgore Ave.
Muncie, IN 47304-4896
765-289-4257
fax: 765-289-6013
(N scale brass locomotives)

ROCO
c/o Wm. K. Walthers, Inc.
5601 W. Florist Ave.
Milwaukee, WI 53218
e-mail: custserv@walthers.com
www.walthers.com
(European-prototype locomotives, rolling stock, structure kits, vehicles, track systems)

SUNSET MODELS, INC.
37 S. Fourth Street
Campbell, CA 95008
408-866-1727
fax: 408-866-5674
e-mail: sdmann@best.com
www.3rdrail.com
(brass locomotives and rolling stock)

TOMIX
c/o Mokei Imports
6950 Kingsbury
St. Louis, MO 63130
314-725-8413
fax: 314-725-0239
(locomotives, rolling stock, structure kits, accessories)

after-market manufacturers and suppliers
of N scale products

ACCURATE LIGHTING
205 West Florida
Appleton, WI 54911
www.accuratelighting.com
(illumination and lighting products, lighted miniscenes)

ACME MODEL ENGINEERING CO.
654 Bergen Blvd.
Ridgefield, NJ 07657
(switch control panels and terminal strips)

AFTER HOURS GRAPHICS
P.O. Box 62373
Sharonville, OH 45262-0373
513-563-7446
fax: 513-563-7448
e-mail: rrdecals@aol.com
(decals)

AIM PRODUCTS
c/o Wm. K. Walthers Inc.
5601 W. Florist Avenue
Milwaukee, WI 53218
e-mail: custserv@walthers.com
www.walthers.com
(tunnel portals, abutments, retaining walls)

AL'S KUSTOM TRAIN CARS
527 Loughton Lane
Arnold, MD 21012
410-757-9497
e-mail: alskustm@erols.net
www.erols.com/alskustm
(custom painted and pad printed N scale rolling stock)

ALLOY FORMS
c/o Wm. K. Walthers Inc.
5601 W. Florist Avenue
Milwaukee, WI 53218
e-mail: custserv@walthers.com
www.walthers.com
(metal scenery products and vehicle kits)

AMACO
c/o Wm. K. Walthers Inc.
5601 W. Florist Avenue
Milwaukee, WI 53218
e-mail: custserv@walthers.com
www.walthers.com
(scenic molding materials and latex products)

AMERICAN MODEL BUILDERS, INC.
1420 Hanley Ind. Ct.
St. Louis, MO 63144
www.laserkit.com
(Laserkit line of N scale structure kits)

AMI
P.O. Box 11861
Clayton, MO 63105
e-mail: info@AMI-Roadbed.com
www.ami-roadbed.com
(roadbed materials, streets, etc. for N scale)

AMSI
c/o Wm. K. Walthers Inc.
5601 W. Florist Avenue
Milwaukee, WI 53218
e-mail: custserv@walthers.com
www.walthers.com
(scenery materials)

W.S. ATARAS ENGINEERING INC.
40 Laughton Street
Upper Marlboro, MD 20774
301-249-5184
fax: 708-570-6140
e-mail: bataras@wsaeng.com
www.wsaeng.com
*(signal control mounting
adapters)*

AZTEC MFG. COMPANY
2701 Conestoga Dr., #113
Carson City, NV 89706
775-883-3327
fax: 775-883-3357
e-mail: aztecmfg@usa.net
www.aztectrains.com
(N scale track cleaning cars)

BACKDROP WAREHOUSE
P.O. Box 27877
Salt Lake City, UT 84127-0877
888-542-5227
801-964-6155
fax: 801-962-4238
e-mail: backdrop@
  backdropwarehouse.com
www.backdropwarehouse.com
(photographic backdrops)

BEV-BEL
c/o MainLine Models
P. O. Box 1002
Hudson, OH 44236-1002
e-mail: Rsemko@stratos.net
www.bev-bel.com
(custom-decorated rolling stock)

BK ENTERPRISES
12874 County Road #314B
Buena Vista, CO 81211-9102
719-395-8076
e-mail: bktruscal@aol.com
(track systems and turnouts)

**BLACK BEAR
CONSTRUCTION CO.**
P.O. Box 26911
Austin, TX 78755-0911
512-467-8400
fax: 512-458-8765
(bridge and trestle kits)

BLAIR LINE
P.O. Box 1136
Carthage, MO 64836
417-359-8300
e-mail: dalerush@blairline.com
www.blairline.com
*(laser-cut structures, signs, and
bridges for N scale)*

BOWSER MFG. CO., INC.
1302 Jordan Ave.
P.O. Box 322
Montoursville, PA 17754
570-368-2379
fax: 570-368-5046
e-mail: bowser@mail.csrlink.net
(rolling stock and accessories)

BRAGDON ENTERPRISES
2960 Garden Tower
Georgetown, CA 95634
530-333-1365
fax: 530-333-1051
e-mail: bragdon@bragdonent.com
www.bragdonent.com
(scenery products)

BRASS CAR SIDES
715 S. 7th Street
St. Peter, MN 56082-1435
507-931-2784
e-mail: dchenry@gac.edu
www.mria.org/companies/
  brasscarsides.html
(brass passenger car sides)

BUSCH
c/o Wm. K. Walthers Inc.
5601 W. Florist Avenue
Milwaukee, WI 53218
e-mail: custserv@walthers.com
www.walthers.com
*(structure kits, vehicles, signals
and lineside accessories, scenery
materials, tunnel portals)*

CABOOSE INDUSTRIES
1861 N. Ridge Drive
Freeport, IL 61032
*(ground throws for use with
turnouts)*

CENTERLINE PRODUCTS INC.
18409 Harmony Road
Marengo, IL 60152
815-923-1105
fax: 815-923-1106
e-mail:
info@centerline-products.com
www.centerline-products.com
(track cleaning rolling stock)

CHAMPION DECAL COMPANY
P.O. Box 1178
Minot, ND 58702
701-852-4938
fax: 701-852-9429
e-mail: champ@minot.com
www.minot.com/~champ
(decals for N scale)

CHOOCH ENTERPRISES
P.O. Box 217
Redmond, WA 98052
425-788-8680 (phone/fax)
e-mail: chooch@jps.net
www.choochenterprises.com
(tunnels and abutments)

CIRCUITRON
211 Rocbaar Drive
Romeoville, IL 60446-1163
*(switch machine motors and
accessories, signals)*

CITY CLASSICS
P.O. Box 16502
Pittsburgh, PA 15242
412-276-1312 (phone/fax)
(structure kits)

CLOVER HOUSE
P.O. Box 62
Sebastopol, CA 95473-0062
(dry transfers)

COLOR-RITE
c/o Wm. K. Walthers Inc.
5601 W. Florist Avenue
Milwaukee, WI 53218
e-mail: custserv@walthers.com
www.walthers.com
(plaster rock molds and "water" simulation kits)

CORNERSTONE SERIES
c/o Wm. K. Walthers Inc.
5601 W. Florist Avenue
Milwaukee, WI 53218
e-mail: custserv@walthers.com
www.walthers.com
(structure kits)

DALLEE ELECTRONICS
246 W. Main Street
Leola, PA 17540
e-mail: info@dallee.com
www.dallee.com
(electronic throttles, control systems, and accessories)

DEL-AIRE PRODUCTS
321 North 40th Street
Allentown, PA 18104
1-888-DEL-AIRE (phone/fax)
e-mail: delaire@fast.net
www.delaire.com
(air-powered switch machines)

DELUXE INNOVATIONS
P.O. Box 4213
Burbank, CA 91503-4213
818-848-DLUX
fax: 818-848-1667
e-mail: deluxeinnovations@
 thethreshold.com
www.deluxeinnovations.com
(rolling stock)

DESIGN PRESERVATION MODELS
P.O. Box 66
Linn Creek, MO 65052
573-346-1234
www.dpm.com
(structure kits and scenic accessories)

DETAIL ASSOCIATES
P.O. Box 5357
San Luis Obispo, CA 93403
805-544-9593
(rolling stock, accessories, detail parts, scenic backdrops)

DIGITRAX
450 Cemetery Street #206
Norcross, GA 30071
770-441-7992
fax: 770-441-0759
e-mail: sales@digitrax.com
www.digitrax.com
(digital control systems)

DM CUSTOM DECALS
2127 South 11th Street
Manitowoc, WI 54220-6513
(custom decals)

DOUGLAS BROOKS CREATIVE MODELS
307 MacKay Ave.
Ventura, CA 93004
http://swiftsite.com/
 dbcreativemodels
(model palm trees—all scales)

EARL R. ESHLEMAN COMPANY
53 Maytown Avenue
Elizabethtown, PA 17022
717-367-6162
(turnouts and linkage components)

ETI
c/o Wm. K. Walthers Inc.
5601 W. Florist Avenue
Milwaukee, WI 53218
e-mail: custserv@walthers.com
www.walthers.com
 (casting resins and polymer coatings)

FINE N-SCALE PRODUCTS
4202 Blue Heron Circle
Anacortes, WA 98221
360-299-4527
fax: 360-588-0247
(N scale rolling stock)

GHQ
28100 Woodside Road
Shorewood, MN 55331
612-374-2693
fax: 612-470-4428
www.ghqmodels.com
(customized power units for N scale locomotives; vehicles)

GLOOR CRAFT MODELS
c/o Wm. K. Walthers Inc.
5601 W. Florist Avenue
Milwaukee, WI 53218
e-mail: custserv@walthers.com
www.walthers.com
(structure kits, rolling stock kits)

GOOD WOOD CO.
P.O. Box 452
Wolf Creek, OR 97497
541-866-2445
(display cases)

GREENWAY PRODUCTS
139 Ramsey Road
Ligonier, PA 15658
724-238-6268
www.greenwayproducts.com
(rolling stock, display cases)

HEICO MODELL
c/o Wm. K. Walthers Inc.
5601 W. Florist Avenue
Milwaukee, WI 53218
e-mail: custserv@walthers.com
www.walthers.com
(freight car loads)

HELJAN
c/o Wm. K. Walthers Inc.
5601 W. Florist Avenue
Milwaukee, WI 53218
e-mail: custserv@walthers.com
www.walthers.com
(structure kits, scenery materials, accessories)

HERPA
Herpa Miniaturemodelle GmbH
Leonrodstrasse 46-47
D-90599 Dietenhofen
Germany
e-mail: herpa@herpa.de
www.herpa.de
(vehicles)

HOMABED
801 Chesley Ave.
Richmond, CA 94801-2135
510-614-7629
www.homabed.com
(roadbed products for N scale track)

IMAGES REPLICAS
P.O. Box 99
E. Norwich, NY 11732
516-822-8259
(N scale powered and dummy subway cars)

INSTANT BUILDINGS
c/o Wm. K. Walthers Inc.
5601 W. Florist Avenue
Milwaukee, WI 53218
e-mail: custserv@walthers.com
www.walthers.com
(structural scenic backdrops)

INSTANT HORIZONS
c/o Wm. K. Walthers Inc.
5601 W. Florist Avenue
Milwaukee, WI 53218
e-mail: custserv@walthers.com
www.walthers.com
(scenic backdrops)

**INTERMOUNTAIN
RAILWAY COMPANY**
30 E. Ninth Ave.
P.O. Box 839
Longmont, CO 80502
800-472-2530
fax: 303-722-8534
e-mail: intermountain@sni.net
www.intermountain-railway.com
(N scale rolling stock)

INTO DETAILS
P.O. Box 255
Amherst, NH 03031-0255
(N scale photo-etched brass accessory kits)

ISLE LABORATORIES
P.O. Box 636
Sylvania, OH 43560
517-486-4055
(scenery products)

ITTY BITTY LINES
c/o Wm. K. Walthers Inc.
5601 W. Florist Avenue
Milwaukee, WI 53218
e-mail: custserv@walthers.com
www.walthers.com
(roadbed)

JAMES PUBLICATIONS
6342 Forest Hill Blvd., PMB 316
West Palm Beach, FL 33415
561-434-2944
e-mail:
info@wildweststructures.com
www.wildweststructures.com
(plans for structure designs)

JL INNOVATIVE DESIGN
c/o Wm. K. Walthers Inc.
5601 W. Florist Avenue
Milwaukee, WI 53218
e-mail: custserv@walthers.com
www.walthers.com
(structure kits, vintage-style signage and advertising)

JNJ TRAINS
c/o Wm. K. Walthers Inc.
5601 W. Florist Avenue
Milwaukee, WI 53218
e-mail: custserv@walthers.com
www.walthers.com
(diesel locomotive shells)

K&S SCENERY PRODUCTS
4848 S. Highland Drive #438
Salt Lake City, UT 84117
(pine tree kits)

KIBRI
c/o Wm. K. Walthers Inc.
5601 W. Florist Avenue
Milwaukee, WI 53218
e-mail: custserv@walthers.com
www.walthers.com
(structure kits, rolling stock, vehicles, accessories, scenery materials)

**LASERKIT/AMERICAN
MODEL BUILDERS**
c/o Wm. K. Walthers Inc.
5601 W. Florist Avenue
Milwaukee, WI 53218
e-mail: custserv@walthers.com
www.walthers.com
(structure kits)

**LENZ AGENCY OF NORTH
AMERICA**
P.O. Box 143
Chelmsford, MA 01824
978-250-1494 (phone/fax)
www.lenz.com
(digital DCC command control systems)

LOGIC RAIL
21175 Tomball Parkway
Houston, TX 77070
281-251-5813
e-mail: lgcrail1@pdq.net
http://freeweb.pdq.net/lgcrail1
(electronic components for N scale)

**MAINLINE & SIDING
STRUCTURES**
392 Morrison Road
Columbus, OH 43213
614-755-5401
fax: 614-755-5402
(structure kits)

MAIN STREET GRAPHICS
P.O. Box 173
Jefferson Valley, NY 10535-0173
(window graphic kits for structures)

MCHENRY COUPLERS
1207 Pebble Point
Goshen, KY 40026
*(metal-coil knuckle spring cou-
plers for locomotives and rolling
stock)*

METAL MINIATURES
c/o Wm. K. Walthers Inc.
5601 W. Florist Avenue
Milwaukee, WI 53218
e-mail: custserv@walthers.com
www.walthers.com
(vehicles)

**MICRO ENGINEERING
COMPANY**
1120 Eagle Road
Fenton, MO 63026
314-349-1112
fax: 314-349-1180
(N scale structure kits)

MICRON ART
8400 Washita Dr.
Austin, TX 78749
512-292-7065
*(brass and metal structures for
N scale)*

MICROSCALE INDUSTRIES INC.
18435 Bandilier Circle
Fountain Valley, CA 92708-7012
714-593-1422
fax: 714-593-1432
e-mail: microscale@aol.com
www.microscale.com
(decals)

**MIDWEST PRODUCTS
COMPANY**
400 S. Indiana Street
Hobart, IN 46342
800-348-3497
e-mail:
info@midwestproducts.com
www.midwestproducts.com
(roadbed)

MILLER ENGINEERING
P.O. Box 282
New Canaan, CT 06840-0282
203-595-0619
e-mail: milleren@microstru.com
www.microstru.com
*(photo-etched kits and illuminat-
ed signage)*

MINIATRONICS
561-K Acorn Street
Deer Park, NY 11729
800-942-9439
631-242-MINI
fax: 631-242-7796
e-mail:
miniatronics@miniatronics.com
www.miniatronics.com
*(illumination and lighting systems
for structures, signals, and trains)*

MLR MANUFACTURING CO.
c/o Wm. K. Walthers Inc.
5601 W. Florist Avenue
Milwaukee, WI 53218
e-mail: custserv@walthers.com
www.walthers.com
(track-laying tools and accessories)

MODEL DIE CASTING, INC.
5070 Sigstrom Drive
Carson City, NV 89706
775-884-4388
fax: 775-884-4391
www.mdcroundhouse.com
(N scale rolling stock)

**MODEL RECTIFIER
CORPORATION**
80 Newfield Avenue
P.O. Box 6312
Edison, NJ 08837
732-225-6360
fax: 732-225-0091
*(power supplies, digital DCC com-
mand control systems)*

MODELWERX
1585 E. Pander St.
Vancouver, BC, Canada V5L 1V9
604-254-0101
fax: 604-254-1108
e-mail: info@promodel.bc.ca
(N scale structure kits)

MOKEI IMPORTS
6950 Kingbury
St. Louis, MO 63130
(assembled N scale structures)

**MOUNTAINS IN MINUTES/
ISLE LABORATORIES**
c/o Wm. K. Walthers Inc.
5601 W. Florist Avenue
Milwaukee, WI 53218
e-mail: custserv@walthers.com
www.walthers.com
*(scenery materials, rock castings,
molding materials, tunnel portals)*

MR. PLASTER
P.O. Box 23066
Toledo, OH 43623-0066
419-472-0718 (phone/fax)
e-mail: info@mrplaster.com
www.mrplaster.com
*(plaster detail and scenery
products)*

THE N SCALE ARCHITECT
3 Oxford Lane
Hackettstown, NJ 07840
908-684-8478
e-mail:
the-n-arch@worldnet.att.net
(craftsman wood kits for N scale)

**NEW YORK RAILWAY
SUPPLY INC.**
9158 Rothbury Drive #183
Gaithersburg, MD 20879
301-947-8075
fax: 301-947-8076
e-mail: sales.service@nyrs.com
www.nyrs.com
(turntable indexing controller)

NJ INTERNATIONAL
77 W. Nicholai Street
Hicksville, NY 11801
516-433-8720
fax: 516-938-5109
www.njinternational.com
*(lighting and signals, switch
motors, structure kits)*

NOCH
c/o Wm. K. Walthers Inc.
5601 W. Florist Avenue
Milwaukee, WI 53218
e-mail: custserv@walthers.com
www.walthers.com
*(trees, figures, scenery materials,
tunnel portals, retaining walls,
structure kits, pre-formed layouts)*

NORTH COAST ENGINEERING
1900 Empire Blvd., Suite 303
Webster, NY 14580
716-671-0370
fax: 716-671-9337
e-mail: jscorse@aol.com
www.tttrains.com/northcoast
(digital DCC decoders
and systems)

**NORTHEASTERN
SCALE MODELS**
99 Cross Street
Methuen, MA 01844
978-688-6019
fax: 978-794-9104
e-mail: info@nesm.com
www.nesm.com
(structure kits)

NORTHWEST SHORT LINE
P.O. Box 423
Seattle, WA 98111-0423
206-932-1087
fax: 206-935-7106
e-mail: info@nwsl.com
www.nwsl.com
(hobby tools and supplies)

NUCOMP MINIATURES
P.O. Box 539
Bluffton, IN 46714
800-710-9034
fax: 219-824-1699
e-mail: sales@nucompinc.com
www.nucompinc.com
(mobile home model kits and
vehicle kits)

N-WAY PRODUCTS
c/o Wm. K. Walthers Inc.
5601 W. Florist Avenue
Milwaukee, WI 53218
e-mail: custserv@walthers.com
www.walthers.com
(signals)

PERIOD MINIATURES
c/o Wm. K. Walthers Inc.
5601 W. Florist Avenue
Milwaukee, WI 53218
e-mail: custserv@walthers.com
www.walthers.com
(structure kits)

PLASTRUCT
1020 S. Wallace Place
City of Industry, CA 91748
800-666-7015
e-mail: plastruct@plastruct.com
www.plastruct.com
(scale plastic building supplies
and lighting kits, scenery
materials, trees)

PECO
Beer, Nr. Seaton
Devon, EX12 3NA England
www.peko-uk.com
(N scale track and turnouts)

PIKESTUFF
c/o Rix Products
3747 Hogue Road
Evansville, IN 47712
812-426-1RIX
fax: 812-423-3174
www.rixproducts.com
(structure kits and scenic
detail parts)

**PIKO MODELLSPIELWAREN
GMBH**
Lutherstrasse 30
Sonneberg 95505
Germany
e-mail: piko@piko.de
www.piko.de
(structure kits)

POLA GMBH
c/o Gebr. FALLER GmbH
Abt. Kundendienst
Kreuzstrasse 9
D-78148 G˛tenbach/Schwarzwald
e-mail: info@pola.de
www.pola.de
(structure kits)

POLYTERRAIN
2105 W. 18th. Street
Fayetteville, AR 72701
501-521-8080
fax: 501-761-3227
e-mail: polyt@pgtc.net
www.polyterrain.com
(scenery products)

PAUL M. PREISER KG
Steinfield Postfach 12-33
Rottenburg D-8803
Germany
(figures and scenic accessories,
vehicles)

PROTOTYPE MODELS
P.O. Box 3394
Bloomington, IL 61702-3394
(craftsman structures and detail
parts for N scale)

QSI
3800 S.W. Cedar Hills Blvd,
Suite 224
Beaverton, OR 97005
(503) 350-0595
fax: (503) 626-9995
e-mail:
qsi_feedback@uwphoto.net
www.qsindustries.com
(sound systems for layout environment enhancement)

RAILROADS UNDER GLASS
East Meredith, NY
607-278-5201/203-877-7086 (all
for appointment)
(custom-built coffee table layouts
for N and other scales)

R&S ENTERPRISES
P.O. Box 643
Jonestown, PA 17038
717-865-3444
www.rrtrack.com
(sectional-track layout design
software)

RAIL GRAPHICS
1183 N. Lancaster Circle
South Elgin, IL 60177
847-742-5404
fax: 847-742-5407
e-mail: railgraf@mcs.net
www.mcs.net/~railgraf
(decals for locomotives
and rolling stock)

RED CABOOSE
c/o Wm. K. Walthers Inc.
5601 W. Florist Avenue
Milwaukee, WI 53218
e-mail: custserv@walthers.com
www.walthers.com
(rolling stock kits)

RICHMOND CONTROLS
P.O. Box 1467
Richmond, TX 77406-1467
e-mail: jjhinds@wt.net
www.richmondcontrols.com
*(locomotive and rolling stock
lighting systems for N scale and
larger)*

RIX PRODUCTS
3747 Hogue Road
Evansville, IN 47712
812-426-1RIX
fax: 812-423-3174
www.rixproducts.com
*(track and switch products,
structure kits, scenic detail parts)*

SANDIA SOFTWARE
9428 Tasco NE
Albuquerque, NM 87111-2222
505-821-0014
fax: 505-821-0038
e-mail:
tracks@sandiasoftware.com
www.cadrail.com
(railroad design software)

SCENIC EXPRESS
1001 Lowry Avenue
Jeannette, PA 15644-2671
800-234-9995
fax: 724-527-5955
e-mail: scenery@ibm.net
www.scenicexpress.com
(scenery materials and tree kits)

SHOWCASE MINIATURES
P.O. Box 753
Cherry Valley, CA 92223
909-845-9914
www.showcaseminiatures.com
*(etched brass structure kits
for N scale)*

SIEVERS BENCHWORK
Jackson Harbor Rd.
Washington Island, WI 54246
920-847-2264
fax: 920-847-2676
*(ready-to-assemble custom
benchwork)*

SIGNAL RESEARCH
P.O. Box 7073
Huntsville, AL 35807
256-650-5311 (phone/fax)
e-mail: SigResrch@aol.com
www.signalresearch.com
(digital block control systems)

SIGNSGALORE
9 Carlson Lane
Palm Coast, FL 32137-8150
904-445-6556
fax: 904-445-6553
e-mail: plocher@aol.com
www.tttrains.com/signsgalore
(signs and structure interior art)

SKD ELECTRONICS
2217 Holly Oak Court
Waldorf, MD 20601
301-705-7734 (phone/fax)
e-mail: traindetec@aol.com
www.traindetec.com
*(infrared train detection and
signal control system)*

SMALL SCALE RAILWAY CO.
22421 Edmunton
St. Clair Shores, MI 48080
fax: 313-881-4445
www.solarverse.com/ssryco
*(sound and lighting units
for N scale)*

SOLIDESIGN
8005 Ore Knob Drive
Fenton, MI 48430
e-mail: sgwright@tir.com
www.raildreams.com
(decals)

SOUNDTRAXX
463 Turner Drive, Suite 104A
Durango, CO 81301
970-259-0690
fax: 970-259-0691
e-mail: sales@soundtraxx.com
www.soundtraxx.com
*(digital DCC decoders and sound
systems)*

SUNLIT VISTAS
c/o Wm. K. Walthers Inc.
5601 W. Florist Avenue
Milwaukee, WI 53218
e-mail: custserv@walthers.com
www.walthers.com
*(tree kits, trees, and scenic
materials)*

SUNRISE ENTERPRISES
P.O. Box 172
Doyle, CA 96109
530-827-2178
fax: 530-827-2658
e-mail: sunrise@psln.com
www.psln.com/sunrise
*(flashing end-of-train device and
other N scale detail parts)*

SWITCHMASTER
c/o Wm. K. Walthers Inc.
5601 W. Florist Avenue
Milwaukee, WI 53218
e-mail: custserv@walthers.com
www.walthers.com
(switch machines and accessories)

SYLVAN SCALE MODELS
32229 Sylvan Rd., RR#2
Parkhill, Ontario
Canada NOM 2KO
www.isp.on.ca/sylvan
*(rolling stock, structures, and
other products for N scale)*

TERRAIN FOR TRAINS
P.O. Box 60456
Pasadena, CA 91116-6456
www.terrainfortrains.com
*(molded model railroad layout
bases)*

THINFILM DECALS
P.O. Box 70323
Pasadena, CA 91117-0323
626-584-5902
(decals)

TOMAR INDUSTRIES
9520 E. Napier Avenue
Benton Harbor, MI 49022
616-944-5129
fax: 616-944-1901
e-mail: tomarup@juno.com
(drumheads, marker lamps)

TRAINTRONICS
c/o Wm. K. Walthers Inc.
5601 W. Florist Avenue
Milwaukee, WI 53218
e-mail: custserv@walthers.com
www.walthers.com
*(block control and crossing-signal
electronics)*

TRC MODELS
Box 29031
Richmond, VA 23242
(bridge kits)

VIRNEX INDUSTRIES
P.O. Box 613
Lake Delton, WI 53940
608-254-4382
*(locomotive traction tires and
tire-installation tools)*

VOLLMER
Porschestrasse 25
D-70435 Stuttgart-Zuffenhausen
Germany
e-mail: vollmer@vollmer-kit.com
www.vollmer-kit.com/
  index_e.htm
(structure kits, scenery materials)

WM. K. WALTHERS INC.
5601 W. Florist Avenue
Milwaukee, WI 53218
e-mail: custserv@walthers.com
www.walthers.com
*(structure kits; comprehensive
N scale catalog)*

WANGROW ELECTRONICS
P.O. Box 98
Park Ridge, IL 60068-0098
e-mail:
systemone@wangrow.com
www.wangrow.com
*(decoders and electronics for
N scale locomotives)*

WIKING
c/o Wm. K. Walthers Inc.
5601 W. Florist Avenue
Milwaukee, WI 53218
e-mail: custserv@walthers.com
www.walthers.com
www.wiking.de
(vehicles)

WILD WEST STRUCTURES
c/o James Publications
6342 Forest Hill Blvd., #316
West Palm Beach, FL 33415
www.wildweststructures.com
(Old West-style buildings)

WOODLAND SCENICS
P.O. Box 98
Linn Creek, MO 65052
573-346-5555
e-mail: webmaster@woodland-
scenics.com
www.woodlandscenics.com
(scenery materials for all scales)

retailers specializing in N scale products

The following retail establishments that have indicated, through their commercial advertising, that they either specialize in N scale products or, in some cases, stock N scale exclusively. There are many other dealers who also carry substantial inventories of N scale (as well as other scales) and these dealers can be found in the combined HO/N scale dealer list that appears following the HO section of this book.

AL **RIO GRANDE ACTION
HOBBIES**
1213 Chesser SE
Huntsville, AL 35803
256-881-2703
www.riograndehobbies.com

CA **THE FREIGHT YARD**
930 East Orangethrope Ave.,
Ste. C
Anaheim, CA 92801
714-680-4791/714-680-0716
fax: 714-680-3811
frtyard@flash.net
www.thefreightyard.com

PEGASUS HOBBIES
930 East Orangethrope Ave.,
Ste. C
Anaheim, CA 92801
714-680-0716
fax: 714-680-3811

TRACKSIDE TRAINS
1675 Rollins Rd., Ste. B-1
Burlingame, CA 94010

CO **TRAIN SHOWCASE**
38 South Sierra Madre
Colorado Springs, CO
80903-3312
719-471-1887

CABOOSE HOBBIES
500 S. Broadway
Denver, CO 80209-4002
303-777-6766
fax: 303-777-0028
www.caboosehobbies.com

N SCALE SUPPLY
4980 Kipling Blvd., #9
Wheat Ridge, CO
80033-6733
303-456-6702
fax: 800-727-7420
e-mail:
sales@nscalesupply.com
www.nscalesupply.com

DE **MITCHELL'S TRAINS,
TOYS & HOBBIES**
Fairfax Shopping Center
2119 Concord Pike
Wilmington, DE 19803
800-726-2119
fax: 302-888-1859
e-mail: trains@mitchells.com
http://mitchells.com

FL **TEXNRAILS**
16115 SW 117th Ave.,
Ste. A-9
Miami, FL 33177-1614
305-255-1434
fax: 305-255-9458
e-mail: sales@texnrails.com
http://texnrails.com

TRAINS OF OCALA
1405 Southwest 6th Ave.
Ocala, FL 34474
352-369-5152
fax: 352-369-5153

IA **JNJ TRAINS**
P.O. Box 1535
Ottumwa, IA 52501-7535
515-682-4986
fax: 515-682-1404
www.netins.net/showcase/
jnjtrains

IL **CHICAGOLAND HOBBY**
6017 Northwest Hwy.
Chicago, IL 60631
773-775-4848
fax: 773-775-6398

END OF TRACK HOBBIES
9706-8 Franklin Ave.
Franklin Park, IL 60131
847-455-2510
fax: 847-455-0340

N SCALE MEMORIES
2450 E. Grass Lake Rd.
Lindenhurst, IL   60046
847-265-3884

IN **'N' GAUGE TRAIN SHOP**
4759 N. Post Rd.
Indianapolis, IN 46226-4133
317-898-4883
(no mail orders)

MA **KEN'S TRAINS**
Mill Village, Route 20
Sudbury, MA 01776-0636
978-443-6883

MD **M.B. KLEIN, INC.**
162 North Gay St.
Baltimore, MD 21202
410-539-6207
fax: 410-685-1357
e-mail: mbkleininc@
starpower.net

ME **TRAIN & TROOPER**
68 Memorial Highway
North Yarmouth, ME 04097
207-829-3211
fax: 207-829-6335
e-mail: trainand@agate.net
www.agate.net/~trainand/
index.html

NH **NEAL'S N-GAUGING
TRAINS**
86 Tide Mill Road
Hampton, NH 03842
603-926-9031
fax: 603-929-0230

NJ **THE N-SCALE DIVISION**
4 Brighton Terrace
Wayne, NJ 07470
973-694-8102
fax: 973-694-8102
e-mail: nscalediv@
hotmail.com

NY **LBC MODEL TRAINS**
121 S. Long
Williamsville, NY
14221-6625
716-631-3081
fax: 716-631-1250

T&S FLY "N" TRAINS
81 Keyel Drive
Rochester, NY 14625
716-381-6216

OK **CHALLENGER N SCALE
HOBBIES**
2230 E. 56th Pl.
Tulsa, OK 74105-6114
918-749-1634

VA **NATIONAL CAPITOL
TRAINS**
9001 Scott Street
Springfield, VA 22153
703-644-0839
e-mail: nctrains@erols.com

NORGE STATION
7405 Richmond Rd.
Williamsburg, VA 23188
757-564-7623

WA **ONLINE TRAINS**
5127 80th St. SW
Lakewood, WA 98499
253-472-7732
e-mail: uprob@wa.freei.net
www.onlinetrains.com

**EXPRESS STATION
MODEL TRAINS**
640 Strander Blvd.
Seattle, WA 98188
800-237-5139

WI **WISCONSIN N SCALE**
5104 S. Packard Ave.
Cudahy, WI 53110-1922
414-769-6376

magazines and periodicals of interest to N scale modelers

N-SCALE MAGAZINE
Hundman Publishing
13110 Beverly Park Road
Mukilteo, WA 98275
800-810-7660
www.nscalemagazine.com
*(Foremost publication devoted
exclusively to N scale. Published
bi-monthly.)*

**MODEL RAILROADER
MAGAZINE**
Kalmbach Publishing Co.
21027 Crossroads Circle
P.O. Box 1612
Waukesha, WI 53187-1612
800-446-5489
fax: 262-796-1615
e-mail: customerservice@
 kalmbach.com
www.modelrailroader.com

**RAILROAD MODEL
CRAFTSMAN MAGAZINE**
108 Phil Harden Rd., Fredon
Township
P.O. Box 700
Newton, NJ 07860-0700
973-383-3355
e-mail:
rmcsubs@rrmodelcraftsman.com
www.rrmodelcraftsman.com

**MODEL RAILROADING
MAGAZINE**
Highlands Station, Inc.
2600 S. Parker Rd., Suite 1-211
Aurora, CO 80014
303-338-1700
fax: 303-338-1949
www.modelrailroadingmag.com

**RAILMODEL JOURNAL
MAGAZINE**
Golden Bell Press
2403 Champa Street
Denver, CO 80205

**MAINLINE MODELER
MAGAZINE**
13110 Beverly Park Rd.
Mulkiteo, WA 98275
425-743-2607
fax: 425-787-9269

**MAINE 2-FOOT QUARTERLY
MAGAZINE**
P.O. Box 133
Washingtonville, OH 44490-0133
330-702-0177
e-mail: m2fq@aol.com

**FINESCALE RAILROADER
MAGAZINE**
Westlake Publishing Company
1574 Kerryglen Street
Westlake Village, CA 91361
805-494-4070
www.finescalerr.com

**NARROW GAUGE AND
SHORTLINE GAZETTE
MAGAZINE**
Benchmark Publications, Ltd.
P.O. Box 26
Los Altos, CA 94023
408-428-0840
fax: 408-428-0715

associations and clubs of interest to N scale hobbyists

NTRAK, INC.
c/o Jim FitzGerald
1150 Wine Country Place
Templeton, CA 93465
805-434-5058
e-mail: ntrak@ntrak.org
www.ntrak.org
*(N scale modular railroading
organization)*

N GAUGE SOCIETY
c/o Ray Cranidge
137 Sheffield St.
Scunthrope
DN15 7LZ England
http://ourworld.compuserve.com/
homepages/NGauge Society
*(International N scale
organization)*

ONETRAK
c/o Jim FitzGerald
1150 Wine Country Place
Templeton, CA 93465
805-434-5058
e-mail: ntrak@ntrak.org
www.ntrak.org
*(variation of the NTRAK modular
railroading concept)*

NCAT
c/o Hal Riegger
522 Johnson Clan Ave.
Gridley, CA 95948
*(coordinating group for N scale
catenary/trolley operations)*

**NATIONAL MODEL RAILROAD
ASSOCIATION (NMRA)**
4121 Cromwell Rd.
Chattanooga, TN 37421
423-892-2846
fax: 423-899-4869
www.nmra.org

web sites of interest to N scale enthusiasts

www.dwmp.com/Nternet
(links to a variety of N scale sites)

www.nscaleauction.com
*(free auction site for N scale,
sponsored by Brooklyn
Locomotive Works)*

www.ehobbies.com
*(model railroad discussion groups
and general interest train topics)*

www.nmra.org
*(National Model Railroad
Association web site. Go to
World Wide Rail Sites directory
for links to N scale sites)*

www.railserve.com
*(links to a variety of railroading/
model railroading sites)*

www.trainweb.com
*(Internet portal site—prototype
and model railroading)*

www.hobbyhighway.com
*(discussion forums and free classi-
fied ads for model railroaders)*

www.internethobbies.com
(online hobby shop—all scales)

www.mria.org
*(Model Railroad Industry
Association—MRIA—site)*

www.ete.org
(European Train Enthusiasts site)

**http://davesrailpix.railfan.net/
models/models.htm**
*(Traction and trolley site; includes
models; 14,000-plus photos)*

www.railnet.net
*(prototype information for
modelers in all scales)*

The potential for creative and highly detailed HO scale model railroading is virtually unlimited, as evidenced by the superb work of photographer and modeler Ken Patterson. In this scene, Western Maryland steam power charges through a late summer landscape.

Photo by Ken Patterson

HO SCALE
(1:87)

B y far the most popular of all the model railroading scales, HO scale dates back to the 1930s, when initial variants of the 1:87 proportion began to appear in early editions of model railroading publications. Its early promise—that of scale realism, proportioned accurately—stood in stark contrast to most model train products that had come before, which, generally, were more toy-like in design. The term "HO" (pronounced aich-oh, and signifying Half-O) comes from its proportional origins being nearly half the size of O scale/gauge (1:48).

HO scale grew in popularity in the post-World War II period, continuing its role as the scale alternative to more popular toy trains like those produced by Lionel, Märklin, Marx, and the A.C. Gilbert Company. But despite its growth and championing by many hobby publications, HO was still somewhat hampered by poor performance and the lack of ready-to-run products.

This began to change as the 1950s drew to a close, as many model companies and even toy manufacturers began to join early icons like Mantua and Athearn in the hunt for "scale" models to fulfill the needs and desires of model railroaders. With the increased attention given by manufacturers in that period, HO product selection grew rapidly, and by the 1960s, the scale had overtaken the once-dominant O gauge as the most popular form of model railroading.

Today, HO enjoys an incredible product selection, ranging from ready-to-run products by industry giants to finescale offerings from small manufacturers. Indeed, one of the strengths of HO continues to be the unending variety of products continually offered by cottage-industry firms, each striving to provide something different and unique to this burgeoning marketplace.

HO model railroading today is a hobby enjoyed by thousands of individuals as well as many groups. Elaborate club layouts are located in cities and towns throughout the nation, and these organizations combine fellowship with prototypical train operations, and an opportunity to participate in the phases of layout building that the individual hobbyist finds most appealing. There's virtually no limit to what can be achieved with the combined talents and energies of a group of dedicated model railroaders. Many of these clubs actively seek and accept new members, regardless of previous experience in the hobby or skill level. To find a club near you, consult the club listings in *Model Railroader* and *Railroad Model Craftsman* magazines. Pay them a visit during one of their regular operating sessions or public open house events, and you're likely to end up hooked on HO model railroading as the hobby for you.

HO SCALE (1:87) RESOURCES

manufacturers of HO scale locomotives and rolling stock

ALPHA MODELS LTD.
P.O. Box 118
Rocky Point, NY 11778
516-744-9420
*(brass locomotives and
rolling stock)*

AMERICAN LIMITED MODELS
P.O. Box 7803
Fremont, CA 94537-7803
fax: 510-794-8488
www.americanlimitedmodels.com
*(locomotives, rolling stock, struc-
ture kits, detail parts, accessories)*

ATHEARN
19010 Laurel Park Road
Compton, CA 90220
310-631-3400
fax: 310-885-5296
e-mail: athearn@athearn.com
www.athearn.com
(locomotives, rolling stock, sets)

ATLAS MODEL RAILROAD CO.
378 Florence Avenue
Hillside, NJ 07205
908-687-0880
fax: 908-851-2550
e-mail: atlasrr@atlasrr.com
www.atlasrr.com
*(locomotives, rolling stock,
track systems, model kits)*

BACHMANN INDUSTRIES INC.
1400 East Erie Avenue
Philadelphia, PA 19124
215-533-1600
fax: 215-744-4699
e-mail: Bachtrains@aol.com
www.bachmanntrains.com
*(locomotives, rolling stock, track
systems, accessories, structure
kits, sets)*

BOWSER MANUFACTURING CO.
P.O. Box 322
Montoursville, PA 17754
570-368-2379
fax: 579-368-5046
e-mail: bowser@mail.csrlink.net
www.bowser-trains.com
*(locomotives, rolling stock,
accessories)*

BRAWA
c/o Wm. K. Walthers Inc.
5601 W. Florist Avenue
Milwaukee, WI 53218
e-mail: custserv@walthers.com
www.walthers.com
*(European-prototype locomotives,
rolling stock, signals and lighting,
scenery materials)*

CHALLENGER IMPORTS LTD.
P.O. Box 93244
Des Moines, IA 50393
515-280-8363
fax: 515-288-7336
www.challengerimports.com
*(brass locomotives and rolling
stock)*

CON-COR
8101 East Research Court
Tucson, AZ 85718-6758
888-255-7826
e-mail: concor@azstarnet.com
www.all-railroads.com
*(locomotives, rolling stock,
structure kits, vehicles)*

FLEISCHMANN
c/o Daylight Distributors
4411 Sepulveda Blvd.
Culver City, CA 90230
310-313-9370
*(European-prototype locomotives
and rolling stock)*

GHB INTERNATIONAL
P.O. Box 4063
Gaithersburg, MD 20885
301-869-3437
fax: 301-869-4358
e-mail: georghb@erols.com
www.ghbintl.com
(traction products)

HALLMARK MODELS
4822 Bryan Street
Dallas, TX 75204
214-821-2558
fax: 214-824-2101
e-mail: hmmcrown@aol.com
www.hallmarkmodels.com
*(brass locomotives and rolling
stock)*

HIGHLINERS
P.O. Box 22435
San Diego, CA 92192
858-453-3942
*(diesel locomotives and diesel
detail parts)*

HOBBYTOWN OF BOSTON
P.O. Box 5135
Hollywood, FL 33083-5135
*(diesel locomotive kits
and drive systems)*

INTERMOUNTAIN RAILWAY
COMPANY
30 E. Ninth Ave.
P.O. Box 839
Longmont, CO 80502-0839
303-772-1901
800-472-2530
fax: 303-772-8534
e-mail: intermountain@sni.net
www.intermountain-railway.com
(locomotives and rolling stock)

INTERNATIONAL HOBBY CORPORATION (IHC)
413 E. Allegheny Avenue
Philadelphia, PA 19134
215-426-2873
fax: 215-634-2122
(locomotives, rolling stock, sets, structure kits, scenic accessories, vehicles)

KATO USA
100 Remington Road
Schaumburg, IL 60173
847-781-9500
fax: 847-781-9570
e-mail: kato@katousa.com
www.katousa.com
(locomotives, rolling stock, passenger cars, track and control systems)

LIFE-LIKE PRODUCTS INC.
1600 Union Avenue
Baltimore, MD 21211
1-800-638-1470
e-mail:
feedback@lifelikeproducts.com
www.lifelikeproducts.com
(locomotives, rolling stock, accessories, structure kits, scenery materials, trees)

MANTUA
P.O. Box 10
412 Grandview Avenue
Woodbury Heights, NJ 08097
800-362-6882 ext. 103 (for catalog request)
856- 853-0300
fax: 856-384-1081
e-mail: webmaster@mantua.com
www.mantua.com
(locomotives, sets, rolling stock)

MÄRKLIN, INC.
16988 W. Victor Road
P.O. Box 510559
New Berlin, WI 53151-0559
414-784-8854
800-321-8811
fax: 414-784-1095
www.marklin.com
(locomotives, rolling stock, track systems, digital DCC command control systems, accessories)

MODEL DIE CASTING INC.
5070 Sigstrom Drive
Carson City, NV 89706
775-884-4388
fax: 775-884-4391
e-mail: customerservice@mdcroundhouse.com
www.mdcroundhouse.com
(locomotives, rolling stock, accessories)

MODEL POWER
180 Smith Street
Farmingdale, NY 11735
516-694-7022
800-628-2803
fax: 516-694-7133
e-mail: mdlpowr@aol.com
www.modelpower.com
(locomotives, rolling stock, sets, structure kits, accessories)

MODEL RECTIFIER CORPORATION
80 Newfield Avenue
P.O. Box 6312
Edison, NJ 08837
732-225-6360
fax: 732-225-0091
(locomotives, power supplies, digital DCC command control systems)

MTS IMPORTS
P.O. Box 50
Middletown, NY 10940
914-342-5623
fax: 914-344-6187
e-mail: mtsimp@warwick.net
www.mtsimports.com
(brass locomotives, traction and rolling stock)

NJ INTERNATIONAL
77 W. Nicholai Street
Hicksville, NY 11801
516-433-8720
fax: 516-938-5109
www.njinternational.com
(brass locomotives and rolling stock, lighting and signals, switch motors, structure kits)

ORIGINAL WHISTLE STOP INC.
2490 E. Colorado Blvd.
Pasadena, CA 91107
626-796-7566
fax: 626-796-8004
e-mail: trainmaster@thewhistlestop.com
www.thewhistlestop.com
(brass locomotives and rolling stock, detail parts, decals)

OVERLAND MODELS INC.
3808 W. Kilgore Avenue
Muncie, IN 47304-4896
765-289-4257
fax: 765-289-6013
(brass locomotives and rolling stock)

PACIFIC FAST MAIL
P.O. Box 57
Edmonds, WA 98020
425-776-3112
fax: 425-775-5075
(brass locomotives and rolling stock)

PRECISION SCALE CO.
3961 Highway 93 North
P.O. Box 278
Stevensville, MT 59870
406-777-5071
fax: 406-777-5074
(brass locomotives and rolling stock, detail parts)

RIVAROSSI
c/o Model Expo Inc.
P.O. Box 229140
3850 N. 29th Terrace
Hollywood, FL 33022
800-222-3876
e-mail: modelexpo1@aol.com
www.modelexpoinc.com
(locomotives, passenger cars, rolling stock)

ROCO
c/o Wm. K. Walthers Inc.
5601 W. Florist Avenue
Milwaukee, WI 53218
e-mail: custserv@walthers.com
www.walthers.com
(European-prototype locomotives, passenger cars, rolling stock, structure kits, vehicles, track systems)

STEWART HOBBIES INC.
140 New Britain Blvd.
Chalfont, PA 18914-1832
215-822-6968
fax: 215-822-7239
www.stewarthobbies.com
(locomotives and rolling stock)

SUNSET MODELS INC.
37 S. Fourth Street
Campbell, CA 95008
408-866-1727
fax: 408-866-5674
e-mail: sdmann@best.com
www.3rdrail.com
(brass locomotives and rolling stock)

TRAINLINE
c/o Wm. K. Walthers Inc.
5601 W. Florist Avenue
Milwaukee, WI 53218
e-mail: custserv@walthers.com
www.walthers.com
(locomotives, rolling stock, sets)

WM. K. WALTHERS INC.
5601 W. Florist Avenue
Milwaukee, WI 53218
e-mail: custserv@walthers.com
www.walthers.com
(locomotives, rolling stock, sets, structure kits, track systems, decals, accessories)

after-market manufacturers and suppliers of HO products

ACCURAIL
P.O. Box 1202
Elburn, IL 60119-1202
630-365-6400
fax: 630-365-6499
e-mail: accurail@elnet.com
www.elnet.com/~accurail
(rolling stock, structure kits, detail parts)

ACCURATE LIGHTING
205 West Florida
Appleton, WI 54911
www.accuratelighting.com
(illumination and lighting products, lighted miniscenes)

ACME MODEL ENGINEERING CO.
654 Bergen Blvd.
Ridgefield, NJ 07657
(switch control panels and terminal strips)

AFTER HOURS GRAPHICS
P.O. Box 62373
Sharonville, OH 45262-0373
513-563-7446
fax: 513-563-7448
e-mail: rrdecals@aol.com
(decals)

AIM PRODUCTS
c/o Wm. K. Walthers Inc.
5601 W. Florist Avenue
Milwaukee, WI 53218
e-mail: custserv@walthers.com
www.walthers.com
(tunnel portals, abutments, retaining walls)

ALCO PRODUCTS
312 Hunter Forge Road
Macungie, PA 18062
610-845-7300
fax: 610-845-7301
(locomotive repowering kits)

A-LINE/PROTO POWER WEST
P.O. Box 7916
1760 White Avenue
La Verne, CA 91750
909-593-2003
fax: 909-593-7733
(locomotive repowering kits)

ALLOY FORMS
c/o Wm. K. Walthers Inc.
5601 W. Florist Avenue
Milwaukee, WI 53218
e-mail: custserv@walthers.com
www.walthers.com
(metal scenery products and vehicle kits)

ALPINE DIVISION SCALE MODELS
c/o Wm. K. Walthers Inc.
5601 W. Florist Avenue
Milwaukee, WI 53218
e-mail: custserv@walthers.com
www.walthers.com
(structure kits)

AMACO
c/o Wm. K. Walthers Inc.
5601 W. Florist Avenue
Milwaukee, WI 53218
e-mail: custserv@walthers.com
www.walthers.com
(scenic molding materials and latex products)

AMERICAN MODEL BUILDERS
1420 Hanley Industrial Court
St. Louis, MO 63144
314-968-3076
fax: 314-968-0799
e-mail: laserkit@aol.com
(wood structure kits, rolling stock kits)

AM MODELS
c/o Tomar Industries
9520 E. Napier Avenue
Benton Harbor, MI 49022
616-944-5129
fax: 616-944-1901
e-mail: tomarup@juno.com
*(structure kits and scenic
accessories)*

AMSI
c/o Wm. K. Walthers Inc.
5601 W. Florist Avenue
Milwaukee, WI 53218
e-mail: custserv@walthers.com
www.walthers.com
(scenery materials)

ARISTO-CRAFT TRAINS
Polk's Model Craft Hobbies
346 Bergen Ave.
Jersey City, NJ 07304
201-332-8100
fax: 800-310-POLK
e-mail: aristo@cnct.com
www.aristocraft.com/aristo
(power and control systems)

**W.S. ATARAS ENGINEERING
INC.**
40 Laughton Street
Upper Marlboro, MD 20774
301-249-5184
fax: 708-570-6140
e-mail: bataras@wsaeng.com
www.wsaeng.com
*(signal control mounting
adapters)*

AZTEC MFG. COMPANY
2701 Conestoga Dr., #113
Carson City, NV 89706
775-883-3327
fax: 775-883-3357
e-mail: aztecmfg@usa.net
www.aztectrains.com
(track cleaning cars in all scales)

BACKDROP WAREHOUSE
P.O. Box 27877
Salt Lake City, UT 84127-0877
888-542-5227/801-964-6155
fax: 801-962-4238
e-mail: backdrop@backdropware-
house.com
www.backdropwarehouse.com
(photographic backdrops)

BETHLEHEM CAR WORLD INC.
263 Parkview Drive
Souderton, PA 18964
(rolling stock kits)

BEV-BEL
c/o MainLine Models
P. O. Box 1002
Hudson, OH 44236-1002
e-mail: Rsemko@stratos.net
www.bev-bel.com
(custom-decorated rolling stock)

BK ENTERPRISES
12874 County Road #314B
Buena Vista, CO 81211-9102
719-395-8076
e-mail: bktruscal@aol.com
(track systems and turnouts)

**BLACK BEAR
CONSTRUCTION CO.**
P.O. Box 26911
Austin, TX 78755-0911
512-467-8400
fax: 512-458-8765
(bridge and trestle kits)

BLAIR LINE
P.O. Box 1136
Carthage, MO 64836-6136
417-359-8300
e-mail: dalerush@blairline.com
www.blairline.com
*(decals, structure kits, signs, scenic
accessories)*

BRAGDON ENTERPRISES
2960 Garden Tower
Georgetown, CA 95634
530-333-1365
fax: 530-333-1051
e-mail: bragdon@bragdonent.com
www.bragdonent.com
(scenery products)

BRANCHLINE TRAINS
333 Park Ave.
East Hartford, CT. 06108
e-mail: bill@branchline-trains.com
www.branchline-trains.com
(rolling stock)

BRASS CAR SIDES
715 S. 7th Street
St. Peter, MN 56082-1435
507-931-2784
e-mail: dchenry@gac.edu
(brass passenger car sides)

**DOUGLAS BROOKS
CREATIVE MODELS**
307 MacKay Avenue
Ventura, CA 93004-1518
805-647-5514
e-mail: DSHDS@aol.com
www.swiftsite.com/dbcreative-
models
(palm tree scenic accessories)

BTS STRUCTURES
P.O. Box 561
Seffner, FL 33583
813-681-7666 (phone/fax)
e-mail: bill@btsrr.com
www.btsrr.com
(structure kits)

**BUILDERS IN
SCALE/SWITCHMASTER**
P.O. Box 460025
Aurora, CO 80046-0025
800-884-1822
fax: 303-680-6088
www.buildersinscale.com
(structure kits and scenic details)

**BUILDING & STRUCTURE
COMPANY**
P.O. Box 1296
Fenton, MO 63026
618-624-6909
fax: 618-624-3590
e-mail: psmith@apci.net
(structure kits)

BURLINGTON ROUNDHOUSE
Corporation
P.O. Box 665
Castle Rock, CO 80104-0665
303-660-2000
fax: 303-688-5069
(structure kits)

BUSCH
c/o Wm. K. Walthers Inc.
5601 W. Florist Avenue
Milwaukee, WI 53218
e-mail: custserv@walthers.com
www.walthers.com
*(structure kits, vehicles, signals
and lineside accessories, scenery
materials, tunnel portals)*

C&BT SHOPS
P.O. Box 647
Ingomar, PA 15127-0647
412-538-4443
fax: 412-366-3870
www.ModelRailroading.org/
  Companies/CBTShops.html
(rolling stock)

CABOOSE INDUSTRIES
1861 N. Ridge Drive
Freeport, IL 61032
(ground throws for use with turnouts)

CAMPBELL SCALE MODELS
P.O. Box 5307
Durango, CO 81301
970-385-7729
fax: 970-385-7724
(structure kits)

CASCADE MODELS
1520 Leadville
Boise, ID 83706
208-343-0113
(brass passenger and freight cars)

C.C. CROW
P.O. Box 1427
Mukilteo, WA 98275
425-355-5622
(structure kits)

CENTERLINE PRODUCTS INC.
18409 Harmony Road
Marengo, IL 60152
815-923-1105
fax: 815-923-1106
e-mail: info@
  centerline-products.com
www.centerline-products.com
(track cleaning rolling stock)

CENTRAL VALLEY
1203 Pike Lane
Oceano, CA 93445
(bridge, fence, ladder, beam kits and detail parts)

CHAMPION DECAL COMPANY
P.O. Box 1178
Minot, ND 58702
701-852-4938
fax: 701-852-9429
e-mail: champ@minot.com
www.minot.com/~champ
(decals)

CHOOCH ENTERPRISES
P.O. Box 217
Redmond, WA 98052
425-788-8680 (phone/fax)
e-mail: chooch@jps.net
www.choochenterprises.com
(tunnels and abutments)

CIBOLO CROSSING
P.O. Bxo 2640
Universal City, TX 78148-1640
210-658-4548
(structure kits)

CIRCUITRON
211 Rocbaar Drive
Romeoville, IL 60446-1163
(switch machine motors and accessories, signals)

CIRCUS CRAFT
c/o Wm. K. Walthers Inc.
5601 W. Florist Avenue
Milwaukee, WI 53218
e-mail: custserv@walthers.com
www.walthers.com
(circus accessories)

CITY CLASSICS
P.O. Box 16502
Pittsburgh, PA 15242
412-276-1312 (phone/fax)
(structure kits)

CLASSIC MINIATURES
c/o Wm. K. Walthers Inc.
5601 W. Florist Avenue
Milwaukee, WI 53218
e-mail: custserv@walthers.com
www.walthers.com
(structure kits)

CLEAR CREEK MODELS/ MASTER CREATIONS N3
c/o Wm. K. Walthers Inc.
5601 W. Florist Avenue
Milwaukee, WI 53218
e-mail: custserv@walthers.com
www.walthers.com
(narrow-gauge rolling stock kits)

CLOVER HOUSE
P.O. Box 62
Sebastopol, CA 95473-0062
(dry transfers)

CM SHOPS
c/o Wm. K. Walthers Inc.
5601 W. Florist Avenue
Milwaukee, WI 53218
e-mail: custserv@walthers.com
www.walthers.com
(rolling stock)

COACH YARD
P.O. Box 593
Del Mar, CA 92014-0593
fax: 626-796-7566
e-mail:
CarMan@TheCoachYard.com
(brass passenger cars)

COLOR-RITE
c/o Wm. K. Walthers Inc.
5601 W. Florist Avenue
Milwaukee, WI 53218
e-mail: custserv@walthers.com
www.walthers.com
(plaster rock molds and "water" simulation kits)

CORNERSTONE SERIES
c/o Wm. K. Walthers Inc.
5601 W. Florist Avenue
Milwaukee, WI 53218
e-mail: custserv@walthers.com
www.walthers.com
(structure kits)

CUSTOM FINISHING
c/o Wm. K. Walthers Inc.
5601 W. Florist Avenue
Milwaukee, WI 53218
e-mail: custserv@walthers.com
www.walthers.com
(metal trackside equipment kits)

CVP PRODUCTS
P.O. Box 835772
Richardson, TX 75083-5772
972-422-2169
www.cvpusa.com
(DCC control systems)

DALLEE ELECTRONICS
246 W. Main Street
Leola, PA 17540
e-mail: info@dallee.com
www.dallee.com
(electronic throttles, control systems, and accessories)

DEL-AIRE PRODUCTS
321 North 40th Street
Allentown, PA 18104
1-888-DEL-AIRE (phone/fax)
e-mail: delaire@fast.net
www.delaire.com
(air-powered switch machines)

DESIGN PRESERVATION MODELS
P.O. Box 66
Linn Creek, MO 65052
573-346-1234
www.dpm.com
(structure kits and scenic accessories)

DETAIL ASSOCIATES
P.O. Box 5357
San Luis Obispo, CA 93403
805-544-9593
(rolling stock, accessories, detail parts, scenic backdrops)

DETAILS WEST
P.O. Box 61
Corona, CA 92878-0061
e-mail: detwest@aol.com
(detail parts)

DIGITRAX
450 Cemetery Street #206
Norcross, GA 30071
770-441-7992
fax: 770-441-0759
e-mail: sales@digitrax.com
www.digitrax.com
(digital control systems)

DM CUSTOM DECALS
2127 South 11th Street
Manitowoc, WI 54220-6513
(custom decals)

DOWNTOWN DECO
4319 Rainbow Drive
Missoula, MT 59803
406-251-8005
(structure kits)

DURANGO PRESS N3
c/o Wm. K. Walthers Inc.
5601 W. Florist Avenue
Milwaukee, WI 53218
e-mail: custserv@walthers.com
www.walthers.com
(narrow and standard gauge rolling stock, structure kits)

DYNA-MODEL PRODUCTS
c/o Wm. K. Walthers Inc.
5601 W. Florist Avenue
Milwaukee, WI 53218
e-mail: custserv@walthers.com
www.walthers.com
(structure kits)

EASTERN CAR WORKS
P.O. Box L 624
Langhorne, PA 19047
www.easterncarworks.com
(passenger car and rolling stock kits)

EEL RIVER MODELS
P. O. Box 659
Ukiah, CA 95482
e-mail: erm@p-b-l.com
www.zapcom.net/~eelrivermodels
(rolling stock)

EKO
c/o Wm. K. Walthers Inc.
5601 W. Florist Avenue
Milwaukee, WI 53218
e-mail: custserv@walthers.com
www.walthers.com
(figures, vehicles, scenic accessories)

EARL R. ESHLEMAN COMPANY
53 Maytown Avenue
Elizabethtown, PA 17022
717-367-6162
(turnouts and linkage components)

ETI
c/o Wm. K. Walthers Inc.
5601 W. Florist Avenue
Milwaukee, WI 53218
e-mail: custserv@walthers.com
www.walthers.com
(casting resins and polymer coatings)

EVERGREEN HILL DESIGNS
31328 N. Brooks Creek Road
Arlington, WA 98223
1-800-337-3547
fax: 360-403-0569
e-mail: davidry@tgi.net
www.osorail.com
(structure kits)

EVERGREEN SCALE MODELS
12808 NE 125th Way
Kirkland, WA 98034
425-823-0458
fax: 425-820-9091
(plastic structure building supplies)

FALLER GMBH
e-mail: info@faller.de
www.faller.de
(structure kits, scenery materials, trees, scenic backdrops, tunnel portals, "water" simulation systems)

FEATHER LITE
c/o Wm. K. Walthers Inc.
5601 W. Florist Avenue
Milwaukee, WI 53218
e-mail: custserv@walthers.com
www.walthers.com
(tunnel portals, abutments, retaining walls)

FINE SCALE MINIATURES
49 Main Street
Peabody, MA 01960-5549
978-531-9418
(limited run custom structure kits)

FUNARO & CAMERLENGO
c/o Wm. K. Walthers Inc.
5601 W. Florist Avenue
Milwaukee, WI 53218
e-mail: custserv@walthers.com
www.walthers.com
(passenger car and rolling stock kits)

GLOOR CRAFT MODELS
c/o Wm. K. Walthers Inc.
5601 W. Florist Avenue
Milwaukee, WI 53218
e-mail: custserv@walthers.com
www.walthers.com
(structure kits, rolling stock kits)

GOOD WOOD CO.
P.O. Box 452
Wolf Creek, OR 97497
541-866-2445
(display cases)

R. J. GOULD
P.O. Box 8976
Albany, NY 12208
e-mail: rjgwvg@earthlink.net
(scenic accessories)

GRANDT LINE PRODUCTS
1040-B Shary Court
Concord, CA 94518
510-671-0143
fax: 510-671-0806
(structure kits and detail parts)

GREAT WEST MODELS
c/o Wm. K. Walthers Inc.
5601 W. Florist Avenue
Milwaukee, WI 53218
e-mail: custserv@walthers.com
www.walthers.com
(structure kits)

GREENWAY PRODUCTS
139 Ramsey Road
Ligonier, PA 15658
724-238-6268
www.greenwayproducts.com
(rolling stock, display cases)

GRS MICRO-LITING
32 Woodlake Drive SE
Rochester, MN 55904
800-676-4252
(lighting kits and lighting-based miniscene kits)

**GUTS, GRAVEL & GLORY
SCENIC SUPPLIES**
c/o Wm. K. Walthers Inc.
5601 W. Florist Avenue
Milwaukee, WI 53218
e-mail: custserv@walthers.com
www.walthers.com
(structure kits)

H&O MARITIME ACCESSORIES
P.O. Box 425
Stockton Springs, ME 04981
800-448-5567
(tugboat kits)

HEICO MODELL
c/o Wm. K. Walthers Inc.
5601 W. Florist Avenue
Milwaukee, WI 53218
e-mail: custserv@walthers.com
www.walthers.com
(freight car loads)

HELJAN
c/o Wm. K. Walthers Inc.
5601 W. Florist Avenue
Milwaukee, WI 53218
e-mail: custserv@walthers.com
www.walthers.com
(structure kits, scenery materials, accessories)

HERPA
Herpa Miniaturemodelle GmbH
Leonrodstrasse 46-47
D-90599 Dietenhofen
Germany
e-mail: herpa@herpa.de
www.herpa.de
(vehicles)

HOBBY LOADS
936 Moyer Road
Newport News, VA 23608
757-877-7152
(coal loads)

HOMABED
801 Chesley Avenue
Richmond, CA 94801-2135
1-888-RRBED4U
www.homabed.com
(Homasote roadbed products)

**INDUSTRIAL HERITAGE
SCALE MODELS**
c/o Wm. K. Walthers Inc.
5601 W. Florist Avenue
Milwaukee, WI 53218
e-mail: custserv@walthers.com
www.walthers.com
(structure kits)

INDUSTRIAL MINIATURES
Rt 1, Box 169
Milbank, SD 57252
(structures)

INSTANT BUILDINGS
c/o Wm. K. Walthers Inc.
5601 W. Florist Avenue
Milwaukee, WI 53218
e-mail: custserv@walthers.com
www.walthers.com
(structural scenic backdrops)

INSTANT HORIZONS
c/o Wm. K. Walthers Inc.
5601 W. Florist Avenue
Milwaukee, WI 53218
e-mail: custserv@walthers.com
www.walthers.com
(scenic backdrops)

ISLE LABORATORIES
P.O. Box 636
Sylvania, OH 43560
517-486-4055
(scenery products)

ITTY BITTY LINES
c/o Wm. K. Walthers Inc.
5601 W. Florist Avenue
Milwaukee, WI 53218
e-mail: custserv@walthers.com
www.walthers.com
(roadbed)

JAEGER
c/o Wm. K. Walthers Inc.
5601 W. Florist Avenue
Milwaukee, WI 53218
e-mail: custserv@walthers.com
www.walthers.com
(freight car load kits)

JAMES PUBLICATIONS
6342 Forest Hill Blvd., PMB 316
West Palm Beach, FL 33415
561-434-2944
e-mail:
info@wildweststructures.com
www.wildweststructures.com
(plans for structure designs)

JL INNOVATIVE DESIGN
c/o Wm. K. Walthers Inc.
5601 W. Florist Avenue
Milwaukee, WI 53218
e-mail: custserv@walthers.com
www.walthers.com
*(structure kits, vintage-style sig-
nage and advertising)*

**JORDAN HIGHWAY
MINIATURES**
c/o Wm. K. Walthers Inc.
5601 W. Florist Avenue
Milwaukee, WI 53218
e-mail: custserv@walthers.com
www.walthers.com
(vehicle kits)

JV MODELS
c/o Wm. K. Walthers Inc.
5601 W. Florist Avenue
Milwaukee, WI 53218
e-mail: custserv@walthers.com
www.walthers.com
(structure kits)

K&S SCENERY PRODUCTS
4848 S. Highland Drive #438
Salt Lake City, UT 84117
(pine tree kits)

KADEE QUALITY PRODUCTS
673 Avenue C
White City, OR 97503-1078
541-826-3883
fax: 541-826-4013
e-mail: mail@kadee.com
www.kadee.com
(rolling stock, couplers)

KIBRI
c/o Wm. K. Walthers Inc.
5601 W. Florist Avenue
Milwaukee, WI 53218
e-mail: custserv@walthers.com
www.walthers.com
*(structure kits, rolling stock, vehi-
cles, accessories, scenery materials)*

**GREG KOMAR
DRY TRANSFERS**
15532 Woodway
Tampa, FL 33613
(dry transfers)

HI-TECH DETAILS
P.O. Box 244
Ukiah, CA 95482
707-462-7680
*(boxcar kit; locomotive detail
parts)*

**LASERKIT/AMERICAN
MODEL BUILDERS**
c/o Wm. K. Walthers Inc.
5601 W. Florist Avenue
Milwaukee, WI 53218
e-mail: custserv@walthers.com
www.walthers.com
(structure kits)

LBF COMPANY
1931 NW Mulholland Drive
Roseburg, OR 97470
541-677-9595
fax: 541-677-1978
e-mail: sales@lbfcompany.com
www.lbfcompany.com
(rolling stock)

**LENZ AGENCY
OF NORTH AMERICA**
P.O. Box 143
Chelmsford, MA 01824
978-250-1494 (phone/fax)
www.lenz.com
*(digital DCC command
control systems)*

**MAINLINE & SIDING
STRUCTURES**
392 Morrison Road
Columbus, OH 43213
614-755-5401
fax: 614-755-5402
(structure kits)

MAIN STREET GRAPHICS
P.O. Box 173
Jefferson Valley, NY 10535-0173
*(window graphic kits for
structures)*

MASTER CREATIONS
3970 N. Highway 89
Prescott, AZ 86301
520-778-0374
fax: 520-778-7448
(structure kits)

MCHENRY COUPLERS
1207 Pebble Point
Goshen, KY 40026
*(metal-coil knuckle spring
couplers for locomotives and
rolling stock)*

MERTEN
c/o Wm. K. Walthers Inc.
5601 W. Florist Avenue
Milwaukee, WI 53218
e-mail: custserv@walthers.com
www.walthers.com
(figures, scenic accessories)

**MICRO ENGINEERING
COMPANY**
1120 Eagle Road
Fenton, MO 63026
314-349-1112
fax: 314-349-1180
*(track and plastic building
supplies)*

MICROSCALE INDUSTRIES INC.
18435 Bandilier Circle
Fountain Valley, CA 92708-7012
714-593-1422
fax: 714-593-1432
e-mail: microscale@aol.com
www.microscale.com
(decals)

**MICRO STRUCTURES/MILLER
ENGINEERING**
c/o Wm. K. Walthers Inc.
5601 W. Florist Avenue
Milwaukee, WI 53218
e-mail: custserv@walthers.com
www.walthers.com
(structure kits)

**MIDWEST PRODUCTS
COMPANY**
400 S. Indiana Street
Hobart, IN 46342
800-348-3497
e-mail:
info@midwestproducts.com
www.midwestproducts.com
(roadbed)

MILLER ENGINEERING
P.O. Box 282
New Canaan, CT 06840-0282
203-595-0619
e-mail: milleren@microstru.com
www.microstru.com
*(photo-etched kits and
illuminated signage)*

MINIATRONICS
561-K Acorn Street
Deer Park, NY 11729
800-942-9439
631-242-MINI
fax: 631-242-7796
e-mail: miniatronics@
    miniatronics.com
www.miniatronics.com
*(illumination and lighting systems
for structures, signals, and trains)*

MLR MANUFACTURING CO.
c/o Wm. K. Walthers Inc.
5601 W. Florist Avenue
Milwaukee, WI 53218
e-mail: custserv@walthers.com
www.walthers.com
*(track-laying tools and
accessories)*

MOUNTAINS IN MINUTES/
ISLE LABORATORIES
c/o Wm. K. Walthers Inc.
5601 W. Florist Avenue
Milwaukee, WI 53218
e-mail: custserv@walthers.com
www.walthers.com
*(scenery materials, rock castings,
molding materials, tunnel portals)*

MR. PLASTER
P.O. Box 23066
Toledo, OH 43623-0066
419-472-0718 (phone/fax)
e-mail: info@mrplaster.com
www.mrplaster.com
*(plaster detail and scenery
products)*

NEW YORK RAILWAY
SUPPLY INC.
9158 Rothbury Drive #183
Gaithersburg, MD 20879
301-947-8075
fax: 301-947-8076
e-mail: sales.service@nyrs.com
www.nyrs.com
(turntable indexing controller)

NOCH
c/o Wm. K. Walthers Inc.
5601 W. Florist Avenue
Milwaukee, WI 53218
e-mail: custserv@walthers.com
www.walthers.com
*(trees, figures, scenery materials,
tunnel portals, retaining walls,
structure kits)*

NORTH COAST ENGINEERING
1900 Empire Blvd., Suite 303
Webster, NY 14580
716-671-0370
fax: 716-671-9337
e-mail: jscorse@aol.com
www.tttrains.com/northcoast
*(digital DCC decoders
and systems)*

NORTHEASTERN SCALE MODELS
99 Cross Street
Methuen, MA 01844
978-688-6019
fax: 978-794-9104
e-mail: info@nesm.com
www.nesm.com
(structure kits)

NORTHWEST SHORT LINE
P.O. Box 423
Seattle, WA 98111-0423
206-932-1087
fax: 206-935-7106
e-mail: info@nwsl.com
www.nwsl.com
(locomotive upgrade products)

NUCOMP MINIATURES
P.O. Box 539
Bluffton, IN 46714
800-710-9034
fax: 219-824-1699
e-mail: sales@nucompinc.com
www.nucompinc.com
*(mobile home model kits and
vehicle kits)*

N-WAY PRODUCTS
c/o Wm. K. Walthers Inc.
5601 W. Florist Avenue
Milwaukee, WI 53218
e-mail: custserv@walthers.com
www.walthers.com
(signals)

OK ENGINES
Box 355
Mohawk, NY 13407
315-866-1807
*(metal passenger car and
locomotive kits)*

OLD & WEARY CAR SHOP
37 Highland Avenue
Piedmont, NY 10968
914-365-1473
e-mail: AL1HDAGENT@ aol.com
www.theoldandwearycarshop.com
(custom-decorated rolling stock)

ON-TRAK MODEL PRODUCTS
P.O. Bxo 1517
Black Mountain, NC 28711-1517
704-669-5444 (phone/fax)
(vehicle kits)

OREGON RAIL SUPPLY
P.O. Box 490
Scappoose, OR 97056
503-543-6466
fax: 503-543-6005
e-mail: orail@oregonrail.com
www.oregonrail.com
(freight cars and signals)

PLASTRUCT
1020 S. Wallace Place
City of Industry, CA 91748
800-666-7015
e-mail: plastruct@plastruct.com
www.plastruct.com
*(scale plastic building supplies and
lighting kits, scenery
materials, trees)*

PECO
c/o Wm. K. Walthers Inc.
5601 W. Florist Avenue
Milwaukee, WI 53218
e-mail: custserv@walthers.com
www.walthers.com
(track systems)

PIKESTUFF
c/o Rix Products
3747 Hogue Road
Evansville, IN 47712
812-426-1RIX
fax: 812-423-3174
www.rixproducts.com
*(structure kits and scenic
detail parts)*

**PIKO MODELLSPIELWAREN
GMBH**
Lutherstrasse 30
Sonneberg 96505
Germany
e-mail: info@piko.de
www.piko.com
(structure kits)

POLA GMBH
c/o Gebr. FALLER GmbH
e-mail: info@pola.de
www.pola.de
(structure kits)

POLYTERRAIN
2105 W. 18th. Street
Fayetteville, AR 72701
501-521-8080
fax: 501-761-3227
e-mail: polyt@pgtc.net
www.polyterrain.com
(scenery products)

PAUL M. PREISER KG
Steinfield Postfach 12-33
Rottenburg D-8803
Germany
*(figures and scenic accessories,
vehicles)*

PRE-SIZE
c/o Wm. K. Walthers Inc.
5601 W. Florist Avenue
Milwaukee, WI 53218
e-mail: custserv@walthers.com
www.walthers.com
*(tunnel portals, abutments,
retaining walls)*

QSI
3800 S.W. Cedar Hills Blvd,
Suite 224
Beaverton, OR 97005
503-350-0595
fax: 503-626-9995
e-mail: qsi_feedback@uwphoto.net
www.qsindustries.com
*(sound systems for layout
environment enhancement)*

R&S ENTERPRISES
P.O. Box 643
Jonestown, PA 17038
717-865-3444
www.rrtrack.com
*(sectional-track layout design
software)*

RAIL GRAPHICS
1183 N. Lancaster Circle
South Elgin, IL 60177
847-742-5404
fax: 847-742-5407
e-mail: railgraf@mcs.net
www.mcs.net/~railgraf
*(decals for locomotives and
rolling stock)*

RAIL POWER PRODUCTS
7283 N. Stagecoach Drive
Park City, UT 84098
435-649-9889 (phone/fax)
*(diesel locomotive bodies and
chassis kits)*

RED CABOOSE
c/o Wm. K. Walthers Inc.
5601 W. Florist Avenue
Milwaukee, WI 53218
e-mail: custserv@walthers.com
www.walthers.com
(rolling stock kits)

RICHMOND CONTROLS
P.O. Box 1467
Richmond, TX 77406-1467
e-mail: jjhinds@wt.net
www.richmondcontrols.com
(lighing kits for rolling stock)

RIGHT-OF-WAY PRODUCTS
23682 Rd. 15-3/4
Chowchilla, CA 93610
559-665-1001
(track component detail parts)

RIX PRODUCTS
3747 Hogue Road
Evansville, IN 47712
812-426-1RIX
fax: 812-423-3174
www.rixproducts.com
*(track and switch products,
structure kits, scenic detail parts)*

RUN 8 PRODUCTIONS
P.O. Box 25224
Rochester, NY 14625
e-mail: windowrun8@aol.com
*(billboards and passenger car
window inserts)*

SANDIA SOFTWARE
9428 Tasco NE
Albuquerque, NM 87111-2222
505-821-0014
fax: 505-821-0038
e-mail:
tracks@sandiasoftware.com
www.cadrail.com
(railroad design software)

SCENIC EXPRESS
1001 Lowry Avenue
Jeannette, PA 15644-2671
800-234-9995
fax: 724-527-5955
e-mail: scenery@ibm.net
www.scenicexpress.com
(scenery materials and tree kits)

SHEEPSCOT SCALE PRODUCTS
c/o Wm. K. Walthers Inc.
5601 W. Florist Avenue
Milwaukee, WI 53218
e-mail: custserv@walthers.com
www.walthers.com
(structure kits)

SHINOHARA
c/o Wm. K. Walthers Inc.
5601 W. Florist Avenue
Milwaukee, WI 53218
e-mail: custserv@walthers.com
www.walthers.com
(track systems)

SHOREHAM SHOPS LIMITED
P.O. Box 22011
Eagan, MN 55122
(brass rolling stock)

SIEVERS BENCHWORK
Jackson Harbor Road
Washington Island, WI 54246
920-847-2264
fax: 920-847-2676
*(benchwork kits for layout
substructures)*

SIGNAL RESEARCH
P.O. Box 7073
Huntsville, AL 35807
256-650-5311 (phone/fax)
e-mail: SigResrch@aol.com
www.signalresearch.com
(digital block control systems)

SIGNSGALORE
9 Carlson Lane
Palm Coast, FL 32137-8150
904-445-6556
fax: 904-445-6553
e-mail: plocher@aol.com
www.tttrains.com/signsgalore
*(scale signs and structure
interior art)*

SKD ELECTRONICS
2217 Holly Oak Court
Waldorf, MD 20601
301-705-7734 (phone/fax)
e-mail: traindetec@aol.com
www.traindetec.com
*(infrared train detection
and signal control system)*

SMALLTOWN USA
c/o Rix Products
3747 Hogue Road
Evansville, IN 47712
812-426-1RIX
fax: 812-423-3174
www.rixproducts.com
*(structure kits and scenic
detail parts)*

**SMOKEY VALLEY RAILROAD
PRODUCTS**
P.O. Box 339
Plantersville, MS 38862
601-566-4480
fax: 601-844-2169
e-mail: larry@smokeyvalley.com
www.smokeyvalley.com
(locomotive kits, detail parts)

SOLIDESIGN
8005 Ore Knob Drive
Fenton, MI 48430
e-mail: sgwright@tir.com
www.raildreams.com
(decals)

SOUNDTRAXX
463 Turner Drive, Suite 104A
Durango, CO 81301
970-259-0690
fax: 970-259-0691
e-mail: sales@soundtraxx.com
www.soundtraxx.com
*(digital DCC decoders
and sound systems)*

SOUTH RIVER MODELWORKS
Bardwells Ferry Road
Conway, MA 01341
413-369-4482
fax: 413-369-4966
e-mail: southriv@javanet.com
www.southrivermodelworks.com
*(limited edition custom
structure kits)*

SS LTD
c/o Wm. K. Walthers Inc.
5601 W. Florist Avenue
Milwaukee, WI 53218
e-mail: custserv@walthers.com
www.walthers.com
(structure kits)

SUNRISE ENTERPRISES
c/o Wm. K. Walthers Inc.
5601 W. Florist Avenue
Milwaukee, WI 53218
e-mail: custserv@walthers.com
www.walthers.com
(signals and lineside accessories)

SWITCHMASTER
c/o Wm. K. Walthers Inc.
5601 W. Florist Avenue
Milwaukee, WI 53218
e-mail: custserv@walthers.com
www.walthers.com
(switch machines and accessories)

**TAURUS PRODUCTS/TROUT
CREEK ENGINEERING**
c/o Wm. K. Walthers Inc.
5601 W. Florist Avenue
Milwaukee, WI 53218
e-mail: custserv@walthers.com
www.walthers.com
(rolling stock kits)

TENSHODO
c/o Wm. K. Walthers Inc.
5601 W. Florist Avenue
Milwaukee, WI 53218
e-mail: custserv@walthers.com
www.walthers.com
(power trucks for locomotives)

THINFILM DECALS
P.O. Box 70323
Pasadena, CA 91117-0323
626-584-5902
(decals)

TICHY TRAIN GROUP
c/o Wm. K. Walthers Inc.
5601 W. Florist Avenue
Milwaukee, WI 53218
e-mail: custserv@walthers.com
www.walthers.com
(rolling stock kits)

**TIMBERLINE SCENERY
COMPANY**
c/o Wm. K. Walthers Inc.
5601 W. Florist Avenue
Milwaukee, WI 53218
e-mail: custserv@walthers.com
www.walthers.com
(trees)

TOMAR INDUSTRIES
9520 E. Napier Avenue
Benton Harbor, MI 49022
616-944-5129
fax: 616-944-1901
e-mail: tomarup@juno.com
(drumheads, marker lamps)

TRAINTRONICS
c/o Wm. K. Walthers Inc.
5601 W. Florist Avenue
Milwaukee, WI 53218
e-mail: custserv@walthers.com
www.walthers.com
*(block control and crossing-signal
electronics)*

TRIDENT
c/o Wm. K. Walthers Inc.
5601 W. Florist Avenue
Milwaukee, WI 53218
e-mail: custserv@walthers.com
www.walthers.com
(vehicles)

TRUCKS-N-STUFF
c/o Wm. K. Walthers Inc.
5601 W. Florist Avenue
Milwaukee, WI 53218
e-mail: custserv@walthers.com
www.walthers.com
(vehicles)

TRU-SCALE MODELS
c/o Wm. K. Walthers Inc.
5601 W. Florist Avenue
Milwaukee, WI 53218
e-mail: custserv@walthers.com
www.walthers.com
(roadbed)

UTAH PACIFIC
c/o Wm. K. Walthers Inc.
5601 W. Florist Avenue
Milwaukee, WI 53218
e-mail: custserv@walthers.com
www.walthers.com
(marker lamps and jewels)

VIRNEX INDUSTRIES
P.O. Box 613
Lake Delton, WI 53940
608-254-4382
(traction tires and tire-installation
tools for Stewart HO & N diesel
locomotives)

VOLLMER
Porschestrasse 25
D-70435 Stuttgart-Zuffenhausen
Germany
e-mail: vollmer@vollmer-kit.com
www.vollmer-kit.com/index_e.htm
(structure kits, catenary systems,
figures, accessories, scenic backdrops, scenery materials, tunnel
portals, retaining walls)

WANGROW ELECTRONICS INC.
P.O. Box 98
Park Ridge, IL 60068-0098
e-mail: systemone@wangrow.com
www.wangrow.com
(digital DCC command control
systems and decoders)

WESTERFIELD
c/o Wm. K. Walthers Inc.
5601 W. Florist Avenue
Milwaukee, WI 53218
e-mail: custserv@walthers.com
www.walthers.com
(rolling stock kits)

WESTON FIGURES
c/o Campbell Scale Models
P.O. Box 5307
Durango, CO 81301
970-385-7729
fax: 970-385-7724
(scale figures)

**WHITEGROUND MODEL
WORKS**
c/o Wm. K. Walthers Inc.
5601 W. Florist Avenue
Milwaukee, WI 53218
e-mail: custserv@walthers.com
www.walthers.com
(structure kits)

WIKING
c/o Wm. K. Walthers Inc.
5601 W. Florist Avenue
Milwaukee, WI 53218
e-mail: custserv@walthers.com
www.walthers.com
www.wiking.de
(vehicles)

WILLIAM. K. WALTHERS INC.
P.O. Box 3039
Milwaukee, WI 53201-3039
414-527-0770
www.walthers.com
(major distributor of model railroad products in all scales)

WILLIAMS BROS. INC.
181 Pawnee Street
San Marcos, CA 92069
619-744-3082
fax: 619-744-1899
(structure and vehicle kits)

WOODLAND SCENICS
P.O. Box 98
Linn Creek, MO 65052
573-346-5555
fax: 573-346-3768
e-mail:
sales@woodlandscenics.com
www.woodlandscenics.com
(structure kits, scenery products,
trees, scenic accessories, rock castings, mini-scenes, tunnel portals,
retaining walls)

dealers in HO model railroad supplies

[A list of more than 1,000 known model railroad retailers follows this section. The majority of these retailers stock HO model railroad equipment and supplies. Refer to this list, and to the Yellow Pages section of the local phone directory, for current hobby supply retailers in your home area, or in the area you are visiting.]

associations and groups of interest to HO scale hobbyists

NATIONAL MODEL RAILROAD ASSOCIATION (NMRA)
4121 Cromwell Rd.
Chattanooga, TN 37421
423-892-2846
fax: 423-899-4869
www.nmra.org

MÄRKLIN ENTHUSIASTS OF AMERICA
c/o Tim Eckert, Sec.
P.O. Box 21753
Charlotte, NC 28221-0153

magazines and periodicals of interest to HO scale model railroaders

MODEL RAILROADER **MAGAZINE**
Kalmbach Publishing Co.
21027 Crossroads Circle
P.O. Box 1612
Waukesha, WI 53187-1612
800-446-5489
fax: 262-796-1615
e-mail:
customerservice@kalmbach.com
www.modelrailroader.com

RAILROAD MODEL CRAFTSMAN **MAGAZINE**
108 Phil Harden Rd., Fredon Township
P.O. Box 700
Newton, NJ 07860-0700
973-383-3355
e-mail:
rmcsubs@rrmodelcraftsman.com
www.rrmodelcraftsman.com

MODEL RAILROADING **MAGAZINE**
Highlands Station, Inc.
2600 S. Parker Rd., Suite 1-211
Aurora, CO 80014
303-338-1700
fax: 303-338-1949
www.modelrailroadingmag.com

MAINLINE MODELER **MAGAZINE**
13110 Beverly Park Rd.
Mulkiteo, WA 98275
425-743-2607
fax: 425-787-9269

MAINE 2-FOOT QUARTERLY **MAGAZINE**
P.O. Box 133
Washingtonville, OH 44490-0133
330-702-0177
e-Mail: m2fq@aol.com

RAILMODEL JOURNAL **MAGAZINE**
Golden Bell Press
2403 Champa St.
Denver, CO 80205

FINESCALE RAILROADER **MAGAZINE**
Westlake Publishing Company
1574 Kerryglen Street
Westlake Village, CA 91361
805-494-4070
www.finescalerr.com

NARROW GAUGE AND SHORTLINE GAZETTE **MAGAZINE**
Benchmark Publications, Ltd.
P.O. Box 26
Los Altos, CA 94023
408-428-0840
fax: 408-428-0715

web sites of interest to HO scale model railroaders

www.railserve.com
(Internet portal site—prototype and model railroading)

www.trainweb.com
(Internet portal site—prototype and model railroading)

www.nmra.org
(National Model Railroad Association home page)

www.hobbyhighway.com
(discussion forums and free classified ads for model railroaders)

www.internethobbies.com
(online hobby shop—all scales)

www.mria.org
(Model Railroad Industry Association—MRIA—site)

www.scintilla.utwente.nl/ marklin
(Märklin Mailing List home page)

http://web.mit.edu/ldsteve/ Public/NAHShome.htm
(North American Hornby Society—Hornby O and Dublo trains)

www.ehobbies.com
(model railroad discussion groups and general interest train topics)

http://home.earthlink.net/ ~esmallshaw
(Earl Smallshaw's HO site; excellent links)

www.ete.org
(European Train Enthusiasts site)

www.nvrra.org
(Nashua Valley Railroad Association web site; with links)

http://members.aol.com/ HVMarklin
(Hudson Valley Märklin Club web site)

http://davesrailpix.railfan.net/ models/models.htm
(Traction and trolley site; includes models; 14,000-plus photos)

www.railnet.net
(prototype information for modelers in all scales)

An HO scale streamliner, adorned in the renowned Santa Fe "Warbonnet" paint scheme, provides an additional blaze of color to this superb scene modeled by Ken Patterson.

Photo by Ken Patterson

N SCALE & HO SCALE
hobby retailers

Following is a list of known retailers in the United States who stock model railroad equipment and supplies. This list includes dealers who sell N scale and/or HO scale trains and related supplies. Since these are the two most popular model railroading scales, most hobby shops carry a representative stock of both scales. Be advised, however, that no dealer could possibly be expected to stock the full range of model railroad equipment, accessories, and supplies available in either N or HO, let alone the full line available for both scales. Nevertheless, many of these retailers can obtain requested items for you from their model railroad distributors.

Be aware, too, that smaller hobby shops tend to come and go. This list may, therefore, identify some shops that are no longer in business, or it may not list some new establishments. For that reason, you should always call ahead before visiting a shop unfamiliar to you, and you should check the local Yellow Pages to find any new hobby retailers in your area.

Finally, be aware that area codes for some phone numbers listed herein may have changed since the date this list was compiled. Generally, a call to an outdated or changed area code will result in a recorded message that provides the current area code. Again, it is best to check the local area Yellow Pages prior to contacting one of these establishments.

major dealer list for N and HO scales

AK **HOBBYCRAFT**
800 East Dimond Boulevard
Anchorage, AK 99515
907-349-5815

MAC'S TRACKS MODEL RAILROADING
9351 Lakeview Court
Juneau, AK 99801
907-789-3371

AL **MODEL CITY MODELS**
#9 Greenbriar Village
1521 Greenbriar Road
Anniston, AL 36207
205-835-5800

HOMEWOOD TOY & HOBBY SHOP
2830 South 18th Street
Birmingham, AL 35209
205-879-3986

BENNETT HOME SUPPLY
410 Second Avenue
Cullman, AL 35055
205-734-2961

CRUMP CAMERA & HOBBY SHOP
806 Bank Street N. E.
Decatur, AL 35601
205-353-3443

H & S HOBBIES
823 Wheeler Avenue
Huntsville, AL 35801
205-534-5081

MOSS VALLEY RAILROAD
320 Church Street
Huntsville, AL 35801
205-536-3303

ACTION HOBBIES
12021 South Memorial Parkway
Huntsville, AL 35803
205-881-2703

MODEL TRAIN SUPPLY
407 St. Clair
Huntsville, AL 35811
205-533-4720

ACMR TRAIN STORE
810 Holcombe Avenue
Mobile, AL 36606
334-476-8866

GM&O "REBEL" HOBBIES
820 Azalea Road
Mobile, AL 36693
334-661-8196

HANGAR ONE HOBBIES
1402 Madison Avenue
Montgomery, AL 36107
334-262-8235

TRAINMASTER OF MONTGOMERY
3641 Debby Drive
Montgomery, AL 36111
205-288-5545

D'LLOYD'S HOBBIES
117 Turman Street
Rainbow City, AL 35901
205-442-1643

AR **BROOKS MODEL HOBBIES**
107 Cherokee Lane
Clarksville, AR 72830
501-754-4936

MICKEY'S MODEL WORKS
2305 Washington Avenue
Conway, AR 72032
501-450-9423

RIVER VALLEY HOBBIES
P.O. Box 425
Dardenelle, AR 72834
501-229-1270

**18TH STREET TRAIN
& HOBBY SHOP**
2105 West 18th Street
Fayetteville, AR 72701
501-521-2091

GOLDEN SPIKE
505 South 17th
Fort Smith, AR 72901
501-785-2557

JACK'S HOBBY SHOP
1200 John Harden Drive
Jacksonville, AR 72076
501-982-6836

MADIJO HOBBY HOUSE
4210 MacArthur Drive
North Little Rock, AR 72118
501-753-0495

LOY'S TOYS
P.O. Box 88
Wesley, AR 72773
501-456-2888

AZ **NORTHWESTERN
ARIZONA MODELS**
2475 Airfield
Kingman, AZ 86401
520-753-1008

ROY'S TRAIN WORLD
1033 South Country
Club Drive
Mesa, AZ 85202
602-833-4353

**CORONADO SCALE
MODELS**
1544 East Cypress Street
Phoenix, AZ 85006
602-254-9656

AN AFFAIR WITH TRAINS
2615 West Bethany Home
Road
Phoenix, AZ 85017
602-249-3781

THE TREASURE HOUSE
15211 North Cave Creek
Road
Phoenix, AZ 85032
602-867-4776

**ARROWHEAD SCALE
MODELS**
662 Holiday Drive
Prescott, AZ 86303
520-445-8409

**CLASSIC TRAINS
INTERNATIONAL**
650 Holiday Drive
Prescott, AZ 86303
520-771-9156

**GERRY'S TRAINS
AND TOOLS**
7337 East Indian Bend Road
Scottsdale, AZ 85250
602-991-2536

CLASSIC HOBBIES
485 East Wetmore
Tucson, AZ 85705
520-293-2022

CRAIG'S HOBBIES
6333 East Broadway
Tucson, AZ 85710
520-885-5036

CRAYCROFT HOBBIES
1611 South Craycroft
Tucson, AZ 85711
520-748-1611

TUCSON HOBBY SHOP
5637 East Speedway
Tucson, AZ 85712
520-722-1931

ARIZONA TRAINS
2420 North Treat Avenue
Tucson, AZ 85716
520-327-4000

FT. LOWELL DEPOT
3501 East Ft. Lowell
Tucson, AZ 85716
800-779-8533

CA **MATCHBOX TRAINS
& HOBBIES**
107 South Garfield
Alhambra, CA 91801
818-282-6136

THE FREIGHT YARD
930 East Orangethorpe
Avenue, Suite C
Anaheim, CA 92801
714-680-4791

TOY TRAIN SHOP
1829 West Lincoln Avenue
Anaheim, CA 92801
714-991-1040

AL'S HOBBY REPAIR
2168 West Broadway
Anaheim, CA 92804
714-535-2854

**THE LITTLE DEPOT
AT HOBBY CITY**
1238-A South Beach
Boulevard
Anaheim, CA 92804
714-828-5080

HOBBY DEPOT
640 West Second Street
Antioch, CA 94509
510-754-0829

HOBBY HOUSE
18245 U. S. Highway 18, #5
Apple Valley, CA 92307
619-242-8618

BOYS AND THEIR TOYS
124 South Elm
Arroyo Grande, CA 93420
805-481-4628

CENTRAL COAST TRAINS
7600 El Camino Real,
Suite #4
Atascadero, CA 93422
805-466-1391

BRAKEMAN'S TRAINS
& HOBBIES
195 Harrison Avenue
Auburn, CA 95603
916-889-1446

B & F TRAIN SHOP
1424 Baker Street
Bakersfield, CA 93305
805-322-7955

NOTHIN' BUT TRAINS
5620 District Boulevard,
Suite 101
Bakersfield, CA 93313
805-397-7151

DEE'S FABRICS & HOBBIES
1316 East Main
Barstow, CA 92311
619-256-6209

BERKELEY HARDWARE
2145 University Avenue
Berkeley, CA 94704
510-845-0410

MOTT'S MINIATURES
DOLL HOUSE SHOP
7900 La Palma Avenue
Buena Park, CA 90620-1912
714-527-1843

EL DORADO TOYS
8725 On The Mall
Buena Park, CA 90620
714-827-0537

THE TRAIN SHACK
1030 North Hollywood Way
Burbank, CA 91505
818-842-3330

BURBANK'S HOUSE
OF HOBBIES
911 South Victory
Burbank, CA 91506
818-848-3674

TRACKSIDE TRAINS
1675 Rollins Road, #B-1
Burlingame, CA 94010
415-692-9724

D & J HOBBY
96 North San Tomas
Aquino Road
Campbell, CA 95008
408-379-1696

THE TRAIN CONNECTION
20832 Roscoe Boulevard
Canoga Park, CA 91306
818-882-8065

BEACHRAIL LINES
71 South Ocean Avenue
Cayucos, CA 93430
805-995-0145

HOBBYTOWN USA
724 Mangrove Avenue
Chico, CA 95926
916-899-2977

IRON HORSE TRAINS
3493 Clayton Road
Concord, CA 94519
510-682-5775

RARA AVIS TRAINS
5650-H Imhoff Drive
Concord, CA 94520
510-685-6566

THE TRAIN CROSSING
1089-C Baker Street
Costa Mesa, CA 92626
714-549-1596

TOYS INTERNATIONAL
3333 Bristol Street
Costa Mesa, CA 92626
714-549-8919

TRAINTOWN
303 South Diamond Bar Blvd.
Diamond Bar, CA 91765
909-612-5781

WOLD'S HOBBIES
7100 Village Parkway
Dublin, CA 94568
510-828-5350

DUNSMUIR HARDWARE
RADIO SHACK
5836 Dunsmuir Avenue
Dunsmuir, CA 96025
916-235-4539

KIT & CABOODLE
550 El Cerrito Plaza
El Cerrito, CA 94530
510-524-9924

BRANCHLINE HOBBIES
250F Crest Street
Escondido, CA 92025
619-489-5020

HOBBY HOUSE
2911 F Street
Eureka, CA 95501
707-445-0310

SCENARIO GAME
& HOBY SHOPPE
39189 Farwell Drive
Fremont, CA 94538
510-792-9333

TOM'S TRAINS
2245 East Hammond Avenue
Fresno, CA 93703
209-266-3192

FRESNO MODEL RAILROAD
744 P Street
Fresno, CA 93721
209-266-2805

ARTHUR'S TOYS
4818 East Tulare Street
Fresno, CA 93727
209-252-9365

ERNIE'S BAKERY
AND TRAINS
4861 East Kings Canyon
Fresno, CA 93727
209-456-1365

BOCK'S TOY & HOBBY STORE
146 North Glendora Avenue
Glendora, CA 91740
818-963-9365

GEOTEK
92 Aero Camino
Goleta, CA 93117
805-961-2178

DYNAMIC HOBBIES
530-1/2 East Floride Avenue
Hemet, CA 92543
714-925-9331

MORGAN'S BIG TRAINS EMPORIUM
7368 Center Avenue
Huntington Beach, CA 92647
714-892-3688

JACKSON STATION TOYS & TRAINS
525-4 South Highway 49
Jackson, CA 95642
209-223-4560

CRESCENTA VALLEY HOBBY & CRAFT
2230 Honolulu Avenue
La Crescenta, CA 91214
818-957-1779

OCEAN VIEW HOBBY
3805 Ocean View Boulevard
La Crescenta, CA 91208
818-957-1779

NARROW GAUGE JUNCTION
250 West Whittier
La Habra, CA 90631
909-861-4856

REED'S HOBBY SHOP
8039 La Mesa Boulevard
La Mesa, CA 91941
619-464-1672

ADDIE'S ATTIC
28200 South State
Highway 189 E110
Lake Arrowhead, CA 92352
909-337-6771

HOBBY WAREHOUSE
4118 East South Street
Lakewood, CA 90712
310-531-1413

THE TRAIN STORE
44845 North Sierra Highway
Lancaster, CA 93534
805-942-1005

THE ELECTRIC TRAIN COMPANY
16200 Hawthorne Boulevard
Lawndale, CA 90260
213-370-3839

ROGER'S RAILROAD JUNCTION
12 West Oak Street
Lodi, CA 95240
209-334-5623

MIKE'S TRAINS & HOBBIES
104 West Ocean Avenue
Lompoc, CA 93436
805-736-6747

ALLIED MODEL TRAINS
4411 South Sepulveda
Boulevard
Los Angeles, CA 90230
310-313-9353

THE RED CABOOSE
2820 G Street
Merced, CA 95340
209-383-2733

THE GREAT TRAIN STORE
150 Great Mall of the
Bay Area
Milpitas, CA 95035
408-956-1797

MODESTO HOBBY & CRAFTS
3500 Coffee Road
Modesto, CA 95355
209-529-7310

PEGASUS HOBBIES
5505 Moreno Boulevard
Montclair, CA 91763
714-982-6507

VALLEY HARDWARE
612 South Myrtle Avenue
Monrovia, CA 91016
818-359-2529

LONGS MODEL RAILROAD SUPPLY
25070 Alessandro Boulevard
Moreno Valley, CA 92388
909-242-5060

SAN ANTONIO HOBBY SHOP, INC.
2550 West El Camino Real
Mountain View, CA 94040
415-941-1278

KENNEDY'S TRAIN SHOP
35201 Newark Boulevard
Newark, CA 94560
510-796-3372

THE ROUNDHOUSE TRAIN STORE
12804 Victory Boulevard
North Hollywood, CA 91606
818-769-0403

CLASSIC HOBBIES & TOYS
9038 Tampa Avenue
Northridge, CA 91324
818-993-5665

A TOY TRAIN DEPOT
681 4th Street
Oakland, CA 94607
510-444-8724

JOHN'S JUNCTION MODEL TRAINS
664 Fourth Street
Oakland, CA 94607
510-893-3370

VILLAGE MODEL SHOP
112 West "B" Street
Ontario, CA 91762
714-983-7317

FRANK'S HOBBY SHOP
666 North Tustin Avenue
Orange, CA 92667
714-639-9901

BIG BOYS TOYS
2127 East Palmdale
Boulevard
Palmdale, CA 93550
805-273-6229

**REALISTIC MINIATURE
TRAINS**
2233 North Palm
Canyon Drive
Palm Springs, CA 92262
619-325-3622

WORLD TRAINS
8311 Rosecrans
Paramount, CA 90723
213-408-0404

**THE ORIGINAL WHISTLE
STOP, INC.**
2490 East Colorado
Boulevard
Pasadena, CA 91107
818-796-7791

MODELS AND MORE
218 Petaluma Boulevard
North
Petaluma, CA 94952
707-762-2378

TRAIN DEPOT
2334 Railroad Avenue
Redding, CA 96001
916-243-1360

**LOCO-BOOSE ELECTRIC
TRAIN SHOP**
260 D Main Street
Redwood City, CA 94063
415-368-1254

THE RAILROAD COMPANY
7107-J Arlington Avenue
Riverside, CA 92503
909-687-2120

PACIFIC COAST HOBBIES
6667 Indiana Avenue, Suite F
Riverside, CA 92506
909-341-0180

RAILROAD HOBBIES
119 Vernon Street
Roseville, CA 95678
916-782-6067

CLASSIC TRAINS
18927 Colima Road
Rowland Heights, CA 91748
818-912-0774

THE GREAT TRAIN STORE
545 Downtown Plaza
Sacramento, CA 95814
916-443-2793

BRUCE'S TRAIN SHOP
2752 Marconi Avenue
Sacramento, CA 95821
916-485-5288

IRON HORSE HOBBIES
3101 Fulton Avenue
Sacramento, CA 95821
916-978-0693

R/C COUNTRY HOBBIES
4191 A Power Inn Road
Sacramento, CA 95826
916-731-5868

GUNNING'S HOBBIES
550 San Anselmo Avenue
San Anselmo, CA 94960
415-454-3087

**BUSY BEE HOBBIES
& CRAFTS**
461 West Highland Avenue
San Bernardino, CA 92405
714-886-2669

J&M HOBBY HOUSE
1660 Laurel Avenue
San Carlos, CA 94070
415-593-5019

**ARTISANS' DEPOT,
TRAIN DIVISION**
170 Avenida Del Mar
San Clemente, CA 92672
714-366-0930

FRANK "THE TRAINMAN"
4207 Park Boulevard
San Diego, CA 92103
619-295-1611

THE WHISTLE STOP
3834 Fourth Avenue
San Diego, CA 92103
619-295-7340

C & C TRAIN REPAIR
4186 Adams Avenue
San Diego, CA 92116
619-281-1284

THE TRAIN STOP
211 West Bonita Avenue
San Dimas, CA 91773
909-599-2602

CHAN'S TRAINS & KITS
2450 Van Ness Avenue
San Francisco, CA 94109
415-885-2899

FRANCISCAN HOBBIES
1920-A Ocean Avenue
San Francisco, CA 94127
415-584-3919

DOODLEBUG HOBBIES
106 Third Street, Suite L
P.O. Box 1235
San Juan Bautista, CA 95045
408-623-1088

FAMILY HOBBY
14288 East 14th Street
San Leandro, CA 94578
510-895-1530

HOBBIES UNLIMITED
17950 Hesperian Boulevard
San Lorenzo, CA 94580
510-278-1150

LAWS HOBBY CENTER
855 Marsh
San Luis Obispo, CA 93401
805-544-5518

TALBOT'S HOBBIES
445 South B Street
San Mateo, CA 94401
415-342-0126

THE HOBBY DEPOT
3016 State Street
Santa Barbara, CA 93105
805-682-1000

THE TRAIN SHOP
1829 Pruneridge Avenue
Santa Clara, CA 95050
408-296-1050

**DLA HO MODEL
RAILROADING**
28130 Ave Crocker #303
Santa Clarita, CA 91355
800-758-3015

ROUNDHOUSE TRAINS
740 Water Street
Santa Cruz, CA 95060
408-423-9239

MOLLY'S CUPBOARD
1666 Copenhagen Drive
Solvang, CA 93463
805-688-8490

SIERRA RAIL SHOP
19233 Rockridge Way
Sonora, CA 95370
209-532-6381

**HOBO JUNCTION MODEL
RAILROADING**
434 North California Street
Stockton, CA 95202
209-466-2572

DELTA DEPOT
5939 Pacific Avenue
Stockton, CA 95207
209-473-3410

**PACIFIC TRAINS
AND GIFTS**
5939 Pacific Avenue
Stockton, CA 95207
209-473-3410

**RICHARD'S MODEL
HOBBIES**
1324 South Mary Avenue
Sunnyvale, CA 94087
408-992-0246

MARTY'S HOBBIES
1728 Moorpark Road
Thousand Oaks, CA 91360
805-497-3664

**ALL ABOARD MODEL
RAILROAD EMPORIUM**
3766 Pacific Coast Highway
Torrance, CA 90505
213-791-2637

TRUCKEE TRAIN & TOY
Truckee Town Square
10156 Donner Pass Road
Truckee, CA 96161
916-587-0941

MOLLY'S CUPBOARD
10122 Donner Pass Road
Truckee, CA 96161
916-587-7544

**THE SQUARE
ROUNDHOUSE**
1468 Lander Avenue
Turlock, CA 95380
209-668-4454

SAN-VAL DISCOUNT, INC.
7444 Valjean Avenue
Van Nuys, CA 91406
818-786-8274

GOLD COAST STATION
3029 East Main Street
Ventura, CA 93003
805-641-9805

**FRIEND'S RIGHT TRACK
HOBBIES**
1818 East Main Street
Ventura, CA 93003
805-643-5338

AT TRAIN -N- WHEELS
2646 Palma Drive, Suite 460
Ventura, CA 93003
805-644-9484

TRICKS & TRACKS
16906 D Street
Victorville, CA 92392
619-952-8075

TRAIN CROSSING
1613 West Garvey Avenue
North
West Covina, CA 91790
818-960-1429

ARNIE'S TRAINS
6452 Industry Way, Unit B
Westminster, CA 92683
714-893-1015

PLANE LOCO FOR HOBBIES
7700 Bell Road, Suite G
Windsor, CA 95492
707-837-0204

YORBA TOY TRAINS
18300 Yorba Linda
Boulevard, #204
Yorba Linda, CA 92686
714-961-8368

THE HOBBY PLACE
21560A Yorba Linda
Boulevard
Yorba Linda, CA 92687
714-779-0946

**YREKA WESTERN
RAILROAD GIFT SHOP**
300 East Miner Street
Yreka, CA 96097
916-842-4146

THE WESTERN DEPOT
1650 Sierra Avenue,
Suite 203
Yuba City, CA 95993
916-673-6776

CO **AMERICAN CLASSIC
TOY TRAINS**
2225 South Peoria Street
Aurora, CO 80014
303-745-9909

EAD'S NEWS
1715 28th Street
Boulder, CO 80302
303-442-5900

TRAIN SHOWCASE
38 South Sierra Madre
Colorado Springs, CO 80903
719-471-1887

DIAMOND FUN SHOPPE
125 East Boulder
Colorado Springs, CO 80903
719-520-0126

KRIS KRINGLE LTD.
2619 West Colorado Avenue
Colorado Springs, CO 80904
719-633-1210

RAILWAY CROSSING
201 South 15th
Colorado Springs, CO 80904
719-634-6007

CUSTOM RAILWAY SUPPLY
432 West Fillmore
Colorado Springs, CO 80907
719-634-4616

PLUM LOCO OF COLORADO
6527 North Academy Boulevard
Colorado Springs, CO 80918
719-594-4123

CABOOSE HOBBIES
500 South Broadway Street
Denver, CO 80209
303-777-6766

DOUGLAS MODELS
130 Lippan Street
Denver, CO 80223
303-629-0921

THE MODELER'S PLACE
351-K West Girard Avenue
Englewood, CO 80110
303-762-8866

LINK & PIN HOBBIES
7868 South Magnolia Way
Englewood, CO 80112
303-741-4712

HOBBY TOWN
2531 D South College Avenue
Fort Collins, CO 80525
303-244-5445

THE HOBBY HUT
811 North 12th Street
Grand Junction, CO 81501
303-242-8761

HIS 'N' HERS MODEL TRAINS
2692 U.S. Highway 50, Suite K
Grand Junction, CO 81503
303-245-5504

DON'S HOBBIES
815 Tenth Street
Greeley, CO 80631
303-353-3115

RAILROAD HOBBIES
2001 North Quail Drive
Lakewood, CO 80215
303-232-0199

COLPAR HOBBIES
3333 South Wadsworth Boulevard
Lakewood, CO 80227
303-989-7008

HOVER STREET HOBBIES
1600 Hover Street, Unit D-5
Longmont, CO 80501
303-776-8292

TSARSKOE SELO
44 East 10th
Silverton, CO 81433
303-387-5487

HOBBY TOWN
6975 West 88th Avenue
Westminster, CO 80021
303-431-0482

MIZELL TRAINS INC.
3051-B West 74th Avenue
Westminster, CO 80030
303-429-4811

CT **BRANFORD HOBBIES**
609 Boston Post Road
Branford, CT 06405
203-488-9865

BERKSHIRE HILLS MODEL RAILWAY SUPPLY
93 Main Street
Canaan, CT 06018
203-824-0527

CANAAN TRAINS AND HOBBIES
27 Railroad Street
P.O. Box 718
Canaan, CT 06018
203-824-7433

HOBBY HOUSE
405 East Putnam Avenue
Cos Cob, CT 06807
203-869-0969

DANBURY HOBBY CENTER
366 Main Street
Danbury, CT 06810
203-743-9052

ICE HOUSE HOBBIES
98 Federal Road
Danbury, CT 06810
203-790-7008

RAILWORKS
5 Padanaram Road
Danbury, CT 06811
203-797-8386

BLINN'S INC.
50 Unquowa Place
Fairfield, CT 06430
203-259-5229

THE GENERAL STORE
119 Samson Rock Park
Madison, CT 06443
203-245-9027

THE TRAIN EXCHANGE AND MINIATURE CORNER
71 Hilliard Street
Manchester, CT 06040
203-646-0610

HOBBY CENTER
426 Williams Street
New London, CT 06320
203-444-2944

HOBBY JUNCTION
56 Danbury Road
Ridgefield, CT 06877
203-438-4452

**SHELTON RAILROAD
SYSTEMS**
15B Elm Street
P.O. Box 2272
Shelton, CT 06484
203-924-8761

VALLEY HOBBIES, INC.
777 Hopmeadow Street
Simsbury, CT 06070
203-651-3234

TRACKSIDE
63 Moxley Road
Uncasville, CT 06382
203-848-0480

J&E TRAIN DEPOT
911 Hartford Turnpike
Vernon, CT 06066
203-870-7311

THE HOBBY GALLERY
1810 Meriden Road
Wolcott, CT 06716
203-879-2316

THE CABOOSE
5 Mohawk Drive
Wolcott, CT 06716
203-879-9797

DC **THE GREAT TRAIN STORE**
50 Massachusetts Avenue
NE 109
Washington, DC 20002
202-371-2881

DE **TRAINS - N - THINGS**
23 Penn Mart Center
New Castle, DE 19720
302-322-8343

FIRST STATE HOBBIES
Lewes Plaza
1604 Savannah Road
Lewes, DE 19958
302-645-7700

**INLET HOBBIES
+ ELECTRONICS**
DuPont Highway
Millsboro, DE 19966
302-934-6538

MITCHELL'S FAMILY STORE
Fairfax Shopping Center
2119 Concord Pike
Wilmington, DE 19803
302-652-3258

FL **D & S HOBBY SHOP**
750 West Hampshire
Boulevard
Beverly Hills, FL 32665
352-527-1500

THE ENGINEHOUSE
1726 SE 44th Terrace
Cape Coral, FL 33904
813-549-4654

DENNIS'S TRAINS
504 Virginia Lane
Clearwater, FL 34624
813-441-9521

TRAINS & TREASURES, INC.
2551 Drew Street, Suite 105
Clearwater, FL 34625
813-799-5447

SPARE TIME HOBBIES
23 Stone Street
Cocoa, FL 32922
407-636-1808

**DUNN TOYS
& HOBBIES, INC.**
154 South Beach Street
Daytona Beach, FL 32114
904-255-3474

HOBBYTOWN USA
2455 West International
Speedway Blvd.
Daytona Beach, FL 32114
904-252-9935

UNIVERSAL HOBBIES, INC.
5443 North Federal Highway
Ft. Lauderdale, FL 33308
954-481-9390

TRADER JACK'S
61 South State Road 7
Fort Lauderdale, FL 33317
305-583-3334

R C HOBBIES
6800 North University Drive
Fort Lauderdale, FL 33321
305-721-5720

**DISCOUNT TRAIN
AND HOBBY**
312 East Oakland Park Blvd.
Fort Lauderdale, FL 33334
305-564-2440

THE TRAIN SHOP
4984 South 25th Street
Fort Pierce, FL 34981
407-464-8411

**CHOO CHOO BARN
& HOBBIES**
5454 South Suncoast Blvd.
Homosassa, FL 32646
904-621-0336

HOBBY WORLD
7273 103rd Street
Jacksonville, FL 32210
904-772-9022

CARS, PLANES, & TRAINS
10290-4 Phillips Highway
Jacksonville, FL 32256
904-926-2233

THE OAKS HOBBY SHOP
U.S. Hwy 41 N, Rt. 3
Box 425
Jasper, FL 32052
904-792-2480

THE HOBBY CENTER
Hwy 192 East Mill Creek
Mall
Kissimmee, FL 34744
407-846-2864

**PERKINS HOBBIES
& COLLECTIBLES**
1117 South Florida Avenue
Lakeland, FL 33803
813-683-3251

THE DEPOT HOBBY SHOP
603 Ridge Road
Lantana, FL 33462
407-585-1982

BIG BOYS R/C & HOBBIES
325 G East Merritt Island
Causeway
Merritt Island, FL 32952
407-454-4214

MICRO MACRO MUNDO
2856 N.W. 72nd Avenue
Miami, FL 33122
305-594-6950

**ORANGE BLOSSOM
HOBBIES**
1975 NW 36th Street
Miami, FL 33142
305-633-1517

OLD TOY TRAINS
12470 NE 7th Avenue
Miami, FL 33161
305-891-6248

READY TO ROLL
831B NW 143rd Street
Miami, FL 33168
305-688-8868

TEXNRAILS
16115 SW 117th Avenue
Miami, FL 33177
305-255-1434

**WEST FLORIDA RAILROAD
MUSEUM**
206 Henry Street
Milton, FL 32570
904-623-3645

HOBBY OASIS
540 Atlantic Boulevard
Neptune Beach, FL 32266
904-249-2066

HOBBY HOUSE
3223 East Silver Springs
Boulevard
Ocala, FL 32670
904-620-8333

TRAINS OF OCALA
1405 Southwest 6th Ave.
Ocala, FL 34474
352-369-5152

ROB'S HOBBY WORLD
8602 SW State Road 200
Ocala, FL 32674
904-854-2799

**FRANK'S TRAINS
& HOBBIES**
3910 Tampa Road
Oldsmar, FL 34677
813-855-1041

A TOY TRAIN STORE, INC.
Oldsmar Flea Market
Oldsmar, FL 34677
813-855-6931

HOBBY WORLD
175 Blanding
Orange Park, FL 32073
904-272-6315

**COLONIAL PHOTO
& HOBBY, INC.**
634 North Mills Avenue
Orlando, FL 32803
407-841-1485

**BIG KIDS WORLD
OF TRAINS, INC.**
1039 North Mills Avenue
Orlando, FL 32803
407-894-4884

RAY'S MODEL TRAINS
8424 East Highway 50
Orlando, FL 32817
407-277-4593

TRAINLAND
Gooding's Plaza
8255 International Drive
Orlando, FL 32819
407-363-9002

WHISTLE STOP HOBBIES
1901 19th Street South
Palm Harbor, FL 34683
813-785-0469

BOBE'S HOBBY HOUSE
5719 North W Street
Pensacola, FL 32505
904-433-2187

AAA TRAINS & HOBBIES
710 North V Street
Pensacola, FL 32505
904-469-0550

H & R TRAINS, INC.
6901 U.S. Hwy 19 North
Pinellas Park, FL 34665
813-526-4682

**WARRICK CUSTOM
HOBBIES**
1025 South University Drive
Plantation, FL 33324
305-370-0708

ROUNDHOUSE SOUTH
4611 Ridgewood Avenue
Port Orange, FL 32127
904-304-7002

WAYSIDE ENGINE CO.
17990 NW 77 Avenue
Reddick, FL 32686
904-591-2001

GATEWAY STATION
6554 Gateway Avenue
Sarasota, FL 34231
941-921-7203

**GULF COAST
MODEL RAILROAD INC.**
3222 Clark Road
Sarasota, FL 34231
941-923-9303

BILL'S TRAIN SHOP
P.O. Box 561
Seffner, FL 33584
813-681-7666

HOBO'S HOBBIES
320 South Ponce De Leon
Boulevard
St. Augustine, FL 32084
904-826-0222

HOBBY CABOOSE
220 B West Tharpe
Tallahassee, FL 32303
904-385-9728

BENJY'S TRAINS & TOYS
8715 40th Street N.
Tampa, FL 33604
813-980-3790

CHESTER HOLLEY MODEL RAILROAD SPECIALIST
3818 South Himes Avenue
Tampa, FL 33611
813-831-7202

HAPPY HOBO TRAINS
4040 West Waters Avenue, #1100
Tampa, FL 33614
813-886-5072

CHOO CHOO CHARLIE'S
3108 State Road 60 East
Valrico, FL 33594
813-681-4439

THE TRAIN DEPOT
900 South Orlando Avenue
Winter Park, FL 32789
407-629-1365

HOBBY INTERNATIONAL
2335 Temple Trail #5
Winter Park, FL 32789
407-644-5990

MAINLINE K&M RAILROAD
5306 Eighth Street
Zephyrhills, FL 33540
813-780-8144

GA **THE GREAT TRAIN STORE**
North Point Mall
Alpharetta, GA 30202
404-751-0943

SOUTHEASTERN HOBBY DEPOT INC.
4246 Peachtree Road
Atlanta, GA 30319
404-262-7508

FAT MAN'S FOREST
1545 Laney Walker Boulevard
Augusta, GA 30904
706-722-0796

HOBBY TOWN USA
Brookwood Square
3999 Austell Road, Suite 701
Austell, GA 30001
404-941-5611

BUFORD JUNCTION
359 Shadburn Avenue
Buford, GA 30518
404-945-3222

GANDY DANCERS
5460 Peachtree Road
Chamblee, GA 30341
404-451-7425

HOBBYTOWN USA
Harmony Place
2301 Airport Thruway
Columbus, GA 31904
706-660-1793

CURRY COMPANY
129 Main Street
LaGrange, GA 30240
706-845-0384

THE TRAIN WORKS
251F Hurricane Shoals Road
Lawrenceville, GA 30245
404-339-7780

KENNESAW TRAINS & HOBBIES, INC.
2844 South Main Street
Kennesaw, GA 30144
770-528-0990

HOBBY SHOP
353 Pat Mell Road
Marietta, GA 30060
404-333-0190

TOY TRAINS 'N THINGS
2055 Beaver Ruin Road
Norcross, GA 30071
404-446-7868

RIVERDALE STATION
6504 Church Street, Suite 8
Riverdale, GA 30274
404-991-6085

BULL STREET STATION
151 Bull Street
Savannah, GA 31402
912-236-4344

B & B SALES CO.
New London Plaza
2332 Henry Clower Boulevard
Snellville, GA 30278
770-972-2328

MEMORY STATION
Highway 441 South
P.O. Box 56
Watkinsville, GA 30677
706-769-8986

HI **AL'S CANE TRAIN HOBBIES**
285 Hukiliki Street, Unit B-106
Kahului, Maui, HI 96732
808-871-8588

IA **MIDWEST TRAINS**
1114 State Street
Bettendorf, IA 52722
319-359-1427

CABOOSE STOP HOBBIES
301 Main Street
Cedar Falls, IA 50613
319-277-1754

BOX KAR HOBBIES
109 Third Avenue SE
Cedar Rapids, IA 52401
319-362-1291

TRAINS & MORE, INC.
541 31st Street
Des Moines, IA 50312
800-443-5460

HOBBY HAVEN
Sherwood Forest Shopping Center
7672 Hickman Road
Des Moines, IA 50322
515-276-8785

H & J HOBBIES
1185 Grand Avenue
Marion, IA 52302
319-373-7897

HOBBY CRAFT SHOP
21 West Main Street
Marshalltown, IA 50158
515-752-9788

EAST SIDE TRAINS
932 B East State Street
Mason City, IA 50401
515-423-1748

JNJ TRAINS
P.O. Box 1535
Ottumwa, IA 52501
515-682-4986

COUNTRY DEPOT
2592 Lincoln Avenue
Oskaloosa, IA 52577
515-673-5927

KRANTZ HOBBY
2014 South St. Aubin Street
Sioux City, IA 51106
712-276-7079

ID **MAC'S**
7316 Fairview
Boise, ID 83704
208-375-3816

**END OF THE LINE MODEL
TRAIN SUPPLY**
1717 South Eagleson Road
Boise, ID 83705
208-377-4320

RAILWAY HOBBIES
1217 Broadway, #103
Boise, ID 83706
208-343-2800

**JIM RICE CUSTOM
PAINTING**
Route 1, Box 39
Harrison, ID 83833
208-689-3256

HATCH'S HOBBIES
2235 East 17th Street
Idaho Falls, ID 83404
208-523-5144

HOBBYTOWN USA
W. 2006 Pullman Road
Moscow, ID 83843
208-882-9369

IL **ACE HARDWARE 200**
994 North Lake Street
Aurora, IL 60506
630-897-9227

**WEST SUBURBAN MODEL
RAILROAD CENTER**
106 South Lincolnway,
Suite E
North Aurora, IL 60542
708-897-2867

THE TRAIN DOCTOR
715 East Main
Belleville, IL 62220
618-233-2824

IRON HORSE HOBBIES, INC.
5555 West St. Charles Road
Berkeley, IL 60163
708-547-7363

**BERWYN'S TOY TRAINS
& MODELS**
2827 South Harlem Avenue
Berwyn, IL 60402
708-484-4384

HOBBY CITY
6910 West Cermak Road
Berwyn, IL 60402
708-795-0280

**ROUNDHOUSE TRAIN
SHOP**
Six Points Road & Alexander
Bloomington, IL 61701
309-827-8703

HOBBYLAND INC.
616 North Main Street
Bloomington, IL 61701
309-828-1442

**DANNY'S TRAINS
AND PLANES**
636 South Main Street
Bourbonnais, IL 60914
815-932-2000

**THE OWL'S ROOST MODEL
RAILROAD SHOP**
263 North Convent
Bourbonnais, IL 60914
815-932-6100

**THE GOLDEN SPIKE
TRAIN SHOP**
6357 West 79th Street
Burbank, IL 60459
708-598-3114

**THE PIZZA & PASTA
EXPRESS**
104 North Division
Carterville, IL 62919
618-985-6262

**CENTRALIA GOLD
AND HOBBY**
119 East Broadway
Centralia, IL 62801
618-533-7296

PRAIRIE GARDENS
3000 West Springfield
Champaign, IL 61821
217-356-5558

ZIENTEK'S MODEL TRAINS
2001 West 18th Street
Chicago, IL 60608
312-226-9720

**ALLIED MODEL TRAINS
& HOBBIES**
2329 West Belmont Avenue
Chicago, IL 60618
312-472-1710

**SF&C MODEL TRAINS
& HOBBYS**
2329 West Belmont Avenue
Chicago, IL 60618
312-472-1710

TRAIN STORE
4147 West 63rd Street
Chicago, IL 60629
312-585-2112

TROST HOBBY SHOP
3111 West 63rd Street
Chicago, IL 60629
312-925-1000

**STANTON HOBBY SHOP,
INC.**
4734 North Milwaukee
Avenue
Chicago, IL 60630
312-283-6446

CHICAGOLAND HOBBY
6017 North Northwest
Highway
Chicago, IL 60631
312-775-4848

PILOT MODEL SHOP
5450 West Belmont Avenue
Chicago, IL 60641
312-736-0451

RAM HOBBY SHOP
6603 West Higgins Avenue
Chicago, IL 60656
312-775-3382

ALL MODELS LTD.
5645 North Lincoln Avenue
Chicago, IL 60659
312-728-3333

**CHICAGOLAND GARDEN
RR SUPPLY**
10801 South Mason Avenue
Chicago Ridge, IL 60415
708-425-6873

**ANDY'S MAIN LINE
TRAINS**
114 West Main
Collinsville, IL 62234
618-344-7795

**WALT'S MODEL
& HOBBY SHOP**
1701 North Larkin Avenue
Crest Hill, IL 60435
815-741-0043

HAMMER'S HOBBIES
1959 East Pershing Road
Decatur, IL 62526
217-875-2627

DES PLAINES HOBBIES
1468 Lee Street
Des Plaines, IL 60018
847-297-2118

PARK LANE HOBBIES
15415 Cottage Grove
Avenue
Dolton, IL 60419
708-849-2595

DOWNERS GROVE HOBBIES
6234 South Main Street
Downers Grove, IL 60516
630-960-5900

TRACK II TRAINS
108 North Main Street
Edwardsville, IL 62025
618-656-6109

B & G TRAIN WORLD
829 Walnut Avenue
Elgin, IL 60120
847-888-2646

AL'S HOBBY SHOP
121 Addison
Elmhurst, IL 60126
630-832-4908

END OF TRACK HOBBIES
9706 Franklin Avenue
Franklin Park, IL 60131
847-455-2510

**REYNAULD'S EURO-
IMPORTS**
227 South Third Street
Geneva, IL 60134
630-262-0771

**SCHUHAM ACE
HARDWARE CO.**
485 West Roosevelt Road
Glen Ellyn, IL 60137
630-467-4800

**BESS TRUE VALUE
HARDWARE**
1850 Glenview Road
Glenview, IL 60025
847-724-2200

DON'S HOBBY WORLD
18415 South Halsted Avenue
Glenwood, IL 60425
708-754-7988

WILL O' THE WIND
603 Harris Avenue
Greenville, IL 62246
618-664-3353

**LA GRANGE HOBBY
CENTER**
25 South LaGrange Road
La Grange, IL 60525
708-354-1220

**THE OAKRIDGE
CORPORATION**
15800 New Avenue
Lemont, IL 60439
630-257-0909

LOMBARD HOBBIES
524 East St. Charles Place
Lombard, IL 60148
630-620-1084

JIM'S HOBBIES LTD.
814B Front Street
McHenry, IL 60097
815-363-0333

**TRAINS & CARS
OF YESTERDAY**
7923 West Golf
Morton Grove, IL 60053
847-470-9500

HIS & HER HOBBYS
15 West Busse Avenue
Mount Prospect, IL 60056
847-392-2668

**RON'S MUNDELEIN
HOBBIES**
431 North Lake Street
Mundelein, IL 60060
847-949-8680

HOBBYTOWN USA
504 South Route 59
Naperville, IL 60540
630-778-8707

LARSEN HOBBY
2571 East Lincoln Highway,
#3
New Lenox, IL 60451
815-485-1991

JEFFREY ALANS
701 Towanda
Normal, IL 61761
309-454-7456

PALATINE HOBBY, LTD.
772 West Euclid Avenue
Palatine, IL 60067
847-359-7888

THE RIGHT TRACK
6521 West 127th Street
Palos Heights, IL 60463
708-388-3008

**HILL'S HOBBY
& COLLECTOR'S SHOP**
10 Prairie Street
Park Ridge, IL 60068
847-823-4464

MIKE'S MAINLINE HOBBIES
1227-D West Glen Avenue
Peoria, IL 61614
309-692-1909

JEFFREY ALANS
4601 North Sheridan Road
Peoria, IL 61614
309-693-7773

VIDEO SERVICES
Model Trains Division
627 Putnam Street
Peru, IL 61354
815-223-1610

TOP HAT HOBBIES, INC.
126 North 5th Street
Quincy, IL 62301
217-222-0040

ROCKFORD HOBBIES INC.
619 South Rockford Avenue
Rockford, IL 61104
815-397-2919

BRASS WHISTLE
630 Hollister Avenue
Rockford, IL 61108
815-398-2877

**CHOO CHOO
CONNECTION**
1228 North Roselle Road
Schaumburg, IL 60195
847-882-7728

**NORTH SHORE HOBBY
& COLLECTOR'S GALLERY**
4901 Oakton Street
Skokie, IL 60077
847-673-4849

**SPRINGFIELD HAMMER'S
HOBBIES**
2448 South 10th Street
Springfield, IL 62703
217-523-0265

THE WHISTLE POST
2347 West Monroe Plaza
Springfield, IL 62704
217-787-0031

JEFFREY ALANS
1602 Wabash
Springfield, IL 62704
217-787-7771

VALLEY ROUNDHOUSE
122 West Saint Paul Street
Spring Valley, IL 61362
815-663-3411

ORLAND HOBBIES
16952 Oak Park Avenue
Tinley Park, IL 60477
708-429-9911

**LARSEN & PETERSEN
PAINT CO.**
2750 Grand Avenue
Waukegan, IL 60085
847-623-0027

TIMELESS HOBBIES
75 Danada Square East
Wheaton, IL 60187
630-690-5542

VENTURE HOBBIES
23 Huntington Lane
Wheeling, IL 60090
847-537-8669

IN **BREMEN HOBBIES
& CRAFTS**
308 North Bowen Avenue
Bremen, IN 46506
800-569-3917

**CLAUSSEN'S HOBBY
& BIKE**
104 West Clark Street
Crown Point, IN 46307
219-663-3086

A A HOBBY SHOP
2023 West Franklin Street
Evansville, IN 47712
812-423-8888

PHIL'S HOBBY SHOP
1722 Lake Avenue
Fort Wayne, IN 46805
219-426-5056

HOBBY LAND
416 Coliseum Boulevard
Fort Wayne, IN 46805
219-483-8186

HOBBYLAND
204 South Main Street
Goshen, IN 46526
219-534-0027

GEORGE'S TRAIN SHOP
6986 North U.S. 24 East
Huntington, IN 46750
219-672-2539

**BILL'S MODEL RAILROAD
WAREHOUSE**
923 North Lynhurst
Indianapolis, IN 46214
317-481-0513

VARRY TRAINS
6742 East Washington Street
Indianapolis, IN 46219
317-375-0832

THE GREAT TRAIN STORE
147 Indianapolis Union
Station
39 West Jackson Place
Indianapolis, IN 46225
317-634-6688

N GAUGE TRAIN SHOP
4759 North Post Road
Indianapolis, IN 46226
317-898-4883

BIG 4-8-8-4 BOY HOBBIES
8893 Pendleton Pike
Indianapolis, IN 46226
317-898-6284

TOM METZLER
HOBBY CENTER
7418 Madison Avenue
Indianapolis, IN 46227
317-784-3580

HOBBYTOWN USA
5385 East 82nd Street
Indianapolis, IN 46250
317-845-4106

TRAIN EXPRESS
4310 West 96th Street
Indianapolis, IN 46268
317-879-9300

TOLIN K&K
403 Arnold Court
Kokomo, IN 46902
317-453-9793

HAWKINS RAIL SERVICES
903 Main Street
Lafayette, IN 47901
317-742-5577

EISELE PHOTOGRAPHY
1810 Ridgemoor Drive
Long Beach, IN 46360
219-874-3058

B & A HOBBIES & CRAFTS
408 Franklin Street
Michigan City, IN 46360
219-874-2382

HOBBYLAND
620 West Edison Road
Mishawaka, IN 46545
219-255-1722

GUPTA HOBBY CENTER
1701 West Jackson Street
Muncie, IN 47303
317-288-6505

NASHVILLE RAILROAD CO.
Antique Alley
Box 1273
Nashville, IN 47448
812-988-1558

CREST ENTERPRISES
HOBBIES
6672 East Poppy Lane
New Carlisle, IN 46552
219-654-8409

SPENCER'S CRAFTS
& HOBBIES
2015-2017 Ewing St. Rd.
Seymour, IN 47274
812-522-7480

MAIN STREET HOBBY
CENTER
108 East Main Street
Syracuse, IN 46567
219-457-4576

VALPARAISO PET
& HOBBY SHOP
18 North Washington
Valparaiso, IN 46383
219-462-8346

KS **GREAT AMERICAN TRAINS**
901 West 8th Street
Coffeyville, KS 67337
316-251-0640

TAYLOR'S TOYS
3120 West 10th Street
Great Bend, KS 67350
316-793-9698

POOLS PLUS INC.
21 East First
Hutchinson, KS 67501
316-662-0202

R/C HOBBIES
115 West 7th Street
Junction City, KS 66441
913-238-1877

DIGITAL TRAIN CONTROLS
5005 West 129th Street
Leawood, KS 66209
913-897-1398

DON'S RAILROAD
HOBBY SHOP
1223 Pierre Street
Manhattan, KS 66502
913-537-7624

AV & C TRAINS
AND SUPPLIES
110 South Main
McPherson, KS 67460
800-324-8023

J'S HOBBY HAVEN
5303 Johnson Drive
Mission, KS 66205
913-432-8820

D&T TOYS/HOBBY SHOP
1021 Washington Road,
Suite 200
Newton, KS
316-284-2030

PEACEVILLE TRAIN SHOP
432 East Santa Fe
Olathe, KS 66061
913-782-6965

THE COLLECTOR'S CHOICE
15105 Metcalf Avenue
Overland Park, KS 66202
913-681-6830

HOBBYTOWN USA
9270 Metcalf
Overland Park, KS 66212
913-649-7979

FUN FOR ALL HOBBIES
2023 SW Gage Boulevard
Topeka, KS 66604
913-272-5772

HOBBY CENTER, INC.
1034 East Harry Street
Wichita, KS 67211
316-269-3063

ENGINE HOUSE HOBBIES
2718 Boulevard Plaza
Wichita, KS 67211
316-685-6608

KY **HOBBYTOWN USA**
500 Winchester Avenue,
#232
Ashland, KY 41101
606-329-1299

JOHNNY'S
3719 Decoursey Avenue
Covington, KY 41015
606-261-6962

HOBBY HANGAR
1862 Petersburg Road
Hebron, KY 41042
606-334-4330

THE HOBBY SHOP
Pennyrile Mall
Hopkinsville, KY 42240
502-886-5747

HOBBYTOWN USA
2329-B Nicholasville Road
Lexington, KY 40503
606-277-5664

A-1 HOBBY
550 South Fifth Street
Louisville, KY 40202
502-584-0251

THE HOBBY HOUSE
4918 Preston Highway
Louisville, KY 40213
502-968-9467

CABOOSE CORNER
2015 Main Street
Paris, KY 40361
606-987-1257

PERRY'S R/C HOBBIES
214 Globe Street
Radcliff, KY 40160
502-351-7223

LA **HARE'S ART & HOBBY**
4529 Lee Street
Alexandria, LA 71302
318-443-2755

THE CAJUN RAILROAD
148 Croydon Avenue,
Suite A
Baton Rouge, LA 70806
504-926-5592

THE TRAIN STATION
1415 South Morrison
Boulevard
Hammond, LA 70403-5705
504-345-7601

KENNER TRAIN SHOP
2000 20th Street
Kenner, LA 70062
504-466-5876

MIKE'S TRAIN SHOP
1916 Williams Boulevard
Kenner, LA 70062
504-466-8531

**RON'S MODEL
RAILROAD SHOP**
1416 South College Road
Lafayette, LA 70518
318-232-5536

HUB HOBBY SUPPLY
2618 South Broad Street
New Orleans, LA 70125
504-822-3914

THE GREAT TRAIN STORE
1 Poydras Street #114
New Orleans, LA 70130
504-581-3531

**COOK'S COLLECTORS
CORNER INC.**
4402 Youree Drive
Shreveport, LA 71105
318-865-7632

ME **FREIGHT STATION**
Taylor Brook Mall
Auburn, ME 04210
207-784-6556

MAINE TRAINS
Route 4A, Hollis
Bar Mills, ME 04004
207-929-3621

IVERS SPECIALTIES
Fields Pond Road
Brewer, ME 04412
207-989-6189

ASK YOUR MOTHER
49 Pleasant Street
Brunswick, ME 04011
207-729-1542

SMALL'S TRAIN REPAIR
273 Tuttle Road
Cumberland, ME 04021
207-829-3757

**EAST BOOTHBAY
GENERAL STORE**
Ocean Point Road
East Boothbay, ME 04544
207-633-4503

THE CRAFT BARN
Mill Mall, Route 1A
Ellsworth, ME 04605
207-667-7257

SCALE RAILS
1934 Log Cabin Road
Kennebunkport, ME 04046
207-967-3024

**MAINE'S
MASSACHUSETTS HOUSE**
P.O. Box 210, Route One
Lincolnville, ME 04849
207-789-5705

TRAIN & TROOPER
13 Memorial Highway
North Yarmouth, ME 04097
207-829-3211

TRAIN TRACK
Belgrade Road
Oakland, ME 04963
207-465-3081

**SULLIVAN PHOTO
& TRAIN CENTER, INC.**
736 Forest Avenue
Portland, ME 04103
207-773-0146

THE CHRISTMAS NOOK
668 Rockland Street
Rockport, ME 04843
207-230-0711

MD **THE SHIP AND SOLDIER
SHOP**
58 Maryland Ave.
Annapolis, MD 21401
410-268-1141

STAR HOBBY
1244 Ritchie Highway
Annapolis (Arnold),
MD 21401
410-544-7547

M. B. KLEIN
162 North Gay Street
Baltimore, MD 21202
410-539-6207

**ANTIQUE TRAIN
& TOY WORLD**
3626 Falls Road
Baltimore, MD 21211
410-889-0040

**STONELEIGH CYCLE
& HOBBY, INC.**
6717 York Road
Baltimore, MD 21212
410-377-4447

**FRENCH'S TRAINS
& HOBBIES, INC.**
30-1/2 North Dundalk
Avenue
Baltimore, MD 21222
410-285-5809

**THE AMERICAN HOBBY
CENTER**
Bel Air Plaza Shopping
Center
565 Baltimore Pike
Bel Air, MD 21014
410-836-5087

**DENNISON'S TRACKSIDE
HOBBIES**
14 South Main Street
Berlin, MD 21811
410-641-2438

PRO CUSTOM HOBBIES
721 Fredrick Road
Catonsville, MD 21228
410-788-8770

**BOXCAR BOBBY
& BILLY BEAR**
102 Country Day Road
Chester, MD 21619
410-643-3103

BURRETT HOBBIES
9920 Rhode Island Avenue
College Park, MD 20740
301-982-5032

HOWARD'S TRAINS
163-A Green Point Road
East New Market,
MD 21631
410-943-4658

LAD'S HOBBY CENTER
3570 St. Johns Lane
Ellicott City, MD 21042
410-750-7228

TRAIN WORKS
2934 Cedarhurst Road
Finksburg, MD 21048
410-526-0018

FOREST HILL STATION
15 East Jarrettsville Road
Forest Hill, MD 21050
410-893-1089

**TRAINS, TOYS
& TREASURES**
1450 West Patrick Street
Frederick, MD 21702
301-662-5202

ENGINE HOUSE HOBBIES
315-G East Diamond Avenue
Gaithersburg, MD 20879
301-590-0816

PASTIMES
531 Quince Orchard Road
Gaithersburg, MD 20878
301-977-7902

**DAD & SONS
DISCOUNT HOBBIES**
205 Thelma Avenue
Glen Burnie, MD 21061
410-761-7810

**MAYBERRY & SONS
TRAINS & HOBBIES**
10527 Summit Avenue
Kensington, MD 20895
301-564-9360

LIONEL BUY & SELL
3610 University Boulevard
Kensington, MD 20895
301-949-4000

PEACH CREEK SHOPS
201 Main Street
Laurel, MD 20707
301-498-9071

DTL/BRUNSWICK SHOPS
#4 South Main Street
Mt. Airy, MD 21771
301-607-8155

TOY TRAFFIC, INC.
18224 Village Mart Drive
Olney, MD 20832
301-774-2444

TOY WORLD
825 F Rockville Pike
Rockville, MD 20852
301-424-0430

TIMONIUM HOBBIES
2189 Greenspring Drive
Timonium, MD 21093
410-560-0142

**CATOCTIN MOUNTAIN
TRAINS & HOBBIES**
1 East Main Street
Thurmont, MD 21788
301-694-8331

MAIL BAG HOBBIES
16817 Gorsuch Mill Road
Upperco, MD 21155
800-821-6377

**DOUG'S HOBBY/MORAN'S
ARTS & CRAFTS**
2935 Crain Highway
Waldorf, MD 20601
301-843-7774

MA **ACTON MODEL
RAILROAD CENTER**
8 Windsor Avenue
Acton, MA 01720
508-264-4020

BEDFORD TRAIN SHOP
32 Shawnsheen Avenue
Bedford, MA 01730
617-275-7525

SCALE MODEL PRODUCTS
63 Hudson Road
P.O. Box 72
Bolton, MA 01740
508-779-5056

CUSTOM TRAIN WORKS
24 Tina Avenue
Brockton, MA 02402
508-580-5644

CRANBERRY JUNCTION HOBBIES
145 South Main Street
Carver, MA 02330
508-866-4223

TRAINS ON TRACKS
21 Summer Street
Chelmsford, MA 01824
508-256-3465

MASTER HOBBIES
565 Main Street
Cherry Valley, MA 01611
508-892-1440

THE TOY SHOP OF CONCORD
4 Walden Street
Concord, MA 01742
508-369-2553

DUXBURY GREEN, INC.
382 Kings Town Way
Duxbury, MA 02332
617-585-2164

JACOB B. PIKE TRAINS
230 Grove Street
East Bridgewater, MA 02333
508-378-2912

THE FAMILY HOBBY SHOP
48 Shaker Road
East Longmeadow,
MA 01028
413-525-7345

FALMOUTH HOBBIES
847 Main Street
Falmouth, MA 02540
508-540-4551

THE TOY DOCTOR OF CAPE COD
17 Meredith Road
Forestdale, MA 02644
508-477-1186

BAY STATE MODELS
8 Rollins Street
Groveland, MA 01834
508-372-8828

HOOT TOOT 'N WHISTLE HOBBIES
49 Russell Street
Hadley, MA 01035
413-585-8668

THE BRASS CABOOSE SHOP
669 West Washington Street
Hanson, MA 02341
617-447-0100

HOBBY BARN
5 Anderson Ave.
Kingston, MA 02364
617-585-2288

SHEPAUG RAILROAD COMPANY
24 Columbia Street
Leominster, MA 01453
508-537-2277

ON TRAK TRAINS
Mayflower Plaza
Manomet, MA 02360
508-224-7020

THE SPARE TIME SHOP
Rt. 20 East
Marlborough, MA 01752
508-481-5786

WEST STREET HOBBIES
Rte 109
Medway, MA 02053
508-533-1231

MODELER'S JUNCTION
88 Lowell Street
Methuen, MA 01844
508-683-0885

MIKE ROSE HOBBIES
545 Chase Road
North Dartmouth,
MA 02747
508-996-9728

LINDSTROMS
50 Elm Street
North Easton, MA 02356
508-238-6224

THE TRAIN PLACE PLUS
247 West Main Street
Northborough, MA 01532
508-393-2487

STRICTLY TRAINS
58 West Main Street
Northborough, MA 01532
508-393-8442

NORTON PROTOTYPE HOBBIES
160 Taunton Avenue
Norton, MA 02766
508-285-6712

NORTH EAST TRAINS
43 Main Street
Peabody, MA 01960
508-532-1615

BRITISH TOY TRAINS
Mayflower Plaza
Plymouth, MA 02360
508-224-7649

BILL'S FRIENDLY TRAIN SHOPPE
414 Center Street
Randolph, MA 02368
617-986-5295

ED'S BOXCAR
611 Center Street
Raynham, MA 02767
508-822-6563

JACK'S TRAINS
Christmas Tree Lane
Rutland, MA 01543
508-886-4394

SHINING TIME HOBBIES
Seekonk Plaza, Rt. 6
Seekonk, MA 02771
508-336-4040

DON MILLS MODELS
235 Taunton Avenue
Seekonk, MA 02771
508-336-5573

THE TRAIN SHOP
Andrew Square
388 Dorchester Street
South Boston, MA 02127
617-268-6194

ACE HOBBIES
Whistlestop Village
670 Depot Street
South Easton, MA 02375
508-238-7350

PIONEER VALLEY HOBBIES
28 Hanover Street
Springfield, MA 01105
413-732-5531

THE HOBBY CONNECTION
4 Franklin Street
Stoneham, MA 02180
617-438-1697

KEN'S TRAINS
Mill Village
Rt. 20
Sudbury, MA 01776
508-443-6883

HOBBY EMPORIUM
440 Middlesex Road
Tyngsboro, MA 01879
508-649-5055

TUCKER'S HOBBIES
8 Bacon Street, Box 1090
Warren, MA 01083
413-436-5318

HENRY'S HOBBY HOUSE, INC.
67 West Boylston Street,
Unit #1
West Boylston, MA 01583
508-835-6165

MY DAD'S TRAINS
310 Franklin Street
P.O. Box 945
Wrentham, MA 02093
508-384-3555

ME **TRAIN & TROOPER**
68 Memorial Hwy.
North Yarmouth, ME 04097
207-829-3211

MI **RIDER'S HOBBY SHOP**
115 West Liberty Street
Ann Arbor, MI 48104
313-668-8950

THE EMPORIUM COMPANY
201 East Douglass Street
Bangor, MI 49013
616-427-8282

MEYER'S TOY WORLD
72 North Avenue
Battle Creek, MI 49017
616-963-2768

CUM CRAFT, INC.
1008 Adams
Bay City, MI 48706
517-892-6177

DAVE'S MODEL TRAINS
10644 Old U.S. 31
Berrien Springs, MI 49103
616-473-5533

RIDER'S HOBBY SHOP
42007 Ford Road
Canton, MI 48187
313-981-8700

J & W MODEL TRAINS, INC.
6450 East Becht Road
Coloma, MI 49038
616-468-5586

ACE HANSES HARDWARE
13320 West Warren
Dearborn, MI 48126-2494
313-846-0900

JACKIES GIFTS
9226 Summit Street
Erie, MI 48133
419-726-4044

THE IMAGINATION STATION
12777 South Saginaw Street
Grand Blanc, MI 48439
810-603-1600

JOE'S HOBBY CENTER
35203 Grand River
Farmington, MI 48024
313-477-6266

RIDER'S HOBBY SHOP
3012 Corunna Road
Flint, MI 48503
313-234-4051

P & D HOBBY SHOP
31902 Groesbeck Highway
Fraser, MI 48026
810-296-6116

HARBOURFRONT HOBBIES AND CRAFTS
707 Washington Street
Grand Haven, MI 49504
616-842-2910

MEYER'S HOBBY HOUSE, INC.
2136 Plainfield Avenue, NE
Grand Rapids, MI 49505
616-363-8347

RIDER'S HOBBY SHOP
2055 28th Street, SE
Grand Rapids, MI 49508
616-247-9933

HOBBY WORLD
2851 Clyde Park SW
Grand Rapids, MI 49509
616-538-6130

COBBLESTONE CRAFTS & HOBBY
210 Central Avenue
Holland, MI 49423
616-396-3029

HOUSE OF HOBBIES
U. S. 31 at Felch
Holland, MI 49424
616-786-3686

STAN'S ROUNDHOUSE
8344 Portage Road
Kalamazoo, MI 49002
616-324-0300

THE TRAIN BARN
10234 East Shore Drive
Kalamazoo, MI 49002
616-327-4016

RIDER'S HOBBY SHOP
4415 South Westnedge
Kalamazoo, MI 49008
616-349-2666

THE HOBBY HUB
526 Frandor Avenue
Lansing, MI 48912
517-351-5843

RIDER'S HOBBY SHOP
1609 East Michigan Avenue
Lansing, MI 48912
517-485-0700

J & D HOBBIES
288 South Main Street
Lapeer, MI 48446
313-664-1414

G&G TRAINS
1800 Baseline Road
Leslie, MI 49251
517-589-5877

MERRI-SEVEN TRAINS
19155 Merriman Road
Livonia, MI 48152
810-477-0550

EARL'S TRAIN WORLD
10560 Cascade Road, S.E.
Lowell, MI 49331
616-868-7495

RIDER'S HOBBY SHOP
32115 John R. Road
Madison Heights, MI 48071
313-589-8111

THE TRAIN DOCTOR
1576 River Road
Millersburg, MI 49759
517-733-2016

TOOT'S TRAIN STATION
6 East First Street
Monroe, MI 48161
313-242-0003

MONROE HOBBIES, INC.
317 South Monroe Street
Monroe, MI 48161
313-242-3130

**MICHIGAN PADDLESPORT
AND HOBBY SHOP**
9260 McGregor Road
Pinckney, MI 48169
313-426-1651

L & J HOBBIES
8847 Portage Road
Portage, MI 49002
616-323-1010

JOE'S HOBBY CENTER
105 South Livernois
Rochester, MI 48063
313-651-8842

ALCOVE HOBBY SHOP
2424 North Woodward
Avneue
Royal Oak, MI 48073
810-545-6237

TRAIN CENTER HOBBIES
4508 North Woodward
Royal Oak, MI 48073
810-549-6500

**BRASSEUR ELECTRIC
TRAINS**
418 Court Street
Saginaw, MI 48602
517-793-4753

**WHISTLE STOP HOBBIES
& TRAINS**
21714 Harper Avenue
St. Clair Shores, MI 48080
313-771-6770

P&G HOBBIES
3975 17 Mile
Sterling Heights, MI 48310
313-264-0060

PROP SHOP HOBBIES
23326 Van Dyke
Warren, MI 48089
810-757-7160

YOUNG'S GARDEN MART
27825 Ryan Road
Warren, MI 48092
313-573-0230

**BOB'S HOBBY
& COLLECTOR'S SHOP**
340 & 358 North Main St.
Watervliet, MI 49098
616-463-7452

DAVE'S HOBBY & TV
29026 Warren Road
Westland, MI 48185
313-422-4464

**NANKIN HARDWARE
& HOBBY**
35101 Ford Road
Westland, MI 48185
313-722-5700

MN **GREAT NORTHERN
HOBBIES**
323 Minnesota Ave.
Bemidji, MN 56601
218-759-0200

THE GREAT TRAIN STORE
#166 Mall Of America
Bloomington, MN 55425
612-851-9988

CARR'S HOBBY
2009 West Superior Street
Duluth, MN 55806
218-722-7129

HOBBY JUNCTION
1340 Duckwood Drive
Eagan, MN 55123
612-687-0975

HUB HOBBY CENTER
82 Minnesota Avenue
Little Canada, MN 55117
612-490-1675

DON'S HOBBY
424 South Front
Mankato, MN 56001
507-387-1330

HOBBY HUT
EasTen Shopping Center
East Highway 10
Moorhead, MN 56560
218-233-5590

BADERS BIKE
& HOBBY CENTER
121 Eighth Street South
Moorhead, MN 56560
218-236-8852

PERRY'S HOBBIES
114 Vernon Avenue
P.O. Box 68W
Morgan, MN 56266
507-249-3173

BECKER'S MODEL
RAILROAD SUPPLY
2140 Silver Lake Road
New Brighton, MN 55112
612-635-9480

OSSEO SPORTS
TRAIN WORLD
340 Central Avenue
Osseo, MN 55369
612-425-7171

HUB HOBBY CENTER
6416 Penn Avenue S
Richfield, MN 55423
612-866-9575

HOBBY DEPOT LTD.
1208 East 66th
Richfield, MN 55423
612-869-4179

HUB HOBBY CENTER
4114 Lakeland Avenue N
Robbinsdale, MN 55422
612-535-5628

MINIATURES-
COLLECTIBLES-HOBBIES
415 South Broadway
Rochester, MN 55904
507-286-9029

MOON'S HOBBY SHOP
Miracle Mile Mini-Mall
Rochester, MN 55902
507-281-8321

BAKER'S CRAFT & HOBBY
Division Place Fashion Center
2738 West Division Street
Saint Cloud, MN 56301
612-252-0460

SCALE MODEL SUPPLIES
458 North Lexington Parkway
Saint Paul, MN 55104
612-646-7781

UNIVERSITY HOBBIES
8185 University Avenue NE
Spring Lake Park, MN 55432
612-780-4189

A&E RAILROAD/
AL'S REPAIR, INC.
Highway 32 South
Thief River Falls, MN 56701
218-681-4251

MO **CHECKERED FLAG**
HOBBY COUNTRY
14755 Manchester Road
Ballwin, MO 63011
314-394-7600

MAINLINE TRAINS
807 Main Street
Blue Springs, MO 64015
816-224-6962

HENZE'S HOBBY HOUSE
715 New Florissant Road
South
Florissant, MO 63031
314-839-0600

THE TRAIN DEPOT
14070 New Halls Ferry Road
Florissant, MO 63033
314-837-5902

UNION STATION HOBBIES
2122-1/2 Main Street
Joplin, MO
417-623-3959

HALLS CROWN CENTER
200 East 25th Street
Kansas City, MO 64108
816-274-4533

HOBBYTOWN USA
217 South M-291 Highway
Lees Summit, MO 64063
816-525-6885

NEWMAN N SCALE
10 Westwood Place
Moberly, MO 65270
816-263-4182

J&L HOBBY & TRAINS
1362 J NW Highway 9
Parkville, MO 64152
816-746-1282

P M TRAINS AND ROCKS
10101 East 64th Street
Raytown, MO 64133
816-358-6160

HOBBYTOWN USA
3312 South Glenstone Avenue
Springfield, MO 65804
417-889-5757

CRC HOBBIES
3300 Dale, Suite 104
St. Joseph, MO 64506
816-233-5956

HOBBYTOWN USA
13875 Manchester Road
St. Louis, MO 63011
314-394-0177

THE GREAT TRAIN STORE
122 St. Louis Union Station
St. Louis, MO 63103
314-231-7731

NORTH CENTRAL HOBBIES
9120 Lackland Road
St. Louis, MO 63114
314-426-0031

ELECTRIC TRAIN OUTLET
8961 Page Avenue
St. Louis, MO 63114
314-428-2211

KIRKWOOD HOBBIES
127 West Jefferson Avenue
St. Louis, MO 63122
314-821-5596

TINKERTOWN INC.
9666 Clayton Road
St. Louis, MO 63124
314-991-4311

TRAINS TO GO
115 West Lockwood
Webster Groves, MO 63119
314-961-9150

MS **THE EMPORIUM**
136 Rue Magnolia
Biloxi, MS 39530
601-432-1326

S & J CUSTOM MODELS
Post Office Box 1207
Biloxi, MS 39533-1207
601-392-3167

HOBBY CORNER
1534 North First Avenue
Laurel, MS 39440
601-649-4501

**CONDUCTOR'S CHOICE
MODEL TRAINS**
189 East Main Street
Verona, MS 38879
601-842-5465

MT **JIM'S JUNCTION**
811-B 16th Street West
Billings, MT 59102
406-259-5354

CENTRAL HOBBIES
1401 Central Avenue
Billings, MT 59102
406-259-9004

**CENTER COURT SPORTS
AND HOBBY**
103 State Street
Hamilton, MT 59840
406-363-0016

VEK RAILWAY SUPPLY
1228 Bozeman Avenue
Helena, MT 59601
800-411-3394

THE RAIL YARD
860 North Meridian Road
Kalispell, MT 59901
406-756-7848

TREASUE CHEST
1612 Benton Avenue
Missoula, MT 59801
406-549-7992

NC **ANTIQUE TRAIN & TOY CO.**
523 Merrimon Avenue
Asheville, NC 28804
704-253-7648

**CAROLINA ART,
CRAFT & HOBBY**
128 Swannanoa River Road
Asheville, NC 28805
704-258-2227

**THE MODELERS HOBBY
SHOP**
4808C Central Avenue
Charlotte, NC 28205
704-537-9963

**GARY'S TRAINS
& HOBBIES**
2711 West Main Street
Elizabeth City, NC 27909
919-333-1721

**A READY TO RUN
HOBBY SHOP**
3600 Hwy 49 South
Harrisburg, NC 28075
704-455-2220

**DR. B'S TOYS
& NATURE SHOP**
418 North Main Street
Hendersonville, NC 28792
704-696-8697

LELAND'S TOY TRAINS
302 South Center Street
Hildebran, NC 28637
704-397-2457

**SOUTHEASTERN
HOBBY SUPPLY**
415 Virginia Avenue
Marion, NC 28752
704-652-3704

DRY BRIDGE STATION
236 North Main Street
Mt. Airy, NC 27030
910-786-9811

THE HOBBY SHOP
2020 Cameron Street
Raleigh, NC 27605
919-833-1123

JOE'S TRAIN REPAIR
404 Shetland Road
Rougemont, NC 27572
919-471-2613

**LITTLE CHOO CHOO
SHOP, INC.**
500 South Salisbury Avenue
Spencer, NC 28159
704-637-8717

TODD'S TRAIN DEPOT,
404 West Wilson Avenue
Wendell, NC 27591
919-365-5006

**THE ANTIQUE BARN
& TRAIN SHOP,**
2810 Forest Hills Road
Wilson, NC 27893
919-237-6778

THE HOBBY CORNER,
464 Knollwood Street,
Winston-Salem, NC 27103
910-768-2345

ND **DAVES HOBBIES**
200 West Main Avenue
Bismarck, ND 58501
701-255-6353

OMNI HOBBY & GIFT
4340 13th Avenue SW
Fargo, ND 58103
701-282-5675

MCGIFFIN'S
1200 South Washington
Grand Forks, ND 58201
701-772-5311

**AEROPORT HOBBY
SHOPPE**
2112 North Broadway
Minot, ND 58701
701-838-1658

NE **OREGON TRAIL HOBBIES**
2970 North 10th Street #4
Gering, NE 69341
308-635-7900

HOBBYTOWN USA
3537 West 13th Street
Grand Island, NE 68803
308-382-3451

HOBBYTOWN USA
East Park Mall
220 North 66th Street
Lincoln, NE 68505
402-434-5056

TRAIN CELLAR
4711 Huntington, #5
Lincoln, NE 68504
402-464-4925

HOUSE OF TRAINS
8106 Maple Street
Omaha, NE 68134
402-391-2311

SCALE-RAIL
4205 South 87th Street,
Box 27242
Omaha, NE 68127
402-339-3380

**TRAINMAN TRADING
POST**
5215 South 21st Street
Omaha, NE 68107
402-734-7233

NH **CUSTOM TRAINS**
Main Street
P.O. Box 48
Bath, NH 03740
603-747-3492

**ROBERTS RAILROAD
& HOBBIES**
Route 106
Concord, NH 03301
603-224-9258

RAILS AND CRAFTS, INC.
637 Main Street
Laconia, NH 03246
603-524-2824

PERKINS ROAD DEPOT
18 Perkins Road
Londonderry, NH 03053
603-432-5054

ARLINGTON STATION
236 Wedgewood Lane
Manchester, NH 03109
603-622-5230

**MOUNTAIN TRAINS
& HOBBIES**
673 Elm Street
Manchester, NH 03101
603-641-1113

MODELS PLUS
72 Main Street
Meredith, NH 03253
603-279-9026

THE BRASS CABOOSE
Norcross Place
North Conway, NH 03860
603-356-9922

**FITTS PHOTO
& HOBBY SHOP**
Village Shopping Center
U.S. Route 1
North Hampton, NH 03862
603-964-9292

THE LOOSE CABOOSE
Rt. 12
North Swanzey, NH 03446
603-357-8821

**ROBERTS RAILROAD
& HOBBIES**
Route 4 at Route 152
Post Office Box 431
Northwood, NH 03261-0431
603-942-5193

MINUTEMAN PAINT SHOP
Gumpus Hill Road
Post Office Box 907
Pelham, NH 03076-0907
603-635-3196

F. C. DUMAINE ENTERPRISES
Sharon Road, RFD 2, Box 347
Petersborough, NH 03458
603-878-2163

STARLIGHT HOBBIES
953 Islington Street
Portsmouth, NH 03801
 603-436-7625

ROBBIE'S HOBBIES
450 South Broadway
Salem, NH 03079
603-894-1179

TREASURED TOYS
5 North Broadway
Salem, NH 03079
603-898-7224

GRANITE STATE HOBBY
855 Stark Highway South
Weare, NH 03281
603-529-1670

**KLICKETY KLACK
RAILROAD**
Jct. Rts. 28-109 & 109A
Wolfeboro Falls, NH 03896
603-569-5384

NJ **THE HOBBY SHOP**
1077C State Highway #34
Aberdeen, NJ 07747
908-583-0505

THE ROUNDHOUSE INC.
400 New Jersey Avenue
Absecon, NJ 08201
609-641-8474

**OCEAN COUNTRY R/C
& TRAINS**
219 Atlantic City Boulevard
Beachwood, NJ 08722
908-505-9477

U.S. #1 HOBBY
Somerset Shopping Center
Bridgewater, NJ 08807
908-218-1515

TONY'S TRAIN TOWN
452 Pompton Avenue
Cedar Grove, NJ 07009
201-857-2337

JERRY'S TRAIN GALLERY
48 River Road
Chatham, NJ 07928
201-635-6235

**THE HOBBY
& GAME ANNEX**
Rt. 24, Chester Mall
Chester, NJ 07930
908-879-4263

**COLLECTORS HOBBY
STORE**
290 Lakeview Avenue
Clifton, NJ 07011
201-772-1220

FUN ATTIC
65 Laneco Plaza
Clinton, NJ 08809
908-735-6750

JUST TRAINS
41 Highway 34
Colts Neck, NJ 07722
908-409-2772

HOBBY HEAVEN
16 North Union Avenue
Cranford, NJ 07016
908-272-7660

F & M HOBBIES
3118 Route 10
Denville, NJ 07834
201-361-0042

ON THE TRACKS
1 Niagara Street
Dumont, NJ 07628
201-385-7161

MEYER'S DISCOUNT STORE
595 Route 18
East Brunswick, NJ 08816
908-257-8800

FOTO DEPOT
110 Route 9 Rd-3
Englishtown, NJ 07726
908-536-0056

LITTLE HOBBY'S
151 Highway 31
Flemington, NJ 08822
908-782-3474

**SPORTS AMERICA
& HOBBY CENTER,**
Route 1305, PO Box 255
Florence, NJ 08518
609-499-2992

CHICKS HOBBY CENTER
924 Berkley Road
Gibbstown, NJ 08027
609-423-0773

FINE SCALE HOBBIES
2048 Highway 31 North
Glen Gardner, NJ 08826
908-537-2226

HAZLET TRAIN SHOP
25 Brailley Lane
Hazlet, NJ 07734
908-264-7429

**D K & B RAILWAY
SUPPLIES**
114 Main Street
Hightstown, NJ 08520
609-448-5070

C B TRAIN DEPOT
107 Prospect Place
Hillsdale, NJ 07642
201-666-9598

JACKSON HOBBY SHOP
West County Line Road
Jackson, NJ 08527
908-364-3334

AAA HOBBIES & CRAFTS
White Horse & Marion
Magnolia, NJ 08049
609-435-1188

STANDARD HOBBY SUPPLY
Post Office Box 801
Mahwah, NJ 07430
800-223-1355

**STAFFORD TRAINS
& HOBBIES**
747 Route 9 North
Manahawkin, NJ 08050
609-597-3626

MAPLEWOOD HOBBY
410 Ridgewood Road
Maplewood, NJ 07040
201-378-3839

HOBBY SHOP
Rt. 34 Strathmore Shopping
Center
Matawan, NJ 07747
908-583-0505

IRON HORSE HOBBIES
116 Flock Road
Mercerville, NJ 08619
609-586-2282

Z & Z HOBBIES
116 Flock Road
Mercerville, NJ 08619
609-586-2282

**MILLBURN TRAIN
& HOBBY CENTER**
158 Spring Street
Millburn, NJ 07041
201-379-4242

THE TRAIN STATION
Romaine Road
Mountain Lakes, NJ 07046
201-263-1979

TRACK N TRAINS, INC.
111 West Broad Street
Palmyra, NJ 08065
609-786-0080

TECH-TOYS
370 Route 46 West
Parsippany, NJ 07075
201-227-7012

TED'S ENGINE HOUSE
6307 Westfield Avenue
Pennsauken, NJ 08110
609-662-0222

BEN FRANKLIN STORE
10 Wanaque Avenue
Pompton Lakes, NJ 07442
201-835-8008

THE TRAIN SHOP
142 Route 23 North
Pompton Plains, NJ 07444
201-696-7708

HI-WAY HOBBY HOUSE
806 U.S. Route 17
Ramsey, NJ 07446
201-327-0075

**AMERICA'S HOBBY
CENTER, INC.**
820 Kinderkamack Road
River Edge, NJ 07661
201-265-2044

CHOO CHOO EDDIES
38 Ames Avenue
Rutherford, NJ 07073
201-438-4588

TOM'S MODEL TRAINS
1791A East Second Street
Scotch Plains, NJ 07076
908-322-6122

**THE BIG LITTLE
RAILROAD SHOP**
5 North Doughty Avenue
Somerville, NJ 08876
908-429-0220

U.S. #1 HOBBY
Hadley Center
South Plainfield, NJ 07080
908-754-7788

**JERSEY SHORE
HOBBY CENTER**
304 Morris Avenue
Spring Lake, NJ 07762
908-449-2383

**DOHERTY'S WHISTLE
STOP TRAINS**
721 Springfield Avenue
Summit, NJ 07901
908-277-4442

SUSSEX COUNTY HOBBY
69 Main Street
Sussex, NJ 07461
201-875-8580

THE HOBBY CENTER
1406-B Stuyvesant Avenue
Union, NJ 07083
908-688-5983

THE GINGERBREAD STOP
174 Mount Bethel Road
Warren, NJ 07059
908-647-1660

E.M.C. TRACKS & TRAINS
235 A. Rt. 23 South
Wayne, NJ 07470
201-628-4838

OSPREY HOBBIES
189 Berdan Avenue,
Suite 177
Wayne, NJ 07470
201-853-6556

TOTOWA HOBBY SHOP
131 Mountain View
Boulevard
Wayne, NJ 07470
201-696-5170

**MODEL RAILWAY
POST OFFICE**
26 Industrial Road
West Milford, NJ 07480
800-328-6776

SATTLER'S HOBBY SHOP
14 Haddon Avenue
Westmont, NJ 08108
609-854-7136

HERE'S JOHHNY'S
807 North Broad Street
Woodbury, NJ 08096
609-848-0018

NM **ALBUQUERQUE HOBBY
COMPANY**
1431 Eubank Boulevard N. E.
Albuquerque, NM 87112
505-275-1882

HOBBIES 'N' STUFF
9577-L Osuna Road N. E.
Albuquerque, NM 87111
505-293-1217

MBJ LOCK & HOBBIES
2626-C San Pedro Drive N.E.
Albuquerque, NM 87110
505-881-9795

SOUTHWEST HOBBIES
2252-D Wyoming Blvd. N.E.
Albuquerque, NM 87112
505-296-3013

TRAINS WEST, INC.
6001 San Mateo Boulevard
NE, Suite B-3
Albuquerque, NM 87109
505-881-2322

THE HOBBY HUT
126 Wyatt Drive
Las Cruces, NM 88005
505-524-0991

TSARSKOE SELO
1 Bursum Road
Mogollon, NM 88050
505-539-2766

NV **B & R RAILWAYS**
3450 South Procyon,
Suite E
Las Vegas, NV 89102
702-251-5787

HOBBYTOWN USA
4719 Faircenter Parkway
Las Vegas, NV 89102
702-259-5295

HOBBYTOWN USA
3121 North Rainbow
Boulevard
Las Vegas, NV 89108
702-655-0693

NORTH STAR DEPOT
1105 North Nellis Boulevard
Las Vegas, NV 89110
702-437-0835

PRC TRAINS, INC.
3920-J West Charleston
Boulevard
Las Vegas, NV 89102
702-258-7768

THE TRAIN ENGINEER
2550 Chandler #53
Las Vegas, NV 89117
702-597-1754

TRAIN EXCHANGE
6008 Boulder Highway
Las Vegas, NV 89122
702-456-8766

THE GREAT TRAIN STORE
2121 South Casino Drive
Laughlin, NV 89029
702-298-6235

**HENSON'S HOBBIES
EMPORIUM**
5045 South McCarran
Boulevard
Reno, NV 89502
702-825-9670

HIGH SIERRA MODELS
3677 Kings Row
Reno, NV 89503
702-747-7444

HOBBIES OF RENO
535 East Moana Lane
Reno, NV 89502
702-826-6006

NY **THE TRAIN MASTER, LTD.**
4 Highland Avenue
Albany, NY 12205
518-489-4777

HobbyTown USA
3332 Sheridan Drive
Amherst, NY 14226
716-833-7700

**B.E.A.M. ELECTRONICS
HOBBIES & VIDEO**
7830 State Route 434
Apalachin, NY 13732
607-625-2222

**C&D JUNCTION
TRAIN SHOP**
4845 Lakewood Ashville Road
Ashville, NY 14710
716-763-4721

RUDY'S HOBBY & ART
35-16 30th Avenue
Astoria, NY 11103
718-545-8280

THE DEPOT
258 Milton Avenue
Ballston Spa, NY 12020
518-885-8789

**JERICHO HOBBY
AND TRAIN CENTER**
252-04 Hillside Avenue
Bellerose, NY 11426
718-347-2160

GEORGE'S CABOOSE
85 Robinson Street
Binghamton, NY 13904
607-771-8358

**HUDSON SHORES MODEL
TRAIN DEPOT**
547-D Western Highway
Blauvelt, NY 10913
914-398-2407

PEARL PHARMACY
717 Burke Avenue
Bronx, NY 10467
718-882-4524

HOBBY KING
2720 Avenue U
Brooklyn, NY 11229
718-648-5399

STANLEY'S
4914 Fourth Avenue
Brooklyn, NY 11220
718-492-9313

TRAIN WORLD
751 McDonald Avenue
Brooklyn, NY 11218
718-436-7072

WALT'S HOBBY SHOP, INC.
7909 Fifth Avenue
Brooklyn, NY 11209
718-745-4991

**GRAND CENTRAL
STATION HOBBIES**
1845 Clinton Street
Buffalo, NY 14206
716-821-1808

K-VAL HOBBIES
277 Hinman Avenue
Buffalo, NY 14216
716-875-2837

**NIAGARA HOBBY
& CRAFT MART**
3366 Union Road
Buffalo, NY 14225
716-681-1666

HARRY'S DEPOT
2425 Middle Country Road
Centereach, NY 11720
516-471-5889

THE HOBBY HOUSE
8623 Main Street
Clarence, NY 14031
716-631-3447

MAINLINE HOBBIES
9135 Sheridan Drive
Clarence, NY 14031
716-632-8816

**SYRACUSE TRAIN
& HOBBY**
8135 Rt. 11
Clay, NY 13041
315-422-3328

LARKFIELD HOBBY CENTER
82 Larkfield Road
East Northport, NY 11731
516-261-5502

DESPATCH JUNCTION
100 Station Road
East Rochester, NY 14445
716-385-5570

SUSIE-Q HOBBY SHOP
Bushville-Swan Lake Road
RD Box 220
Ferndale, NY 12734
914-292-0921

D-J MODEL TRAINS
397 Reynolds Road
Fort Edward, NY 12828
518-793-2167

NASSAU HOBBY CENTER
43 West Merrick Road
Freeport, NY 11520
516-378-9594

LAKE CITY HOBBIES
30 Cherry Street
Geneva, NY 14456
315-781-0807

TRAINS PLUS
12 Warren Street
Glens Falls, NY 12801
518-761-0173

ARTCRAFT
5914 Camp Road
Hamburg, NY 14075
716-649-3079

THE HAMBURG MODEL RAILROAD STATION
4 Scott Street
Hamburg, NY 14075
716-649-3568

HOBBY IMAGES
89 Jerusalem Avenue
Hicksville, NY 11801
516-822-8259

RIDGE ROAD STATION
16131 West Ridge Road
Holley, NY 14470
716-638-6000

THE CABOOSE, INC.
208 Wall Street
Huntington, NY 11743
516-427-8288

ROCK RIVER MODEL HOBBIES
7762 Rock River Road
Interlaken, NY 14847
607-532-9489

SAUNDERS GREENHOUSE & HOBBIES
1279 Dryden Road
Ithaca, NY 14850
607-273-6331

THE TRAIN SHOP
210 Grand Avenue
Johnson City, NY 13790
607-797-9035

J AND J'S HOBBIES, INC.
37 North Front
Kingston, NY 12401
914-338-7174

PERFORMANCE HOBBY
900 Ulster Avenue
Kingston, NY 12401
914-338-0035

LAKE LUZERNE TRAIN & HOBBY
1933 Lake Avenue,
Box 465, Route 9N
Lake Luzerne, NY 12846
518-696-4905

DOLLHOUSE JUNCTION
679 Hawkins Avenue
Lake Ronkonkoma,
NY 11779
516-467-1222

JP'S TRAINS
277 Troy Schenectady Road
Latham, NY 12110
518-782-0981

KURTS TRAINS & HOBBIES
9440 Perry Road
Le Roy, NY 14482
516-768-2835

HOJACK HOBBIES
400 Buckley Road
Liverpool, NY 13088
315-457-2226

TRAINLAND
293 Sunrise Highway
Lynbrook, NY 11569
516-599-7080

POPS HOBBIES
2657 State Highway 310
Madrid, NY 13660
315-322-7677

MILLER'S
335 Mamaroneck Avenue
Mamaroneck, NY 10543
914-698-5070

AREA HOBBIES, INC.
15 West Main Street
Middletown, NY 10940
914-343-7141

CITY DEPOT MODEL RAILROAD STORE
334 East Main Street
Middletown, NY 10940
914-341-0838

TONY'S TRAIN STATION
841 Rt. 211 East
Middletown, NY 10940
914-692-5330

WILLIS HOBBIES
285 Willis Avenue
Mineola, NY 11501
516-746-3944

AMERICA'S HOBBY CENTER INC.
146 West 22nd Street
New York, NY 10011
212-675-8922

RED CABOOSE
23 West 45th Street
New York, NY 10036
212-575-0155

STUYVESANT BICYCLE & TOY
349 West 14th Street
New York, NY 10014
212-254-5200

THIRD STREET DEPOT
507 Third Street
Niagara Falls, NY 14301
716-285-2043

NORWOOD HOBBY SHOP
2-4 South Main Street
Norwood, NY 13668
315-353-6621

MILL SIDE TRAINS
783 Ridge Road
Ontario, NY 14519
315-524-8515

LACKAWANNA MODEL TRAIN SHOP
523 East High Street
Painted Post, NY 14870
607-962-5164

CATSKILL HOBBIES
Mountain Turnpike
Palenville, NY 12463
518-678-9397

DUFFY'S TRAINS
Rd 3 Box 3 Route 57
Phoenix, NY 13135
315-695-4375

SUNRISE TRAIL HOBBY SUPPLY DEPOT
33 Cain Drive
Plainview, NY 11803
516-454-4827

LEWIS STONE'S RAILROAD PAINT SHOP
126 Main Street, Box 157
Ravena, NY 12143
518-756-2056

NAGENGAST HARDWARE
6802 Fresh Pond Road
Ridgewood, NY 11385
718-821-0958

THE WHISTLE STOP
1967 Ridge Road E
Rochester, NY 14622
716-467-7590

EASTERN HOBBIES, INC.
718 Route 25A
Rocky Point, NY 11778
516-821-3175

ADIRONDACK HOBBIES
2331 Alton Street
Schenectady, NY 12309
518-393-8836

MOHAWK VALLEY RAILROAD CO.
2037 Hamburg Street
Schenectady, NY 12304
518-372-9124

THE MODEL RAILWAY STATION
49 Mohawk Avenue
Scotia, NY 12305
518-382-1714

THREE GUY'S HOBBIES
99 East Main Street
Smithtown, NY 11787
516-265-8303

CENTRAL HOBBY SUPPLY
716 West Manlius Street
Syracuse, NY 13057
315-437-6630

RENSSELAER RAILROAD SHOP
Davison Hall, RPI,
Burdett Avenue
Troy, NY 12180
518-276-2764

K & K TRAIN AND HOBBY
2019 Sunset Avenue
Utica, NY 13502
315-733-6677

VILLAGE HOBBIES
2011 Genesee Street
Utica, NY 13501
315-733-0611

VALLEY MODEL TRAINS
91 Market Street
Wappingers Falls, NY 12590
914-297-7511

NOEL ARNOLD
84 Twin Arch Road
Washingtonville, NY 10992
914-496-5185

EAST DYKE DEPOT
332 East Dyke Street
Wellsville, NY 14895
716-593-0005

TIM'S HOBBY SHOP
2226 Union Road
West Seneca, NY 14224
716-656-1790

WESTCHESTER HOBBIES
102 East Post Road
White Plains, NY 10601
914-949-7943

LBC MODEL TRAINS
5544 Main Street
Williamsville, NY 14204
716-631-3081

OH **ROB'S TRAINS**
361 East Main Street
Alliance, OH 44601
216-823-7222

RENNBRANDT HOBBY
197 Best Street
Berea, OH 44017
216-234-7186

LANDSCAPE RAILROADS & HOBBIES
2681 East Main Street
Bexley, OH 43209
614-235-5105

AMER'S HOBBY SHOP
6010 Market Street
Boardman, OH 44512
330-758-2810

SCHAFFNER'S
2207 North Cleveland Avenue NW
Canton, OH 44709
216-452-4444

GOLF MANOR HOBBIES
2235 Losantiville Avenue
Cincinnati, OH 45237
513-351-3849

WESTERN HILLS PHOTO & HOBBY
6319 Glenway Avenue
Cincinnati, OH 45211
513-661-2141

DEPOT TRAIN & HOBBY
4342 West 130th Street
Cleveland, OH 44135
216-252-8880

HOBBY SOFTWARE
3976 East 71st Street
Cleveland, OH 44105
216-641-3151

HOBBYS ETC.
23345 Lorain Road
Cleveland, OH 44126
216-979-1900

HOUSE OF TRAINS
272 East 156th Street
Cleveland, OH 44110
216-383-9494

THE BLUE CABOOSE
4290 Indianola Avenue
Columbus, OH 43214
614-447-1707

HOBBYLAND
Graceland Shopping Center
140 Graceland Boulevard
Columbus, OH 43214
614-888-7500

STRETE HOBBIES
3655 Sullivant Avenue
Columbus, OH 43228
614-279-6959

THE TRAIN STATION
4430 Indianola Avenue
Columbus, OH 43214
614-262-9056

HECTOR TRAIN STATION
18767 Rd. 18-E
Continental, OH 45831
419-596-3824

TRAINS, ETC.
2046 East Bailey Road
Cuyahoga Falls, OH 44221
216-922-4020

WHISTLE STOP HOBBY SHOP
2146 Front Street
Cuyahoga Falls, OH 44221
216-928-8984

DAYTON MODEL RAILWAYS/ SMITTY'S HOBBY SHOP
3706 Wilmington Pike
Dayton, OH 45429
937-299-1121

TIN PLATE STATION
6342-B Far Hills Avenue
Dayton, OH 45459
513-428-9667

PANDY'S GARDEN CENTER
41600 Griswold Road
Elyria, OH 44035
216-324-4314

THINGS UNIQUE
21946 Lorain Road
Fairview Park, OH 44126
216-333-5210

HUDSON TOY TRAIN & HOBBY
144 North Main Street
Hudson, OH 44236
216-653-2997

WINGS HOBBY SHOP, INC.
17112 Detroit Avenue
Lakewood, OH 44107
216-221-5383

SMOKESTACK HOBBY SHOP
368 Lincoln Avenue
Lancaster, OH 43130
614-653-0404

TRAIN TOWN HOBBY
520 East Hume Road
Lima, OH 45806
419-221-3388

HOMETOWN HOBBY & SUPPLY
1203 West Hunter Street
Logan, OH 43138
614-385-3239

THE CORNER STORE
1249 Colorado Avenue
Lorain, OH 44052
216-288-2351

JOHN'S HOBBY SHOP
15 North Main Street
Mansfield, OH 44902
419-526-4426

J & M HOBBIES
1238 Conant Street
Maumee, OH 43537
419-893-2621

SOUTHLAND TRAIN & HOBBY
Southland Shopping
Center Arcade
6863 Southland Drive
Middleburg Heights,
OH 44130
216-843-5929

SOUTH PARK HOBBIES
1825 Tytus Avenue
Middletown, OH 45042
513-424-5124

DAVIS ELECTRONICS, INC.
217 Main Street
Milford, OH 45150
513-831-6425

TRAINS, PLANES & HOBBY THINGS
88 West Granville Road
New Albany, OH 43054
614-855-8058

PLANES, TRAINS & ARTISTS' THINGS
121 South Broadway
New Philadelphia, OH 44663
216-364-4789

NICK'S SALES & SERVICE
7251 Middlebranch Avenue
NE
North Canton, OH 44721
216-494-0125

TRAINS-N-THINGS
6587 Whipple Avenue NW
North Canton, OH 44720
330-499-1666

CROUSE MILL TRUE VALUE INC.
11788 Market Street
North Lima, OH 44452
216-549-2143

PAUL'S HOBBIES
46 East Main
Norwalk, OH 44857
419-668-3019

DOUBLE D HOBBY SUPPLIES
7727-B West Camp Perry
Western Road
Oak Harbor, OH 43449
419-898-2110

GRAND PACIFIC JUNCTION MODEL RAILROAD
8072 Columbia Road
Olmsted Falls, OH 44138
216-235-4777

HOBBYLAND
6589 East Main Street
Reynoldsburg, OH 43068
614-866-5011

ST. MARYS HOBBY CENTER
118 West Spring Street
St. Marys, OH 45885
419-394-5909

MOSBLACK HOBBY
257 East State Street
Salem, OH 44460
216-337-0006

SIDNEY HOBBY SHOP
301 North Ohio Street
Sidney, OH 45365
937-492-6688

CROSS CREEK ENGINEERING
7188 Pawnee Road,
Post Office Box 191
Spencer, OH 44275
216-667-2833

HOME HOBBIES & CRAFTS
229 East Home Road
Springfield, OH 45503
513-390-0687

SEMAPHORE TRAIN & HOBBY, INC.
5700 Monroe Street
Sylvania, OH 43560
419-885-1533

JACKIES GIFTS
4825 Summit Street
Toledo, OH 43611
419-726-4044

RICK'S TOY TRAINS
4807 Lewis Avenue
Toledo, OH 43612
419-478-0171

STEVE'S FALLEN FLAGGS HOBBIES
5414 Monroe Street
Toledo, OH 43623
419-843-3334

COUNTRY LOOKS TRAINS
5022 Glady Creek Drive
Urbana, OH
937-652-3433

FAMILY HOBBY SHOP
304 North Dixie Drive
Vandalia, OH 45377
513-898-5247

DAD'S TOY SHOP
123 West Auglaize Street
Wapakoneta, OH 45895
419-738-2007

TRUMBULL CAMERA AND HOBBY
8400 East Market Street
Warren, OH 44484
330-856-5225

SHIRAY'S
19930 State Route 117
Waynesfield, OH 45896
419-568-8055

HOBBYLAND, N ORTHWEST SQUARE
6650 Sawmill Road
West Worthington,
OH 43235
614-766-2300

WORTHINGTON HOBBY HOUSE
646 North High Street
Worthington, OH 43215
614-888-7715

BOARDMAN HOBBY CENTER
6820 Market Street
Youngstown, OH 44512
216-758-1522

OK **S & S HOBBIES AND CRAFTS**
108 South Main Street
Broken Arrow, OK 74012
918-251-0330

J & J TRAINS
125 Hal Muldrow Drive
Norman, OK 73069
405-573-9633

WHISTLE STOP TRAINS
1313 West Britton Road
Oklahoma City, OK 73114
405-842-4846

WOODWARD'S
Quailbrook Center
4401 West Memorial Road
Oklahoma City, OK 73134
405-751-4994

THE TRAIN HOUSE
Rt. 1 Box 488
Ramona, OK 74061
918-336-5821

ACTION HOBBIES
4955-C South Memorial
Drive
Tulsa, OK 74145
918-663-8998

CHALLENGER N SCALE HOBBIES
2230 East 56th Place
Tulsa, OK 74105
918-749-1634

**DISCOUNT TRAIN
& MODEL**
8988-X South Sheridan
Road
Tulsa, OK 74133
918-495-1525

TRAIN AND TOY HOUSE
3302 South Peoria
Tulsa, OK 74105
918-742-6378

OR **TAMMIES HOBBIES**
12024 S. W. Canyon Road
Beaverton, OR 97005
503-644-4535

D'S TOYS AND HOBBIES
3312 North Highway 97
Bend, OR 97701
541-389-1330

TRUMP'S HOBBIES
2401 NW Kings Boulevard
Corvallis, OR 97330
541-753-7540

VILLAGE DEPOT
725 Row River Road
Cottage Grove, OR 97424
541-942-5117

**BIG WHEEL MODEL
TRAINS**
1091 Coburg Road
Eugene, OR 97401
541-344-7300

EUGENE TOY & HOBBY
32 East 11th Avenue
Eugene, OR 97401
541-344-2117

EVERGREEN ROUNDHOUSE
3010-C Pacific Avenue
Forest Grove, OR 97116
503-357-8055

AL'S BIKE & TOY
808 Klamath Avenue
Klamath Falls, OR 97601
541-884-4512

HOBBY HABIT
411 Fir
La Grandee, OR 97850
800-963-9602

THE HOBBY TREE
335 East Main Street
Medford, OR 97501
541-773-7002

**QUALITY FARM TOYS
& HOBBIES**
701 Main Street
Oregon City, OR 97045
503-650-8023

HOBBIES UNLIMITED
4503 North Interstate Avenue
Portland, OR 97217
503-287-4090

THE HOBBY SMITH
4148 NE Hancock Street
Portland, OR 97212
503-284-1912

HOBBY WAREHOUSE
8532 S.W. Apple Way
Portland, OR 97225
503-292-3790

VIC'S HOBBY SUPPLY
606 NE Broadway
Portland, OR 97232
503-281-1032

WHISTLE STOP TRAINS
14037 S.E. Stark Street
Portland, OR 97233
503-252-7118

ALL ABOARD HOBBIES
427 SE Main Street
Roseburg, OR 97470
541-672-0280

SKYSPORT
4564 Commercial Street SE
Salem, OR 97302
503-363-4345

ROOKIES & RAILS
13500 SW Pacific Highway,
Suite 26
Tigard, OR 97223
503-639-3325

PA **7TH STREET DEPOT**
619 North 7th Street
Allentown, PA 18102
610-433-2868

**ALLENTOWN TOY TRAIN
SERVICE**
125-1/2 North 11th Street
Allentown, PA 18102
610-821-0740

BLOCH'S HOBBY SHOP
1015 Union Boulevard
Allentown, PA 18102
610-432-9975

**ON THE RIGHT TRACK
HOBBIES**
1814 Union Avenue
Altoona, PA 16601
814-942-4835

**ARDMORE HOBBIES
& CRAFTS**
Ardmore West Shopping
Center
Ardmore, PA 19003
610-896-6615

CHRISTMAS CITY HOBBIES
316 South New Street
Bethlehem, PA 18015
610-974-9590

THE HOBBY STOP
184 East Market Street
Blairsville, PA 15717
412-459-0211

**THE MAIN HOBBY
CENTER INC.**
Rt. 6 Scranton Carbondale
Highway
Blakely, PA 18447
717-489-8857

MAINLINE HOBBY SUPPLY
15015 BuchananTrail East
Blue Ridge Summit,
PA 17214
717-794-2860

NICHOLAS SMITH TRAINS
2343 West Chester Pike
Broomall, PA 19008
610-353-8585

NORTH-END HOBBIES & CRAFTS
75 North Main Street
Chambersburg, PA 17201
717-261-1946

UPTOWN SALES, INC.
33 North Main Street
Chambersburg, PA 17201
800-548-9941

TAYLOR'S HOBBY WORLD
312 South State Street
Clarks Summit, PA 18411
717-587-0181

309 TRAIN SUPPLY
34 Bethlehem Pike
Colmar, PA 18915
215-822-9293

SOTTUNG'S SERVICENTER
808 Girard Avenue
Croydon, PA 19021
215-788-5353

D&S NURSERY & MODEL HOBBIES
813 Route 15 North
Dillsburg, PA 17019
717-432-3866

HERB'S HOBBIES & CRAFTS
200 West State Street
Doylestown, PA 18901
215-345-7123

EARLINGTON TRAIN SPECIALISTS
Allentown & Morwood Roads
Earlington, PA 18918
215-723-5120

BOB'S TRAINS
15 Crystal Street
East Stroudsburg, PA 18301
717-421-6505

THE HOBBY HUT
209 5 Mi N Marshall's Crk,
RD 6
East Stroudsburg, PA 18301
717-588-3383

HOBBY HANGOUT AND CRAFT CENTER
3701 William Penn Highway
Easton, PA 18042
610-252-6871

FISHER'S EFFORT STATION
Route 115,
Post Office Box 137
Effort, PA 18330
610-681-4654

TRAIN CITY
3133 Zuck Road
Erie, PA 16506
814-833-8313

THE TRAIN SHOP
3310 Buffalo Road
Erie, PA 16510
814-899-2157

CRANBERRY HOBBY DEPOT
20327 Perry Highway
Evans City, PA 16033
412-776-3640

FAIRCHANCE PHARMACY
90 Church Street
Fairchance, PA 15436
412-564-2128

TOY TRAIN STATION
21 East Street Road
Feasterville, PA 19053
215-322-5182

MODELLBAHN OTT HOBBIES, INC.
1145 East Philadelphia Avenue
Gilbertsville, PA 19525
610-367-5925

TOMMY GILBERT'S MODEL RAILROAD SUPPLY
346 East Water Street
Gettysburg, PA 17325
717-337-1992

KING GARDEN PALACE
Rd 14 Rt 130 E
Greensburg, PA 15601
412-834-0202

JIM'S TRAIN SHOP
Route 56 West
Homer City, PA 15748
412-479-2026

CLASSIC HOBBIES INC.
2056 Countyline Road
Huntingdon Valley, PA 19006
215-396-7912

NIEDZALKOSKI'S TRAIN SHOP
214 South 4th Street
Jeannette, PA 15644
412-523-8035

BLIND JUNCTION HOBBIES
326 Hosack Road
Jackson Center, PA 16133
412-376-2703

JENKINTOWN HOBBY CENTER
Greenwood & Leedom Streets
Jenkintown, PA 19046
215-884-7555

MY BROTHER'S HOBBIES
360 Goucher Street
Johnstown, PA 15905
814-288-3894

U.S. #1 HOBBY
King of Prussia Plaza
King of Prussia, PA 19406
610-992-9099

SMITTY'S HOBBY & CRAFT
1226 Millersville Pike
Lancaster, PA 17603
717-393-2521

HENNING SCALE MODELS, INC.
126-128 South Line Street
Lansdale, PA 19446
215-362-2442

PENN VALLEY HOBBY CENTER
837 West Main Street
Lansdale, PA 19446
215-855-1268

**ADAM & EVE'S PET
& HOBBY**
Latrobe 30 Shopping Plaza
Latrobe, PA 15650
412-539-7130

FORSTER'S TRAIN SHOP
140 Mary Street
Lemont, PA 16851
814-237-7899

KEYSTONE HOBBY CENTER
239 South Third Street
Lemoyne, PA 17043
717-763-7534

HOBBYCRAFTERS
5907 Emilie Road
Levittown, PA 19057
215-949-3730

GRANDPA CHOO CHOO'S
703 Buffalo Road
Lewisburg, PA 17837
717-524-4802

ELLIE'S LOKIE SHOP
135 West Mahanoy Avenue
Mahanoy City, PA 17948
717-773-2174

RULE'S MODEL TRAINS
43 Market Square
Manheim, PA 17545
717-664-5155

**LITTLE TOWN TOYS
& TRAINS**
220 Center Street
Meyersdale, PA 15552
814-634-8863

**LORETTA'S MAIN LINE
TRAINS**
Water & Union Streets
Middletown, PA 17057
717-944-2336

LOCO LOUIE'S
718 McDade Boulavard
Milmont Park, PA 19033
610-583-7711

**ENGLISH'S MODEL
RAILROAD SUPPLY**
21 Howard Street
Montoursville, PA 17754
717-368-2516

THE STATION
213 Ninth Street
New Cumberland, PA 17070
717-774-7096

**PAUL'S MODEL RAILROAD
SHOP**
201 Lincolnway West
New Oxford, PA 17350
717-624-7567

**LESHERS VARIETY
& HOBBIES**
21 North Seventh Street
Perkasie, PA 18944
215-257-4055

ALFRED CAPPELLI, JR.
313 Market Street
Philadelphia, PA 19106
215-629-1757

BIG BOY'S TOYS
134 Rector Street
Philadelphia, PA 19127
215-483-3512

**GREAT TRADITIONS TOY
TRAINS & SPORTS CARDS**
11706 Bustleton Avenue
Philadelphia, PA 19116
215-698-1993

**S & H HARDWARE
& SUPPLY**
6700 Castor Avenue
Philadelphia, PA 19149
215-745-9375

BRENTWOOD HOBBIES
3629 Brownsville Road
Pittsburgh, PA 15227
412-885-1723

JOHN A. SACCO, JR.
30 Ingram Avenue
Pittsburgh, PA 15205
412-921-1554

MODELPORT, INC.
309 High Street
Pottstown, PA 19464
610-323-6753

J & D WHISTLE STOP
106 East Broad Street
Quakertown, PA 18951
215-538-0501

G & K HOBBY CENTRE
720 Gordon Street
Reading, PA 19601
610-374-8598

**IRON HORSE HOBBY
HOUSE**
60 South Sixth Street
Reading, PA 19602
610-373-6927

KEYSTONE RAIL
RD #2, Box 479 Brewer Road
Rochester, PA 15074
412-728-3995

THE GREAT TRAIN STORE
211 The Mall at Steamtown
Scranton, PA 18503
717-963-0963

NITTANY LINE HOBBIES
253-B Benner Pike
State College, PA 16801
814-235-1661

STRASBURG TRAIN SHOP
Route 741 East, Box 130
Strasburg, PA 17579
717-687-0464

**ANTHRACITE MODEL
TRAINS**
43 East Ludlow Street
Summit Hill, PA 18250
717-645-9133

PROPS AND WHEELS
Broad and Nescopeck Streets
Tamaqua, PA 18252
717-668-2288

DON'S TRAIN SHED
Old Keyes Road
Tioga, PA 16946
717-835-5371

**WALTERS MODEL
RAILROAD SUPPLY**
Rd#4 Box 289-A
Titusville, PA 16354
814-827-2461

BLIND JUNCTION HOBBIES
1 Main Street Depot
Volant, PA 16156
412-533-2372

BRANDYWINE HOBBIES
1502 Westchester Pike
Westchester, PA 19382
610-696-9049

**THE TRAIN SHOPPE
AND HOBBY CENTER**
334 North Penna Avenue
Wilkes-Barre, PA 18702
717-824-7688

G & L HOBBY SHOP
1706 West Market Street
York, PA 17404
717-843-2520

RI **APPONAUG COLOR SHOP**
1364 Greenwich Avenue
Apponaug, RI 02886
401-737-5506

A.A. HOBBIES
885 Dyer Avenue
Cranston, RI 02920
401-943-9990

**SHIPPEETOWN MODEL
SHOP, INC.**
184 Danielson Pike
Foster, RI 02825
401-647-2640

DARLINGTON HOBBIES
506 Armistice Boulevard
Pawtucket, RI 02861
401-722-7574

THE TRAINSHED
562 Kingstown Road
Wakefield, RI 02879
401-789-1420

SC **HOBBYTOWN USA**
3122 North Main Street,
Belvedere Plaza
Anderson, SC 29621
864-261-8479

CREATIVE PASTIME SHOP
1011 Third Avenue
Conway, SC 29526
803-248-2600

**RAIL & SPIKE TRAINS
& HOBBIES**
6788 L Calhoun Memorial
Highway
Easley, SC 29640
864-850-0237

GREAT ESCAPE
Pleasantburg Shopping
Center
1426 Laurens Road
Greenville, SC 29607
803-235-8320

HOBBYTOWN USA
101 Verdae Boulevard #340
Greenville, SC 29607
864-627-9633

ED'S HOBBY SHOP
702 Main Street
Myrtle Beach, SC 29577
803-448-8685

THE GREAT TRAIN STORE
1350 21st Avenue N.,
Building H, Space #136
Myrtle Beach, SC 29577
803-444-0844

THE UNION STATION
785 Murrah Road
North Augusta, SC 29841
803-279-5975

GOLDEN STRIP HOBBIES
315-G Fairview Road
Simpsonville, SC 29681
803-963-7149

**NEW BROOKLAND
RAILROAD & HOBBY**
405 State Street
West Columbia, SC 29169
803-791-3958

SD **WEST RIVER DEPOT**
3110 North Haines Avenue
Rapid City, SD 57701
605-342-0291

**DONOVANS HOBBY
CENTER**
Independence Plaza
3813 South Western Avenue
Sioux Falls, SD 57105
605-338-6945

UNIVERSAL HOBBY SHOP
222 South Main
Sioux Falls, SD 57102
605-338-8623

TN **DAS HOBBY HAUS**
5364 Mountain View Road
Antioch, TN 37013
615-731-3827

CHATTANOOGA DEPOT
3701 Ringgold Road
Chattanooga, TN 37412
615-622-0630

RAILROAD HOBBIES, INC.
4321-A Ringgold Road
Chattanooga, TN 37412
615-622-8847

DAS HOBBY HAUS
1616 Fort Campbell Boulevard
Clarksville, TN 37042
615-553-0350

ED'S SOUTHERN TRAINS
217 East Main Street
Johnson City, TN 37604
615-929-2290

JACK'S TRAINS
200 Wesley Street
Johnson City, TN 37601
615-282-9108

SERIOUS HOBBIES
3101 Browns Mill Road
Johnson City, TN 37604
423-984-9900

AAA MODEL SUPPLY
2045B Brookside Lane
Kingsport, TN 37660
423-378-3330

HUTTON'S HOBBIES
7525 Maynardville Pike
Knoxville, TN 37938
615-922-9811

**TENNESSEE MODEL
HOBBIES**
8903 Oak Ridge Highway
Knoxville, TN 37931
423-927-2900

CHURCH HARDWARE
690 East Raines Road
Memphis, TN 38116
901-332-1144

**MODEL RAILROAD
& HOBBY SHOP**
3436 Park Avenue
Memphis, TN 38111
901-324-7245

**WORLD OF GAMES
AND HOBBIES**
2796 South Perkins
Memphis, TN 38118
901-365-2080

**AARDVARK'S MODEL
TRAIN SHOP**
3607 Gallatin Road
Nashville, TN 37216
615-228-4639

DAN'S TRAINS
Emory Road at I-75 North
Powell, TN 37849
615-938-7212

TX **DISCOUNT MODEL
TRAINS**
4641 Ratliff Lane
Addison, TX 75248
214-931-8135

HOBBY TIME
1409 South Harrison Street
Amarillo, TX 79101
806-376-6643

KING'S HOBBY SHOP
8810 North Lamar Boulevard
Austin, TX 78753
512-836-7388

VILLAGE HOBBY SHOP
2700 West Anderson, #801
Austin, TX 78757
512-452-6401

HOBBY MAKER
1424-F Airport Freeway
Bedford, TX 76022
817-267-0991

BELLAIRE ROUNDHOUSE
5314 Bellaire Boulevard
Bellaire, TX 79720
713-667-7762

I&I HOBBY CENTER
6707 Chimney Rock Road
Bellaire, TX 77401
713-661-7137

ON TRACK LTD.
707 Navidad #1801
Bryan, TX 77801
409-823-2366

B&H TRAINS
2033 Airline Road,
Suite B-2
Corpus Christi, TX 78412
512-985-8383

TRAINS, ETC.
3929 Herndon
Corpus Christi, TX 78411
216-922-4020

**BOBBYE HALL'S HOBBY
HOUSE**
4822 Bryan Street
Dallas, TX 75204
214-821-2550

**CLASSIC TRAINS
& HOBBIES**
11333 East Northwest
Highway
Dallas, TX 75238
214-349-7573

COLIBRI'S
5600 West Lovers Lane,
Suite 139
Dallas, TX 75209
214-352-3394

**COLLECTIBLE TOYS
& TRAINS**
109 Medallion Center
Dallas, TX 75214
214-373-9469

PHIL'S HOBBIES
2740 Valwood Parkway
#105
Dallas, TX 75234
214-243-3603

JERRY'S HOBBIES & GIFTS
2201 I-35E, Suite #L22
Denton, TX 76205
817-591-8038

SILVER SPIKE HOBBIES
525 North Elm Street
Denton, TX 76201
817-383-3914

**WOODIE'S MODEL
TRAIN SHOP**
4010 Polk Avenue
El Paso, TX 79930
915-566-0235

OLD TIME HOBBIES
5030 Trail Lake Drive
Fort Worth, TX 76133
817-292-1322

DASCO
215 Edgewood Drive
Fredericksburg, TX 78624
210-997-7089

J & S HOBBIES
321 Marshall Plaza
Grand Prairie, TX 75051
214-262-5313

THE ENGINE TENDER
West Avenue
Holliday, TX 76366
817-586-1655

G. & G. MODEL SHOP
2522 Times Boulevard
Houston, TX 77005
713-529-7752

HOBBYTOWN USA
The Commons at
Willowbrook
7676 FM 1960 West
Houston, TX 77070
713-955-7097

J.R.'S HOBBY DEPOT
7317 South Kirkwood Road
Houston, TX 77072
713-568-8754

LARRY'S HOBBIES,
156-F 1960 East,
Houston, TX 77073
713-443-7373

TRAINS & PLANES HOBBIES
9737 Westheimer Road
Houston, TX 77042
713-977-1402

TRAINSOURCE: TEXAS
3264 South Loop West
Houston, TX 77025
713-662-0809

RICKS AND ASSOCIATES
5930-D Star Lane
Houston, TX 77057
713-784-7360

MIKE'S HOBBY SHOP
212 Main Street
Humble, TX 77338
713-446-7550

M-A-L HOBBY SHOP
108 South Lee Street
Irving, TX 75060
214-438-9233

HOBBY CENTER
414 North 8th Street,
Post Office Box 849
Killeen, TX 76541
817-634-0488

**ROY'S HOBBIES
& ELECTRONICS**
217 East Kleberg,
Kingsville, TX 78363
512-592-3149

THE TRAINCELLAR
9 North Heron Drive
La Marque, TX 77568
409-935-8029

SOUTHWEST TRAINS
540 Surf, Suite 118
Lewisville, TX 75067
214-221-5891

**COLLECTOR SHOP
AND HOBBIES**
1220 North Town East
Boulevard
Mesquite, TX 75150
214-613-2051

DIBBLE'S HOBBIES
1029 Donaldson Avenue
San Antonio, TX 78228
210-735-7721

HOBBY CENTER, INC.
3441 Fredericksburg Road
San Antonio, TX 78201
210-735-4218

HOBBY STOP
19 Breese Boulevard
San Antonio, TX 78209
210-828-9117

REBEL HOBBIES
6441 Blanco Road
San Antonio, TX 78216
210-828-9117

SPRING CROSSING
1420 Spring Cypress
Spring, TX 77373
281-353-9484

STAR HOBBIES
1200 Hwy 100
South Padre Island/
Port Isabel, TX 78578
210-943-7546

UT **HAMMOND HOBBIES
& TOYS**
5 Points Mall
Bountiful, UT 84010
801-295-5351

MAC'S #101
2135 South Orchard Drive
Bountiful, UT 84010
801-298-7999

ALMOSTA JUNCTION
1161 South State
Clearfield, UT 84015
801-776-1656

**HAMMOND HOBBIES
& TOYS**
Layton Hills Mall
Layton, UT 84041
801-544-4543

**HAMMOND HOBBIES
& TOYS**
Newgate Mall
Ogden, UT 84405
801-393-6490

**WARRENS TRAIN SHOP,
UNION STATION**
25th & Wall
Ogden, UT 84401
801-627-6900

HOBBY STOP
327 East 1200 South #7
Orem, UT 84058
801-226-7947

DOUGLAS MODELS
2065 East 33rd South Street
Salt Lake City, UT 84109
801-487-7752

GREAT ESCAPE HOBBIES
1773 West 4160 South
Salt Lake City, UT 84119
801-966-7785

**HAMMOND HOBBIES
& TOYS**
Cottonwood Mall
4835 Highland Drive,
2nd Floor
Salt Lake City, UT 84117
801-278-0157

**HAMMOND HOBBIES
& TOYS**
Crossroads Mall
50 S. Main Street,
Lower Level
Salt Lake City, UT 84144
801-531-6074

**HAMMOND HOBBIES
& TOYS**
Family Center
1088 E 7200 S Midvale
Salt Lake City, UT
801-561-3821

MAC'S #103
725 East 10600 South
Sandy, UT 84070
801-572-1188

**MODEL RAILROAD
STATION HOBBY SHOP**
9425 S Union Square
Sandy, UT 84070
801-572-6082

WEST VALLEY HOBBIES
1765 West 5400 South
Taylorsville, UT 84118
801-964-1700

MAC'S #102
7046 South Redwood Road
West Jordan, UT 84084
801-566-9009

VA **OBIES TRAINS**
6461 Edsall Road, Suite 405
Alexandria, VA 22312
703-658-9520

BLUE RIDGE DEPOT
510 Blue Ridge Boulevard
Blue Ridge, VA 24064
703-977-6320

PIPER HOBBY
13892 Metrotech Drive
Chantilly, VA 22021
703-803-3103

THE TRAIN JUNCTION
2116-B Berkmar Drive
Charlottesville, VA 22901
804-974-9499

**ARLINGTON HOBBY
CRAFTERS**
Willston Center
6176 Arlington Boulevard
Falls Church, VA 22044
703-532-2224

HOBBIES
2368 Plank Road
Fredericksburg, VA 22401
540-372-6578

BOBBY'S TOY TRAINS
The Wigwam,
U.S. Route 1 North
10412 Washington Hwy,
Suite 4
Glen Allen, VA 23059
804-550-1272

LEESBURG HOBBY CENTER
521-D East Market Street
Leesburg, VA 22075
703-777-1477

TRAINS ETC.
7740 Gunston Plaza
Lorton, VA 22079
703-550-1779

TRAINS UNLIMITED
6010 Fort Avenue
Lynchburg, VA 24502
804-239-8377

KMA JUNCTION
9786 Center Street
Manassas, VA 22110
703-257-9860

TRAIN DEPOT
7214 New Market Court
Manassas, VA 22110
703-335-2216

J & J TRAINS
111 East Main Street
Martinsville, VA 24115
703-638-3439

CHESTERFIELD HOBBIES
13154 Midlothian Turnpike
Midlothian, VA 23113
804-379-9091

**CRAFTECH HOBBY SHOP
P-4**
9475 Bacon Avenue
Norfolk, VA 23511
757-444-3846

TOY CRAFT
8481 Chesapeake Boulevard
Norfolk, VA 23518
757-587-4710

WALT'S HOBBY SHOP
2791 South Crater Road
Petersburg, VA 23805
804-861-1333

THE HOBBY CENTER
8908 West Patterson Avenue
Richmond, VA 23229
804-750-1973

THE TOY CENTER, INC.
5811 Patterson Avenue
Richmond, VA 23226
804-288-4475

THE TOY CENTER, INC.
10441 Midlothian Turnpike
Richmond, VA 23235
804-323-5773

KEN'S TRAINS
2328 Orange Avenue N.E.
Roanoke, VA 24012
703-343-1057

THE RAIL YARD
6711-A Williamson Road
Roanoke, VA 24019
703-362-1714

ROANOKE RAILS
113 Norfolk Avenue S. W.
Roanoke, VA 24011
703-342-5930

GRANDDAD'S HOBBY SHOP
5260-A Port Royal Road
Springfield, VA 22151
703-426-0700

STAUNTON TRAINS & HOBBIES
123 West Beverley Street
Staunton, VA 24401
703-885-6750

THE ROUNDHOUSE
3845 Bonney Road
Virginia Beach, VA 23452
757-340-7980

TSG HOBBIES
251 West Lee Highway,
Suite 683
Warrenton, VA 20186
540-347-9212

NORGE STATION
7405 Richmond Road
Williamsburg, VA 23188
757-564-7623

THE "RIP TRACK"
2885 PS Business Center
Woodbridge, VA 22192
703-590-6901

B&M HOBBIES
100 Elm Lake Way
Yorktown, VA 23693
757-867-6669

VT **SOMEDAY ISLE TOYS & TRAINS**
12 Elliott Street
Brattleboro, VT 05301
802-254-6201

AL'S TRAIN SHOP
56 Home Avenue
Burlington, VT 05401
802-658-4935

THE STEAM SHACK
14 Engrem Avenue
Rutland, VT 05701
802-775-2736

ELLIS PAINT, WALLPAPER & GLASS
85 Eastern Avenue
St. Johnsbury, VT 05819
802-748-3806

BILL PARKER'S TRAIN SHOP
12 Juniper Hill Road
Springfield, VT 05156
802-886-8151

C & J HOBBIES
Rt. 7, Box 2510
Vergennes, VT 05491
802-877-2997

SMITH-THOMPSON RAILROAD GIFTS & COLLECTIBLES
P.O. Box 828
White River Jct, VT 05001
802-296-3001

WA **WAGNER'S HOBBY HOUSE**
131 East Main Street
Auburn, WA 98002
206-939-2515

THE INSIDE GATEWAY
14725 NE 20th
Bellevue, WA 98007
206-747-2016

EAGLES HOBBIES
221 West Holly
Bellingham, WA 98225
360-671-1913

GOLD HILL STATION
111 Grand Avenue
Bellingham, WA 98225
206-671-8802

THE WHISTLESTOP AT COUNTRY VILLAGE
23706 Bothell-Everett Highway
Bothell, WA 98021
206-488-3499

SIDE-TRACKED HOBBIES
101 Cottage, Suite F
Cashmere, WA 98815
509-782-4919

HOBBYTOWN USA
177 NE Hampe Way
Chehalis, WA 98532
206-740-1818

NORTHWEST TRAIN DEPOT
1671 North National Avenue
Chehalis, WA 98532
206-748-6536

EVERETT HOBBYCRAFT
2531 Broadway
Everett, WA 98201
206-252-6130

M & M DEPOT
2032 Main Street,
Post Office Box 1828
Ferndale, WA 98248
206-384-2552

THE TRAIN STATION AT FANTASTICKS
135 Vista Way
Kennewick, WA 99336
509-735-1750

EASTSIDE TRAINS
217 Central Way
Kirkland, WA 98033
206-828-4098

GREAT THINGS AND TRAINS
4127 Pacific Avenue
Lacey, WA 98503
206-459-7854

HOBBYTOWN USA
310 Triangle Mall
Longview, WA 98632
206-636-2543

PACIFIC SCALE MODELS
503 Cherry
Olympia, WA 98501
206-352-9261

PACIFIC RIM HOBBY
228 West 1st Street
Port Angeles, WA 98362
800-994-6229

BEHIND THE TIMES
118 Water Street
Port Townsend, WA 98368
206-385-4754

ATTIC FANATIC MODEL TRAINS
19910 Viking Avenue
Poulsbo, WA 98370
360-779-3200

KITSAP MODEL TRAINS
19910 Viking Avenue
Poulsbo, WA 98370
360-779-3200

POULSBO PACIFIC
19559 Viking Avenue
Poulsbo, WA 98370
360-779-2122

TRACKSIDE TRAINS
201 3rd Street SE
Puyallup, WA 98372
206-845-9759

KING STREET STATION
176 Union Avenue NE
Renton, WA 98059
206-227-9530

AMERICAN EAGLES INC.
12537 Lake City Way NE
Seattle, WA 98125
206-440-8448

DON'S HOBBIES
4746 University Vill. Pl. NE
Seattle, WA 98105
206-525-7700

NORTH END TRAIN CENTER
12333 Lake City Way, NE
Seattle, WA 98125
206-362-4959

THE TRAIN CENTER
3310 West Lynn Street
Seattle, WA 98199
206-283-7886

PARKWATER DEPOT
4909 East Trent Avenue
Spokane, WA 99212
509-535-1043

SPRAGUE HOBBY DEPOT
East 8023 Sprague Avenue
Spokane, WA 99212
509-928-7062

SUNSET JUNCTION MODEL TRAINS
East 213 Sprague Avenue
Spokane, WA 99202
509-838-2379

AMERICAN EAGLES TACOMA
5412 South Tacoma Way
Tacoma, WA 98409
206-474-5765

PACIFIC RAILWAY HOBBIES
5115 100th Street, S.W., #7
Tacoma, WA 98499
206-581-4453

TACOMA TRAINS
2521 North Proctor Street
Tacoma, WA 98406
206-756-7517

EXPRESS STATION HOBBIES
640 Strander Boulevard
Tukwila, WA 98188
206-228-7750

THE CLOVER LEAF
4110 Main Street
Union Gap, WA 98903
509-453-8959

A-TRAIN HOBBY
13503-B SE Mill Plain
Boulevard, Suite 6
Vancouver, WA 98684
206-944-5403

DON'S TRAIN DEPOT
303 Southpark Drive
Wapato, WA 98951
509-877-2836

BOXCAR HOBBIES
6607 Oliver Drive
Yakima, WA 98901
509-457-8590

WI **SETCO HOBBY TRAINS**
1818B North Richmond
Street
Appleton, WI 54911
414-954-9044

TRAIN HOUSE HOBBIES
602 West Third Avenue
Brodhead, WI 53520
608-897-4909

SOMMERFELD'S TRAINS & HOBBIES
12620 Hampton Avenue,
Butler, WI 53007
414-783-7797

CUDAHY NEWS & HOBBY CENTER
4758 South Packard Avenue
Cudahy, WI 53110
414-769-1500

WISCONSIN N SCALE
4872 South Packard Avenue
Cudahy, WI 53110
414-769-6376

BOB'S HOBBY JUNCTION
3621 East Hamilton
Eau Claire, WI 54701
715-832-4445

HOBBY MASTER
3944 Anderson Drive
Eau Claire, WI 54703
715-835-5004

NEW HOBBY SHOP
1234 South Military Avenue
Green Bay, WI 54304
414-498-2025

DREAMERS HOBBIES
4458 South 108th Street
Greenfield, WI 53228
414-425-3467

THE HOBBY SHOP
2203 West Court Street
Janesville, WI 53545
608-752-3445

IRON RAILS OF KENOSHA
2031 22nd Avenue
Kenosha, WI 53140
414-552-8075

ABC HOBBIES
1627 Losey Boulevard S
LaCrosse, WI 54601
608-788-8222

THE PET-HOBBY CENTER
506 Main Street
LaCrosse, WI 54601
608-784-1161

**CAPITOL MODEL RR
SUPPLY COMPANY**
6666 Odana Road,
Suite 101
Madison, WI 53719
608-231-9940

**HOBBY CRAFT
OF MADISON, INC.**
6632 Odana Road
Madison, WI 53719
608-833-4944

HOBBY HORSE
1769 Thierer Road
Madison, WI 53704
800-604-6229

MIDVALE HOBBY SHOP
702 North Midvale
Boulevard
Madison, WI 53705
608-238-2233

**JERRY'S BAY VIEW
HOBBY SHOP**
2633 South Kinnickinnic
Avenue
Milwaukee, WI 53207
414-482-1566

TERMINAL HOBBY SHOP
5619 West Florist Avenue
Milwaukee, WI 53218
414-461-1050

THE HOBBY DEPOT
835 17th Street
Monroe, WI 53566
608-325-5107

THE TRAIN DEPOT
119 Oakton Avenue
Pewaukee, WI 53072
414-695-2363

EXPRESS DEPOT
1100 Main Street
Stevens Point, WI 54481
715-342-9019

ABC R/C
244 West Main Street
Waukesha, WI 53186
414-542-1245

**JETCO'S HIAWATHA
HOBBIES**
1701 Summit Avenue
Waukesha, WI 53188
414-544-4131

POPE'S HOBBYLAND
640 South Third Avenue
Wausau, WI 54401
715-842-4371

WEST BEND HOBBIES INC.
144 North Main Street
West Bend, WI 53095
414-334-0487

S scale and gauge—traditionally associated with American Flyer trains of the 1940s and 1950s—is today benefitting from a number of excellent new products being offered by several manufacturers. Among them is S-Helper Service, whose high-quality lineup of S scale locomotives and rolling stock is evident in this catalog photograph.

Photo courtesy of Don Thompson, S-Helper Service

S SCALE & S GAUGE
(1:64)

"S" is both a modeling scale and a modeling gauge, a fact that newcomers to the hobby sometimes find a bit confusing. S gauge track measures about 7/8 of an inch between the rails, and the scale of the models (assuming that they represent standard gauge prototypes) is 1:64.

The roots of this "ideal" modeling scale extend back to England, where, as far back as the 1930s, some model railroaders believed there was a need for a more convenient and space-saving model railroading scale somewhere between HO scale and O scale. The result of their efforts was 3/16-inch scale (a proportion of 1:64).

Within a short time, 3/16-inch scale had migrated to the U.S., where the Cleveland Model & Supply Co. took up the banner and began making its "C-D" (for Cleveland Designed) line of 3/16-inch products. Within a few year, the National Model Railroad Association (NMRA) granted recognition to the scale, and renamed it "S" —primarily for the "s" components in three-six-teenths, the scale designation, and the seven-eighths measure of the track gauge.

S gauge trains gained in popularity and acceptance in the U.S. through the efforts of Albert Carlton Gilbert—the A.C. Gilbert of Erector Set fame. In the period leading up to, and through, World War II, Gilbert searched for a product line that could go head-to-head against his staunch competitor, Lionel Trains, and Lionel's renowned O gauge trains. Gilbert saw some S scale products displayed at the Chicago Worlds Fair, and he recognized that these items offered a great-to-work-with modeling scale that was larger than HO, but still somewhat smaller than O gauge. In 1946, Gilbert launched his American Flyer line of S gauge electric trains.

By the midpoint of the twentieth century, and for some years before and after, A.C. Gilbert's American Flyer S gauge trains provided erstwhile competition to Lionel's O gauge models. But despite the latter firm's non-prototypical three-rail track system—the target of considerable ribbing from Flyer fans of that era—Lionel Trains ultimately prevailed, and the staunch competitor bought out the entire Flyer line, walking away with the American Flyer trademark and tooling.

Nevertheless, S scale/gauge has retained a very devoted and supportive following over the years. Its fans truly do regard "S" as something of an "ideal" size of model train—big enough to see and to work with, but small enough to provide more railroading action in a limited amount of space. Today, a number of manufacturers, including the current Lionel LLC, which now owns the American Flyer trademark, continue to support this scale and its related track gauge with growing numbers of new items.

S scale/gauge enthusiasts are themselves generally classified into two distinct, but somewhat overlapping camps: Hi-Railers and scale modelers. Hi-Railers are those who hold true to the heritage of the American Flyer line of toy electric trains, with its higher-than-prototypical rail, and the liberties taken in terms of scale proportions so the locomotives and rolling stock can operate on the tight curves associated with toy train track.

The S scale modelers are generally considered to be those who adhere to finely-detailed and accurately proportioned models created in true 1:64 proportions. Furthermore, the track that the scale modelers use is also more true-to-scale in terms of its rail height—a factor that limits the ability of Hi-Rail models to operate on a scale layout unless the wheels are changed.

Model railroaders in the other popular scales have been known to refer to "S" as the "scratch-builder's scale" because of the lack of products available for S scale. However, today that is no longer the case, and increasing numbers of manufacturers—both large and small—are devoting expanded resources to providing S scale modelers with virtually everything needed to assure a satisfying, creative, and productive hobby experience. The resources listed on these pages provide ample evidence of that fact.

To be sure, "S" is neither gone nor forgotten!

S SCALE & S GAUGE RESOURCES

manufacturers of S scale/gauge locomotives and rolling stock

AMERICAN FLYER TRAINS
Lionel LLC
50625 Richard W. Blvd.
Chesterfield, MI 48051-2493
810-940-4100
e-mail: talktous@lionel.com
www.lionel.com
(American Flyer S gauge trains)

AMERICAN MODELS
10087 Colonial Industrial Dr.
South Lyon, MI 48178
248-437-6800
fax: 248-437-9454
www.americanmodels.com
(S gauge locomotives, rolling stock, and related parts and accessories)

GREENBRIER RAILROAD MODELS
distributed by B. T. S.
c/o P.O. Box 561
Seffner, FL 33583
813-681-7666
e-mail: bill@btsrr.com
(imported brass S scale locomotives)

PENNSYLVANIA HERITAGE MODELS (PHM)
R.D. 4, Box 139
Birdsboro, PA 19508
800-238-0072
Tom@paheritagemodels.com
(S gauge Budd RDC cars)

RIVER RAISIN MODELS
6160 Upper Straits Blvd.
West Bloomfield, MI 48324
246-366-9621
(imported S gauge steam locomotive models)

S-HELPER SERVICE, INC. (SHOWCASE LINE)
2 Roberts Road
New Brunswick, NJ 08901
www.showcaseline.com
(S gauge locomotives and rolling stock)

SOUTHWIND MODELS
P.O. Box 3175
Plant City, FL 33564-3175
813-752-1636
fax: 813-752-0656
(imported S scale locomotives)

S SCALE AMERICA
1468 Lee St.
Des Plaines, IL 60018
847-297-2118
fax: 847-297-4976
(S scale locomotives)

SUNSET MODELS
www.sunsetmodels.com
(imported brass S scale/gauge locomotives)

after-market manufacturers and suppliers

AMI
P.O. Box 11861
Clayton, MO 63105
e-mail: AMI1@ninenet.com
www.tttrains.com/ami
(roadbed products for S gauge track)

BK ENTERPRISES
12874 County Road 314B
Buena Vista, CO 81211-9102
719-395-8076
(precision built S scale turnouts)

BOWSER MFG. CO.
21 Howard St.
P.O. Box 322
Montoursville, PA 17754-0322
717-368-2516
(S gauge turntables)

B.T.S.
P.O. Box 561
Seffner, FL 33583-0561
813-759-6300
fax: 813-759-8218
e-mail: bill@btsrr.com
(craftsman structure kits)

CARL'S TOY TRAINS
P.O. Box 443
Medford, MA 02155
800-RIVETIN
www.tiac.net/users/carls
(riveting tools for Am. Flyer S gauge trains)

CHARLIE'S TRAINS
P.O. Box 158-F
Hubertus, WI 53033
414-628-1544
(light bulbs for American Flyer trains)

CLOVER HOUSE
Box 62M
Sebastopol, CA 95473-0062
(S scale dry transfers)

CRYSTAL RIVER PRODUCTS
P.O. Box 598
Conifer, CO 80433
(S scale structure kits)

CTT, INC.
109 Medallion Center
Dallas, TX 75214
(S scale/gauge layout design products)

DES PLAINES HOBBIES
1468 Lee St.
Des Plaines, IL 60018
(custom S gauge rolling stock)

DIGITRAX COMMAND CONTROL
450 Cemetery St., #206
Norcross, GA 30071
770-441-7992
fax: 770-441-0759
www.digitrax.com
(command control components)

DOUGLAS BROOKS CREATIVE MODELS
307 MacKay Ave.
Ventura, CA 93004
http://swiftsite.com/dbcreative-models
(model palm trees—all scales)

DOWNS MODEL RAILROAD COMPANY
314 Lehigh Avenue
Gloucester City, NJ 08030-1217
856-742-0790
fax: 856-742-1864
(wheels and wheelsets for S gauge trains)

GARGRAVES TRACKAGE CORPORATION
Dept. S
8967 Ridge Road
North Rose, NY 14516-9793
315-483-6577
fax: 315-483-2425
www.GarGraves.com
(S gauge switches and track components)

GILBERT REPRODUCTIONS
288 Lancaster Ave.
Malvern, PA 19355
610-296-9428
fax: 610-725-0332
www.webvalley.com/sss_trains
(reproduction American Flyer accessories and tools)

GLENN SNYDER DISPLAY SYSTEMS
260 Oak St.
Buffalo, NY 14203
877-852-4676
fax: 716-852-4677
e-mail: glenn@gsds.com
www.gsds.com
(train display shelves)

HOMABED
801 Chesley Ave.
Richmond, CA 94801-2135
888-772-3348
www.homabed.com
(Homasote roadbed for S gauge track)

KADEE QUALITY PRODUCTS CO.
Dept. 1-S
673 Avenue C
White City, OR 97503-1078
541-826-3883
fax: 541-826-4013
(S scale couplers)

K-LINE ELECTRIC TRAINS
P.O. Box 2831
Chapel Hill, NC 27515
800-866-9986
fax: 919-929-4050
general questions: info@k-line-trains.com
service: service@k-linetrains.com
www.k-linetrains.com
(S gauge track components)

LEHIGH VALLEY MODELS
1225 N. Arch St.
Allentown, PA 18104
(S scale rolling stock kits, trucks, and other vehicles)

MAINSTREETER TRAINS
3895 Colony Paks Drive
Eugene, OR 97405
(car loads and related accessories for American Flyer rolling stock)

MIDNIGHT FLYER PRODUCTS
P.O. Box 41431
Cleveland, OH 44141
(reproduction skirts for American Flyer passenger cars)

MODEL RECTIFIER CORPORATION (MRC)
80 Newfield Avenue
P.O. Box 6312
Edison, NJ 08837
732-225-6360
fax: 732-225-0091
(transformers and power packs for all scales)

M.T.H ELECTRIC TRAINS
7020 Columbia Gateway Dr.
Columbia, MD 21046-1532
888-640-3700
www.mth-railking.com
(Z-4000 transformer for S gauge AC operations)

NASG CLEARINGHOUSE
c/o William Mark, Jr.
438 Rossway Road
Pleasant Valley, NY 12569
914-635-8553
*(coupler height gauge; caps,
T-shirts, other apparel items)*

NORTHWEST SHORT LINE
Box 423
Seattle, WA 98111-0423
206-932-1087
fax: 206-935-7106
(locomotive gears)

ODDBALLS DECALS
26550 227th St.
McLouth, KS 66054
(S scale decals)

PENNSY 'S' MODELS
P.O. Box 5252
Deptford, NJ 08096
856-848-5133
e-mail: info@pennsymodels.com
(S scale rolling stock)

PORT LINES HOBBY SUPPLIES
6 Stoneybrook Dr.
Newburyport, MA 01950-3408
978-465-8798
fax: 978-465-8798
orders only: 888-708-0782
e-mail: portlines@mediaone.com
www.portlines.com
*(S gauge locomotives, rolling
stock, accessories, and parts)*

RAIL RAX
786 Seely Ave.
Aromas, CA 95004
800-830-2843
(display shelves)

RAILROAD PRYNTERS
Dept. S2
P.O. Box 13113
San Luis Obispo, CA 93406
*(S scale signs, building paper,
structure materials)*

REM'S RAILROAD MODELS
536 E. Perry Rd., Suite #6
Grand Blanc, MI 48439
810-785-1088
fax: 810-785-1088
e-mail: remheck@earthlink.net
(S scale rolling stock kits)

R.F. GIARDINA, CO. (RFG)
P.O. Box 562
Oyster Bay, NY 11771
fax: 516-922-1364
*(American Flyer and S
gauge/scale model train parts,
electronics, and supplies)*

RICK JOHNSON
19333 Sturgess Drive
Torrance, CA 90503
310-371-9668
*(molded rubber roadbed for S
gauge track)*

RR-TRACK
R&S Enterprises
P.O. Box 643
Jonestown, PA 17038
717-865-3444
www.rrtrack.com/rrtrack
*(Sectional track layout planning
software)*

R.S.S.V.P. MODELS
P.O. Box 345, Dept. S
Tyngsboro, MA 01879
(S gauge rolling stock)

RUSS BURNS (AFL PARTS)
2109 Pineview Court
Marilla, NY 14102
716-652-1110
*(reproduction parts for American
Flyer and other S scale/gauge
trains)*

S SCALE LOCO & SUPPLY
P.O. Box 550
Richland Town, PA 18955
fax: 610-346-9178
e-mail:
testingspecialties@nni.com
*(detail parts for S scale
equipment)*

SCENERY UNLIMITED
7236 W. Madison St.
Forest Park, IL 60130
708-366-7763
*(wide variety of S scale products,
parts, Shinohara track, and
accessories)*

SIEVERS BENCHWORK
Jackson Harbor Rd.
Washington Island, WI 54246
*(ready-to-assemble custom
benchwork)*

TRAIN REPAIR PARTS
Div. of Hobby Surplus Sales
287 Main St.
P.O. Box 2170
New Britain, CT 06050
www.TrainRepairParts.com
*(repair parts for American Flyer
trains)*

TRAINTRACKER
BangZoom Software, Inc.
14 Storrs Ave.
Braintree, MA 02184
781-849-9977
fax: 781-849-7555
e-mail:
traintracker@bangzoom.com
www.bangzoom.com/TT
(software for toy train inventory)

WILLARD ANIMATIONS
96 Greenwich Drive
Westampton, NJ 08060
609-265-0321
*(custom modular O gauge
animations)*

WOODLAND SCENICS
P.O. Box 98
Linn Creek, MO 65052
573-346-5555
e-mail: webmaster@woodland-
scenics.com
www.woodlandscenics.com
*(variety of scenery materials for
all scales)*

major retailers of S scale/gauge products

This list of S scale/gauge retailers includes dealers who support the hobby through published (in print and/or on line) advertising of their product lines, and whose advertising indicates that they stock or specialize in S scale/gauge products. This list should not be considered all-inclusive. There may be other retailers in your local area who are not listed here, but who do stock S scale/gauge products—consult your phone directory Yellow Pages. Support of your local dealer is always strongly encouraged.

For names and addresses of "authorized" sales or service stations, contact the product manufacturer, or check the manufacturer's web site on the Internet.

AR **TED'S TRAINS & TOYS**
15579 Mariano Rd.
Bentonville, AR 72712
501-273-9915

AZ **ARIZONA TRAINS**
2420 North Treat Ave.
Tucson, AZ 85716
520-325-2321
fax: 520-325-2905
e-mail: aztrains@earthlink.net
www.aztrains.com

CA **TOY TRAIN SHOP**
1829 W. Lincoln
Anaheim, CA 92801
714-991-1040
www.toytrainshop.com

TRACKSIDE TRAINS
1675 Rollins Rd, #B-1
Burlingame, CA 94010-2320
650-692-9724

NORCAL TRAINS & TRUCKS
2797 Depot Rd., #16
Hayward, CA 94545
510-887-7115

THE ELECTRIC TRAIN COMPANY
16200 Hawthorne Blvd.
Lawnsdale, CA 90260
310-370-3839

ALLIED MODEL TRAINS
4411 S. Sepulveda Blvd.
Los Angeles, CA 90230
310-313-9353

PALMDALE HOBBIES
2127 E. Palmdale Blvd.
Palmdale, CA 93550
805-273-6229

THE ORIGINAL WHISTLE STOP INC.
2490 E. Colorado Blvd.
Pasedena, CA 91107
626-796-7791
www.the whistlestop.com

CLASSIC TRAINS
18927 E. Colima Rd.
Rowland Heights, CA 91748-2942
626-912-0774
fax: 626-912-1033
www.classictrains.com

THE TRAIN STOP
211 W. Bonita Ave.
San Dimas, CA 91773
909-599-2602

CHAN'S TRAINS & KITS
2450 Van Ness & Union St.
San Francisco, CA 94109
415-885-2899

FRANCISCAN HOBBIES
11920-A Ocean Ave.
San Francisco, CA 94127
415-584-3919

TALBOT'S
445 South "B" Street
San Mateo, CA 94401
415-342-0267

CO **CABOOSE HOBBIES**
500 S. Broadway
Denver, CO 80209-4002
303-777-6766
fax: 303-777-0028
www.caboosehobbies.com

COLORADO S-SCALE
Connection
250 Broadway
Denver, CO 80203
303-777-2880

MIZELL TRAINS
3051 W. 74th Ave.
Westminster, CO 80030
303-429-4811

CT **BERKSHIRE HILLS HOBBY SUPPLY**
93 Main St., P.O. Box 939
Canaan, CT 06018
860-824-0527

AMATO'S TOY & HOBBY
283 Main St.
New Britain, CT 06051
860-229-9096

TRAIN COLLECTOR
P.O. Box 764
North Haven, CT 06473
203-239-1346
http://members.aol.com/AFSTrains/TrainCollector.html

J&E TRAIN DEPOT
911 Hartford Tpl. (Rt. 30)
Vernon, CT 06066
203-870-7731

DE **TRACKSIDE HOBBIES**
2622 Capitol Trail
Newark, DE 19711
302-266-8063

FL **DISCOUNT TRAIN
& HOBBY**
312 E. Oakland Park Blvd.
Ft. Lauderdale, FL 33334
954-561-0403
fax: 954-564-5367
e-mail: dtl@ix.netcom.com

HOLLYWOOD STATION
1917 Hollywood Blvd.
Hollywood, FL
954-921-2700
e-mail: trainman@
  bellsouth.net
www.hollywood-station
  .com

THE DEPOT HOBBY SHOP
Lantana Shopping Center
603 Ridge Rd.
Lantana, FL 33462
561-585-1982

**ORANGE BLOSSOM
HOBBIES**
1975 NW 36th St.
Miami, FL 33142
305-633-1517

READY-TO-ROLL
831 N. W. 143rd St.
Miami, FL 33168
305-688-8868

B.T.S.
P.O. Box 561
Seffner, FL 33583-0561
813-759-6300
fax: 813-759-8218
e-mail: bill@btsrr.com

**MILLER TOY TRAIN
REPAIR**
5157 Harbinger Rd.
Spring Hill, FL 34608
352-686-7587

H & R TRAINS, INC.
6901 U.S. 19 at Haines Rd.
Pinellas Park, FL 33781
727-526-4682
fax: 813-526-3439
www.hrtrains.com

GA **TOY TRAINS 'N THINGS**
2055 Beaver Ruin Rd.
Atlanta (Norcross), GA
30071
770-446-7868

**LAKESHORE HOBBY
& CRAFT**
275 Pearl Nix Parkway
Gainesville, GA 30501
770-532-4016

LEGACY STATION LTD.
251F Hurricane Shoals Rd.
Lawrenceville, GA 30045
770-339-7780
www.trainworks.com

IA **BOONE HOBBIES**
804 Story St.
Boone, IA 50362
515-432-2361

CABOOSE STOP HOBBIES
301 Main St.
Cedar Falls, IA 50613
319-277-1754

RED'S TRAIN SHOP
3135 Highway 117 N.
Colfax, IA 50054
515-674-3813

**FARNSWORTH
ELECTRONICS**
201-209 E. Mullan Ave.
Waterloo, IA 50704
319-234-6681

IL **HANNAH'S HOME
ACCENTS**
455 Lake St.
Antioch, IL 60002
888-78HOMES

HOBBY CITY
6910 W. Cermak Rd.
Berwyn, IL 60402
708-795-0280

DES PLAINES HOBBIES
1468 Lee St.
Des Plaines, IL 60018
847-297-2118
www.desplaineshobbies
  .com

SCENERY UNLIMITED
7236 W. Madison
Forest Park, IL 60130
708-366-7763

ILLIANA SHORT LINE
3304 Ridge Rd.
Lansing, IL 60438
708-474-9999

**W. SUBURBAN MODEL
RR CENTER**
105 S. River Rd., Suite E
N. Aurora, IL 60542

**HILL'S HOBBY
& COLLECTORS' SHOP**
10 Prairie Ave.
Park Ridge, IL 60068
847-823-4464
www.hillshobby.com

DURST CO. TRAINS
1112 W. University Ave.
Urbana/Champaign, IL
61801
217-367-3600

TIMELESS HOBBIES
75 Danada Sq. East
Wheaton, IL 60477
630-897-2867

IN **BIG FOUR HOBBIES**
1005 E. Main St.
Indianapolis, IN 46186
317-837-1024

KS **DESTINATION TRAIN
CENTER**
13444 Santa Fe Trail Dr.
Lenexa, KS 66215
913-541-8800
www.mindspring.com/
~dtc1

ENGINE HOUSE HOBBIES
2718 Boulevard Plaza
Wichita, KS 67211
316-685-6608

LA **PONCHARTRAIN HOBBY
SHOP**
3755 Ponchartrain Dr.
Slidell, LA 70458
504-649-1199

MA **BEDFORD TRAIN SHOP**
32 Shawsheen Ave.
Bedford, MA 01730
617-275-7525

CHARLES RO SUPPLY, CO.
662 Cross St.
P.O. Box 100
Malden, MA 02148
781-321-0090
fax: 781-321-6459
www.charlesro.com

MODELER'S JUNCTION
88 Lowell St.
Methuen, MA 01844
978-683-0885

**PORT LINES HOBBY
SUPPLIES**
6 Stoneybrook Dr.
Newburyport, MA 01950
978-465-8798
fax: 978-465-8798
orders only: 888-708-0782
e-mail: portlines@aol.com
http://trainweb.com/
cro-con/portlines.html

**BILL'S FRIENDLY TRAIN
SHOPPE**
414 Center Street
Randolph, MA 02368
617-986-5295

JACK'S TRAINS
1 Christmas Tree Lane
Rutland, MA 01543
508-886-4394

PIONEER VALLEY HOBBIES
28 Hanover Street
Springfield, MA 01105
413-732-5531

MD **M.B. KLEIN**
162 N. Gay St.
Baltimore, MD 21202
301-529-6207

FOREST HILL STATION
15 E. Jarrettsville Rd.
(at Rte. 24)
Forest Hill, MD 21050
410-893-1089

**TRAINS, TOYS
& TREASURES**
1507 W. Patrick St.
Frederick, MD 21702
301-662-5202
301-662-0411

THE TRAIN ROOM
360 S. Burhans Blvd.
Hagerstown, MD 21740
301-745-6681

TRAIN DEPOT
214 S. Main St.
Mt. Airy, MD 21771
301-607-8155

JOEY'S TRAINS
2441-B Mountain Rd.
Pasadena, MD 21122-1211
410-439-9510
www.joeystrains.com

**CATOCTIN MOUNTAIN
TRAINS & HOBBIES**
3 W. Main St.
Thurmont, MD 21788
800-532-6589/
301-694-8331
trainspj@aol.com

ME **ON TRACK TRAINS**
Rte 11
Limerick, ME 04048
207-793-4484

MAINE-LY TRAINS
Rt. 22
South China, ME 04358
207-445-3695

**NORM'S O SCALE
(TRAINS & MORE)**
50 Main Mall Rd.
South Portland, ME 04106
207-772-2211

MI **MADISON HARDWARE**
1915 W. Fort Street
Detroit, MI 48216-1817
313-965-9888/
313-965-4382

MYERS HOBBY HOUSE
2136 Plainfield NE
Grand Rapids, MI 49505

MICHIGAN MODELS
2311 Strathmore
Lansing, MI 48910-2885
517-482-2048

MERRI SEVEN TRAINS
19155 Merriman Rd.
Livonia, MI 48152
810-474-5373

**MICHIGAN MODEL TRAIN
CENTER**
9260 McFregor Rd.
Pinckney, MI 48169
734-426-1651

L&J HOBBIES
8847 Portage Rd.
Portage, MI 49002
616-323-1010

**BRASSEUR ELECTRIC
TRAINS**
410 Court St.
Saginaw, MI 48602-4209
517-793-4753

**BOB'S HOBBIES
& COLLECTIBLES**
115 N. Main St.
Water Vliet, MI 49098
616-463-7452

EUREKA TRAINS
1219 Eureka
Wyandotte, MI 48192
313-284-0521

MN **ELLINGTON CRAFT
VILLAGE**
7799 East Rose St.
Owatonna, MN 55060
507-451-0466
www.ellingtoncraft.com

HUB HOBBY CENTER
6416 Penn Ave. South
Richfield, MN 55423
612-866-9575

MO **CHANDLER'S HOBBY
SHOP**
RR1
Holliday City, MO 65258
660-266-3415

**MARTY'S MODEL
RAILROADS**
9622 Gravois Rd.
St. Louis, MO 63123
314-638-8250

NC **TRAINS LIMITED**
5600 Albemarle Rd.,
Suite 300
Charlotte, NC 28212
704-566-9007

THE INSIDE TRACK
1615 W. Friendly Ave.
Greensboro, NC 27403
919-275-5727

DRY BRIDGE STATION
236 N. Main St.
Mount Airy, NC 27030
336-786-9811
e-mail: mikek@
    drybridgestation.com
www.drybridgestation.com

JOE'S TRAIN REPAIR
404 Shetland Rd.
Rougemont, NC 27572
919-471-2613

TODD'S TRAIN DEPOT
3169 Wendell Blvd.,
Box 849
Wendell, NC 27591
919-365-5006

NH **MANSFIELD HOBBIES**
31 Mill Road
Kingston, NH 03848
603-642-5215

NJ **MIKE'S COINS
& COLLECTIBLES**
2900 Dune Drive, Suite 3
Avalon, NJ 08202
609-967-4484

TONY'S TRAIN TOWN
575 Pompton Ave.
Cedar Grove, NJ 07009
201-857-2337

FLYERTOWN MUSEUM
2044 Rt. 9
Clermont, NJ 08210
609-624-3173

CHICK'S HOBBY CENTER
924 Berkley Rd.
Gibbstown, NJ 08027
609-423-0773

DKB RAILWAY SUPPLIES
114 Main St.
Hightstown, NJ 08520
609-448-5070
http://members.aol.com/
MLANDP/dkbpg1.htm

THE TRAIN STORE
553 Bound Brook Rd.
Middlesex, NJ 08846
732-424-1055

TRAINS 'N THINGS
936 E. Weymouth Rd.
Vineland, NJ 08360
856-697-8844
www.trainsnthings.com

LASKEY'S TRAINS
5A Star Plaza
Washington, NJ 07887
908-835-0799

HOBBIES, ETC.
240 South Broad St.
Woodbury, NJ 08096
609-384-7740

NM **WESTERN STATIONERS**
703 N. Bullard St.
Silver City, NM 88061
505-538-5324

NV **TRAIN EXCHANGE**
6008 Boulder Hwy
Las Vegas, NV 89122
702-456-8766

NY **RLR RAILROAD**
15 Jackson St.
Batavia, NY 14020
716-344-1729

**BINGHAMTON MODEL
RR SUPPLY**
93 Front St.
Binghamton, NY 13905
607-722-9239

**GOLDEN SPIKE
INTERNATIONAL**
1700 Grand Concourse
Bronx, NY 10457
718-294-1614
fax: 718-294-5319
www.goldentrains.com

TRAINWORLD
751 McDonald Ave.
Brooklyn, NY 11218
718-436-7072
fax: 718-972-8514
www.trainworldny.com

AURORA RAILS
2268 Blakely Rd
East Aurora, NY 14052
716-652-5718

DESPATCH JUNCTION
100 Station Road
East Rochester, NY 14445
716-385-5570

NASSAU HOBBY CENTER
43 W. Merrick Rd.
Freeport, NY 11520
516-378-9594

HAMBURG MODEL RR STATION
4 Scott St.
(Erie Lackawanna Station)
Hamburg, NY 14075
716-649-3568

TRAINLAND
293 Sunrise Hwy.
Lynbrook, NY 11563
516-599-7080
fax: 718-972-8514
www.trainworldny.com

THE RED CABOOSE
23 West 45th St.
New York, NY 10036
212-575-0155

NORTH SYRACUSE TRAIN SHOP
6037 East Taft Rd.
North Syracuse, NY 13212
315-458-6753

NORWOOD HOBBY SHOP
2-4 South Main St.
Norwood, NY 13668
315-353-6621
www.norwoodhobby.com

LACKAWANNA TRAIN SHOP
86 Victory Highway
Painted Post, NY 14870
607-962-5164

MOHAWK VALLEY RAILROAD CO.
2937 Hamburg St.
Schenectady, NY 12304
518-372-9124

LEBLANC COMPANY
28 Hamlin Pl
Staten Island, NY 10302
701-872-7612

TWIN RAIL HOBBIES
2703 Hurd and Parks Rd.
Swan Lake, NY 12783
914-295-9546

DAVE'S S GAUGE HOBBIES
8226 Main St.
Williamsville, NY 14221
716-632-6102

OH **TRAIN AMERICA**
4199 Boardman-Canfield Rd.
Canfield, OH 44406
330-533-7181
www.trainamerica.com

THE BLUE CABOOSE
4290 Indianola Ave.
Columbus, OH 43214
614-447-1707

TINPLATE STATION
6342-B Far Hills Ave.
Dayton, OH 45459
937-428-9667

G&M TRAINS & HOBBY
301 S. 4th Street
Martins Ferry, OH 43935
740-633-6055

PUTT TRAINS
P.O. Box 463
Orwell, OH 44076

RICK'S TOY TRAINS
4807 Lewis Ave.
Toledo, OH 43612
419-478-0171

OR **PACIFIC RAIL SHOP**
230 North 2nd Ct.
Coos Bay, OR 97420
541-267-6664

THE OLD TOY TRAIN TRADING CO.
665 Virginia
P.O. Box 1112
North Bend, OR 97459
541-756-4594
fax: 541-756-4594

WHISTLE STOP TRAINS
11724 SE Division St.
Portland, OR 97266
503-761-1822
fax: 503-761-1861

PA **ALLENTOWN TOY TRAIN SERVICE**
125-1/2 North 11th St.
Allentown, PA 18102-3843
610-821-0740

ENGLER'S TRAIN DEPOT
2733 W. Emmaus Ave.
Allentown, PA 18103
610-791-9512

WIKE'S HOBBY SHOP
1251 E. Main St.
Anniville, PA 17003
717-867-2318

DAVE'S HOBBIES
1548 Bristol Pike
Bensalem, PA 19020
215-638-0083

MAINLINE HOBBY SUPPLY
15066 Buchanan Trail East
Blue Ridge Summit, PA 17214

NICHOLAS SMITH TRAINS
2343 W. Chester Pike
Broomall, PA 19008
610-353-8585

WAGNER & SONS, INC.
28 E. Willow St.
Carlisle, PA 17013
717-258-0839

SOPP'S HOBBY SHOP
11 Olde Ridge Village
Chadds Ford, PA 19355
610-558-3050

FRED'S TRAIN PARTS
2102 Concord Road
Chester, PA 19013
610-494-4578/
610-497-2670
fax: 610/494-7769

CHARLES SIEGAL'S TRAIN CITY
3133 Zuck Rd.
Erie, PA 16506
814-833-8313

TOM'S TRAINS
288 Lancaster Ave.
Frazer, PA 19355
610-296-9428

ALL ABOARD RAILROAD
1952 Landis Valley Rd.
Lancaster, PA 17601
717-392-1568

BILL PARRIS HOBBY SUPPLIES
205 Golf Club Drive
Langhorne, PA 19047
215-757-1034

ELLIE'S LOKIE SHOP
135 W. Mahanoy Ave.
Mahanoy City, PA 17948
717-773-2174

MAHANOY CITY HOBBIES
1038 E. Centre St.
Mahanoy, PA 17948
570-773-2349

ENGLISH'S MODEL R.R. SUPPLY
21 Howard St.
Montoursville, PA 17754
717-368-5046

B&E JUNCTION
2 Lincoln Hwy/Rte. 30
New Oxford, PA 17350
717-624-4327

TOY TRAIN STATION
21 E. Street Rd.
Philadelphia (Feasterville),
PA 19053
215-322-5182

IRON HORSE HOBBY SHOP
1950 Painters Run Road
Pittsburgh, PA 15241
412-221-2250

COVENTRY TRAINS
653 Laurelwood Rd.
Pottstown, PA 19465
610-323-7792

RI **APPLE VALLEY HOBBIES**
9 Cedar Swamp Rd.
Smithfield, RI 02917
401-231-7790

LARRY'S OUTBOARD & HOBBIES
65 Bordens Ln
Tiverton, RI 02878
401-624-6244

SC **CREATIVE PASTIMES**
1011 3rd Ave.
Conway, SC 29526
843-248-2600

RAIL & SPIKE TRAINS & HOBBIES
6788-L Calhoun Mem. Hwy.
Easley, SC 29640
864-850-0237

TN **PETERSON'S TRAIN STORE**
2613 McGavock Pike
Nashville, TN 37214
615-391-3516

TX **SADDLE HOUSE**
Rt. 5, Box 367A
Bryan, TX 77807
419-778-0732

COLLECTIBLE TRAINS & TOYS
109 Medallion Center
Dallas, TX 75214
214-373-9469
e-mail: ctt@airmail.net
www.trainsandtoys.com

TRAINSOURCE TEXAS
3264 S. Loop West,
South Main
Houston, TX 77025
713-662-0809

LONE STAR TRAINS & COLLECTIBLES
4133 Naco-Perrin
San Antonio, TX 78217
210-655-4665

WACO HOBBY STOP
3253 Village Park Dr.
Waco, TX 76708
254-756-1518
www.pufferbellys.com

UT **BOOMER TRAINS LLC**
6229 S. Highland Dr.
(2000 E)
Salt Lake City, UT 84121
801-272-1711

VA **TRAIN JUNCTION**
3550 Seminole Tr.
Charlottesville, VA 22911
804-550-0739

LEVENTON HOBBY SUPPLY
P.O. Box 1525
Chehalis, VA 98532
360-748-3643/
360-748-6236
fax: 360-748-7507

ARLINGTON HOBBY CRAFTERS
230 West Broad Street
Falls Church, VA 22046
703-532-2224

BOBBY'S TOY TRAINS
10412 Washington Hwy.
Glen Allen, VA 23059
804-974-9499

CHESTERFIELD HOBBIES
13154 Midlothian Tpke.
Village Marketplace
Shopping Center
Midlothian, VA 23701
804-979-9091
www.chesterfieldhobbies.
com

GRANDAD'S HOBBY SHOP
5260-A Port Royal Road
Springfield, VA 22151
703-426-0700

WA **THE INSIDE GATEWAY**
14725 SE Stark St.
Bellvue, WA 98007
425-747-2016

LEVENTON HOBBY SUPPLY
P.O. Box 1525
Chehalis, WA 98532
360-748-3643/
360-748-6236
fax: 360-748-7507

EASTSIDE TRAINS
217 Central Way
Kirkland, WA 98033
425-828-4098

TRACKSIDE TRAINS
202 East Pioneer Ave.
Puyallup, WA
253-845-9759
fax: 253-845-4781
e-mail:
trainman@nwrain.com
www.tracksidetrains.net

PACIFIC RAILWAY HOBBIES
5115 100th St. SW
Tacoma, WA 98499
206-581-4453

WI **SOMMERFELD'S TRAINS & HOBBIES**
12620 W. Hampton Ave.
Butler, WI 53007
414-783-7797
fax: 414-783-9815

HOBBY DEPOT
1524 E. Sumner St.
Hartford, WI 53027
414-670-6242

TERMINAL HOBBIES
5601 W. Florist Ave.
Milwaukee, WI 53218
800-487-2467
c/o: www.walthers.com

JETCO'S HIAWATHA HOBBIES
1701 Summit Ave.
Waukesha, WI 53188
558-544-4131

WV **BRADY HARDWARE**
642 Main St.
Barboursville, WV 25504
304-736-1521

WEST VIRGINIA HOBBY AND CRAFT
Putnam Shopping Center
Teays, WV 25569
304-757-6474

associations and clubs of interest to N scale/gauge hobbyists

TOY TRAIN OPERATING SOCIETY (TTOS)
25 W. Walnut St., Suite 308
Pasadena, CA 91103
626-578-0673
www.ttos.org

A. C. GILBERT HERITAGE SOCIETY
1440 Whalley, PMB 252
New Haven, CT 06515
www.acghs.org

NATIONAL ASSOCIATION OF S-GAUGERS (NASG)
c/o Michael Paschall
2300 Bethelview Road, Suite 110
Cumming, GA 30040-9474
www.trainweb.com/nasg

LIONEL COLLECTORS CLUB OF AMERICA (LCCA)
P.O. Box 479
La Salle, IL 61301
www.lionelcollectors.org

LIONEL RAILROADERS CLUB
(sponsored by Lionel LLC)
50625 Richard W. Blvd.
Chesterfield, MI 48051-2493
810-940-4100
e-mail: talktous@lionel.com
www.lionel.com

NATIONAL MODEL RAILROAD ASSOCIATION (NMRA)
4121 Cromwell Rd.
Chattanooga, TN 37421
423-892-2846
fax: 423-899-4869
www.nmra.org

TRAIN COLLECTORS ASSOCIATION (TCA)
National Business Office
P.O. Box 248
Dept. 10
Strasburg, PA 17579
www.traincollectors.org

magazines, periodicals, books and videos
for S scale/gauge hobbyists

NASG DISPATCH MAGAZINE
(subscription included in NASG
membership)
c/o Michael Paschall
2300 Bethelview Road, Suite 110
Cumming, GA 30040-9474
www.trainweb.com/nasg

S GAUGIAN MAGAZINE
Heimburger House Publishing Co.
7236 W. Madison St.
Forest Park, IL 60130
708-366-1973
http://trainweb.com/sgaugian

**CLASSIC TOY TRAINS
MAGAZINE**
Kalmbach Publishing Co.
21027 Crossroads Circle
P.O. Box 1612
Waukesha, WI 53187-1612
800-446-5489
www.classtrain.com

SN3 MODELER MAGAZINE
Heimburger House Publishing Co.
7236 W. Madison St.
Forest Park, IL 60130
708-366-1973
http://trainweb.com/Sn3modeler

**A.C. GILBERT'S FAMOUS
AMERICAN FLYER TRAINS**
Heimburger House Publishing Co.
7236 W. Madison St.
Forest Park, IL 60130
708-366-1973

**SCENERY UNLIMITED S/SN3
SCALE**
Model Railroad Catalog and
Reference Manual book
7236 W. Madison St.
Forest Park, IL 60130
708-366-1973

**AMERICAN FLYER AND "I LOVE
TOY TRAINS" VIDEOS**
TM Books & Videos
Box 279
New Buffalo, MI 49117
800-892-2822
fax: 219-879-7909
e-mail: tmbooks@aol.com
www.tmbooks-video.com

**THE ALMOST COMPLETE
GUIDE TO AMERICAN FLYER
SETS**
Flyernut Publishing
c/o Robert J. Tufts
4719 Logwood Lane
Chantilly, VA 20151

**O'BRIEN'S COLLECTING TOY
TRAINS: IDENTIFICATION AND
VALUE GUIDE**
Krause Publications
700 E. State St.
Iola, WI 54990
715-445-2214/800-258-0929
fax: 715-445-4087
www.krause.com/Books

**GREENBERG'S POCKET PRICE
GUIDE TO AMERICAN FLYER:
1946-2000**
Kalmbach Publishing Co.
21027 Crossroads Circle
P.O. Box 1612
Waukesha, WI 53187-1612
800-446-5489
www.kalmbach.com/books

**GREENBERG'S GUIDE TO
AMERICAN FLYER S GAUGE:
VOL 1—MOTIVE POWER AND
ROLLING STOCK**
Kalmbach Publishing Co.
21027 Crossroads Circle
P.O. Box 1612
Waukesha, WI 53187-1612
800-446-5489
www.kalmbach.com/books

**NARROW GAUGE AND SHORT
LINE GAZETTE MAGAZINE**
4966 El Camino Real, #101
Los Altos, CA 94022
650-941-3823
fax: 650-941-3845
e-mail: gazette@worldnet.att.net
www.ngslgazette.com

TCA QUARTERLY
(Official quarterly journal, plus
extra issue in April, of the Train
Collectors Association.
Subscription included with membership.)
300 Paradise Lane
Ronks, PA 17572-9537
717-687-8623
fax: 717-687-0742
www.traincollectors.org

TTOS BULLETIN
(Official bi-monthly journal of the
Toy Train Operating Society.
Subscription included
with membership.)
25 W. Walnut St., Suite 308
Pasadena, CA 91103
626-578-0673
fax: 626-578-0750
e-mail: ttos@ttos.org
www.ttos.org

TM BOOKS & VIDEOS
Box 279
New Buffalo, MI 49117
800-892-2822
fax: 219-879-7909
e-mail: tmbooks@aol.com
www.tmbooks-video.com
(toy train videos, value guides,
and reference books. Call for
catalog.)

GREENBERG BOOKS
Kalmbach Publishing Co.
21027 Crossroads Circle
P.O. Box 1612
Waukesha, WI 53187-1612
800-446-5489
www.books.kalmbach.com
(Greenberg line of toy train price guides and reference books. Call for catalog.)

ANTIQUE TRADER BOOKS/ KRAUSE BOOKS
Krause Publications
700 E. State St.
Iola, WI 54990
888-457-2873
www.krause.com/Books
(Publisher of toy train and model railroad price and reference guides. Call for catalog)

web sites of interest to S scale/gauge hobbyists

www.trainweb.org/s-trains
Paul Yorke's S gauge/S scale "S-Trains" Web Site
(Detailed information and links for American Flyer and other S scale/S gauge enthusiasts. Comprehensive one-stop Internet site for the S gauge hobbyist.)

www.trainweb.com
(Major sections include prototype and model railroad information, including rail travel, railfan, model railroading, rail industry, rail search, rail forums, 360x360 photos, and live web cams. Provides links to manufacturers, dealers, and other relavent sites.)

www.tttrains.com
(Information for model railroaders in all scales; links to manufacturers, dealers, and organizations.)

www.trainweb.com/crocon/ sscale.html
(S scale model railroading home page.)

wwwO.delphi.com/railroad
Delphi Railroading Forum
(Site for general railroad/railfan/ model railroad topics.)

www.tmbooks-video.com
Toy Train Revue On-Line
(News and information from the world of toy trains.)

www.railserve.com
RailServe Home Page
(On-line directory to rail-related content on the Internet.)

www.ehobbies.com
(model railroad discussion groups and general interest train topics)

www.eppraisals.com
(On-line appraisal services, including toy and model trains.)

www.ebay.com
(Internet auction site)

www.amazon.com/auctions
(Internet auction site)

www.boxlot.com
(Internet auction site)

www.collect.com
(Internet auction site)

High-stepping motive power from M.T.H. Electric Trains in action on Rob Adelman's beautifully detailed O gauge Hi-Rail empire. The term "Hi Rail" is used by three-rail O gauge modelers to describe layouts which are constructed to resemble and operate like the real thing, aside from the larger-than-scale track profile.

Photo courtesy of Rob Adelman

O SCALE/GAUGE
(1:48)

I In the annals of model railroading, O scale/gauge will likely be remembered as the "Comeback Kid" of the hobby. To understand what has happened in this scale in recent years, it's best to start with a look back at the pre-World War II era.

In the period leading up to the Second World War, O scale (scale models) and O gauge (toy trains) dominated the marketplace—inspired, in large part, by the presence of Joshua Lionel Cowen's renowned Lionel Corporation and its line of high-quality O gauge electric toy trains. Cowen did his best, through astute business savvy and skillful marketing tactics, to assure that no Christmas was complete without a Lionel Electric Train circling the family tree. In the years leading up to the war, O gauge surely reigned supreme as king of the model railroading world.

But things began to change shortly after the war, and O scale/gauge model railroading quickly lost ground to HO, which featured models approximately half the size of their O scale counterparts. The evolution of plastics, along with improvements in mass manufacturing processes, meant that HO trains could be produced in large quantities, and at less cost, than comparable O-size models. This helped spur the growth HO model railroading, and by the early 1950s that scale effectively dominated the marketplace—a ranking it holds to this day.

Over time, O scale/gauge dropped even further in terms of popularity and market share— down to a distant third place behind N scale, which is half the size of HO. Lionel's fortunes plummeted, and in 1969 the firm was sold to General Mills, the breakfast food folks. Ownership of the familiar orange-and-blue Lionel trademark has even changed hands a couple of times since, and it is now owned by an East Coast investment group which today manufactures trains under the Lionel LLC banner. And here's where the story of "O" takes an interesting turn!

In the late 1980s, Lionel Trains, Inc., owners of the trademark at the time, negotiated an arrangement with Mike Wolf, a young Maryland-based entrepreneur, which called for Wolf to handle overseas development and manufacturing of Lionel's "Classics" line of trains— reproductions of some of the original Lionel Corporation's early Standard gauge and O gauge tinplate trains and accessories. For several years, this arrangement between Lionel Trains, Inc., and what was then known as Mike's Train House, worked well enough for both parties. But in 1992, the cooperative arrangement between Lionel and Mike Wolf soured. Wolf subsequently launched his own enterprise: M.T.H. Electric Trains. And the rest, as they say, is history!

M.T.H. Electric Trains has grown over the short period of seven-or-so years into a dominant player in the O scale/gauge marketplace. Some suggest that M.T.H. has even replaced Lionel as the sales leader in that segment of the industry. Regardless of the actual numbers, it's probably safe to assert that O gauge (the three-rail segment of the hobby) has certainly narrowed the gap between it and the still-number-two player in the hobby: N scale.

Wolf's success in the marketplace has also impacted other manufacturers of O gauge equipment, spurring them to offer new and improved products in an effort to compete effectively. Today, there are no less than six major players vying for the O gauge market, and their ranks are swelled even further by specialized manufacturers such as Marx Trains, whose products appeal to the nostalgia market for O gauge toy trains. And, all of these manufacturers are actively supported by a growing number of after-market suppliers who provide an ever-expanding assortment of peripheral items to support O gauge railroading. If there ever was a time in the history of the hobby to be involved in O scale/gauge, this certainly is that time!

O SCALE/GAUGE RESOURCES
(three-rail O27 & O gauge, and 1:48 O scale)

manufacturers of O scale/gauge locomotives and rolling stock

ATLAS O, LLC
603 Sweetland Ave.
Hillside, NJ 07205
908-687-9590
fax: 908-687-6282
e-mail: Help@AtlasO.com
www.atlasO.com

BACHMANN INDUSTRIES, INC.
(On30 scale)
1400 East Erie Ave.
Philadelphia, PA 19124
215-533-1600
fax: 215-744-4699
e-mail: Bachmanntrains@aol.com
www.bachmanntrains.com

BOWSER MFG. CO., INC.
1302 Jordan Ave.
P.O. Box 322
Montoursville, PA 17754
570-368-2379
fax: 570-368-5046
e-mail: bowser@mail.csrlink.net
www.bowser-trains.com

K-LINE ELECTRIC TRAINS
P.O. Box 2831
Chapel Hill, NC 27515
800-866-9986
fax: 919-929-4050
general questions: info@k-line-trains.com
service: service@k-linetrains.com
Collector's Club: kcc@k-line-trains.com
www.k-linetrains.com

KOHS & COMPANY, INC.
(O scale)
P.O. Box 689
Clarkston, MI 48347
248-625-6396
fax: 248-625-7994
e-mail: gwk@kohs.com
www.kohs.com

LIONEL LLC
50625 Richard W. Blvd.
Chesterfield, MI 48051-2493
810-940-4100
e-mail: talktous@lionel.com
www.lionel.com

MARX TRAINS
209 East Butterfield Rd., #228
Elmhurst, IL 60126
630-941-3843
fax: 630-941-3829
e-mail: marxusa@aol.com
www.marxtrains.com

M.T.H. ELECTRIC TRAINS
7020 Columbia Gateway Drive
Columbia, MD 21046-1532
410-381-2580
fax: 410-381-6122
dealer locator: 888-640-3700
www.mth-railking.com

PECOS RIVER BRASS
560 E. Church
Lewisville, TX 75057
972-219-0202
e-mail:
john@pecosriverbrtass.com
www.pecosriverbrass.com
(custom brass locomotives, rolling stock, and structures)

WEAVER MODELS
P.O. Box 231
Northumberland, PA 17857
570-473-9434
fax: 570-473-3293
e-mail: qcweaver@ptd.net
www.weavermodels.com

WILLIAMS ELECTRIC TRAINS
8835-F Columbia 100 Pkwy.
Columbia, MD 21045
410-997-7766
fax: 410-997-6196
www.williamstrains.com

3RD RAIL
Division of Sunset Models, Inc.
37 South Fourth St.
Campbell, CA 95008
408-866-1727
fax: 408-866-5674
www.3rdrail.com

after-market manufacturers and suppliers

AM HOBBIES
14 N. Main St.
Mullica Hill, NJ 08062
609-478-6029
(custom painted rolling strock)

ARDUK ENGINEERING
P.O. Box 734
Pekin, IL 61555
309-346-9607
e-mail: ardukinc@aol.com
(O gauge test benches)

ARTTISTA ACCESSORIES
105 Woodring Lane
Newark, DE 19702
302-455-0195
fax: 302-455-0197
(O scale figures, animals, etc.)

AUTOMOBILIA LIMITED
P.O. Box 3014
Malvern, PA 19355-0714
800-343-9353
fax: 610-644-0560
www.automobilialimited.com
(O scale vehicles and custom-decorated O gauge rolling stock)

AZTEC MFG. COMPANY
2701 Conestoga Dr., #113
Carson City, NV 89706
775-883-3327
fax: 775-883-3357
e-mail: aztecmfg@usa.net
www.aztectrains.com
(track cleaning cars in all scales)

BACKDROP WAREHOUSE
P.O. Box 27877
Salt Lake City, UT 84127-0877
888-542-5277
fax: 801-962-4238
e-mail: backdrop@
  backdropwarehouse.com
www.backdropwarehouse.com
(scenic murals and backdrops for all scales)

BRENNAN'S MODEL RAILROADING
1600 Arlington Ave.
Independence, MO 64052
816-252-4605
http://members.primary.net/
  ~brensan
(O scale track ballast)

BURNS MANUFACTURING
P.O. Box 5301
Rocky Point, NY 11778
516-821-1644
(electronic train detectors, flashers, station stoppers, controllers)

CENTERLINE PRODUCTS, INC.
18409 Harmony Road
Marengo, IL 60152
www.centerline-products.com
(rail-cleaning cars)

CHARLES C. WOOD & CO.
P.O. Box 179
Hartford, OH 44424
330-772-5177
e-mail: chas 327@aol.com
(train enamel for collectible toy trains)

CLARKE SPARES & RESTORATIONS (TINTOWN)
90 West Swamp Rd.
Doylestown, PA 18901
215-348-0595
fax: 215-348-4160
(all-metal tinplate structures)

CLASSIC CASE COMPANY
P.O. Box 395
Rolling Prairie, IN 46371
800-897-3374
e-mail: classic@ccase.com
www.ccase.com
(display cases for O gauge trains)

DALLEE ELECTRONICS, INC.
246 W. Main St.
Leola, PA 17540
717-661-7041
www.dallee.com
(digitized sound and detection systems, throttles, flashers, etc.)

DEL-AIRE PRODUCTS
321 N. 40th St.
Allentown, PA 18104
610-391-0412
(air-powered turnout control systems)

DIE-CAST DIRECT, INC.
1009 Twilight Trail, Dept. CT9911
Frankfort, KY 40601-8432
502-227-8697
www.diecastdirect.com
(die-cast vehicles for O gauge layouts)

DIGITAL DYNAMICS
48 E. Starrs Plain Rd.
Danbury, CT 06810
203-792-7106
fax: 203-792-3338
e-mail: info@digitaldynam.com
www.digitaldynam.com
(Command control upgrades for Lionel TMCC, RailSounds, and other manufacturers' systems)

DOUGLAS BROOKS CREATIVE MODELS
307 MacKay Ave.
Ventura, CA 93004
http://swiftsite.com/
  dbcreativemodels
(model palm trees—all scales)

GARGRAVES TRACKAGE CORPORATION
8967 Ridge Rd.
North Rose, NY 14516-9793
315-483-6577
fax: 315-483-2425
www.GarGraves.com
(track and switches)

GLENN SNYDER DISPLAY SYSTEMS
260 Oak Street
Buffalo, NY 14203
716-852-4676/716-648-5817
fax: 716-852-4677
e-Mail: glenn@gsds.com
www.gsds.com
(wall-mounted train display shelves)

HOBBY INNOVATIONS (VINYLBED)
1789 Campbell Rd.
Mountain City, TN 37683
423-727-8000
(vinyl roadbed)

IC CONTROLS
P.O. Box 296
New Boston, MI 48164
734-697-4153
fax: 734-697-2033
www.iccontrolsinc.com
(TMCC compatible control products)

INDUSTRIAL RAIL
(distributed by UMD)
United Model Distributors, Inc.
301 Holbrook Drive
Wheeling, IL 60090
(O and O27 gauge rolling stock)

JOHNNY "O"
11016 Burbank Road
Burbank, OH 44214
330-624-0942
www.johnnyogauge.com
(assembled wood structures for O gauge)

JULES TOY TRAINS
3500 Winding Creek Road
Sacramento, CA 95864
916-489-2966
fax: 916-489-3497
e-mail: julestoys@aol.com
(ceiling-mounted track systems)

LASTER HOBBIES
P.O. Box 51253
Philadelphia, PA 51253
888-469-0404
(layout accessories and tinplate tools)

MCDONALD MODELS
895 Prospect Blvd.
Waterloo, IA 50701
319-233-0545
(custom-painted rolling stock)

MODEL BUILDING SERVICES
264 Marrett Rd.
Lexington, MA 02421-7024
781-860-0554
e-mail:
aaronannstu@worldnet.att.net
http://home.att.net/
~aarnannstu/mbs.html
(structure kit assembly services)

MODEL RECTIFIER CORPORATION (MRC)
80 Newfield Ave.
Edison, NJ 08837
www.modelrec.com
(transformers and power packs for all scales)

OLSEN'S TOY TRAIN PARTS
2192 McKinley Ave.
Lakewood, OH 44107
shop: 13521 Lakewood Hts. Blvd.
Cleveland, OH 44107
216-671-1980
fax: 216-671-2205
www.olsenstoy.com
(toy train repair parts)

ONE TRACK MIND
Box 1353
Hartselle, AL 35640
256-773-0078
(custom painted rolling stock)

OTT MACHINE SERVICES, INC.
P.O. Box 1701
Lombard, IL 60148
630-889-8030
fax: 630-119-0114
(sound systems for three-rail AC-powered diesel and steam locomotives)

PHOENIX TRAINS
P.O. Box 56
Vernon, CT 06066-0056
860-872-1014
e-mail: phoenixtra@aol.com
(parts for Marx trains)

QSINDUSTRIES, INC.
3800 S.W. Cedar Hills Blvd.,
Suite 224
Beaverton, OR 97005
503-350-0595
fax: 503-626-9995
www.qsindustries.com
(Sound systems for locomotives and rolling stock)

RAIL RAX
786 Seely Ave.
Aromas, CA 95004
800-830-2843
(wall-mounted display shelves for O gauge trains)

R. BISHOP MODEL CRAFTERS
P.O. Box 82
Grafton, VT 05146
802-843-1012
e-mail: info@modelcrafters.com
www.modelcrafters.com
(military train models)

RETRO DISPLAYS
P.O. Box 992
Park Ridge, IL 60068
(display layouts)

RICK JOHNSON
19333 Sturgess Drive
Torrance, CA 90503
310-371-9668
(molded rubber roadbed products)

ROBERT GROSSMAN COMPANY
1967 Chelford Rd.
Richmond Hts., OH 44143
216-738-0602
fax: 216-738-0603
e-mail: marxman@aol.com
(Marx train parts)

ROSS CUSTOM SWITCHES
P.O. Box 110
North Stonington, CT 06355
800-331-1395
fax: 860-536-5108
(custom switches and three rail track)

RR-TRACK
R&S Enterprises
P.O. Box 643
Jonestown, PA 17038
717-865-3444
www.rrtrack.com/rrtrack
(sectional track layout planning software)

S&W PARTS SUPPLY
4928 Folse Dr.
Metarie, LA 70006-1158
504-887-0104
fax: 504-456-6597
(Lionel and American Flyer parts and service)

SCALE MODELS, ARTS & TECHNOLOGIES, INC.
P.O. Box 600505
N. Miami Beach, FL 33160
305-949-1706
fax: 305-947-7458
www.smarttinc.com
(custom model railroad layout builders)

SIEVERS BENCHWORK
Jackson Harbor Rd.
Washington Island, WI 54246
(ready-to-assemble custom benchwork)

STAINLESS UNLIMITED
P.O. Box 224
Augusta, MO 63332
636-228-4767/636-742-5880
www.stainlessunlimited.com
(stainless steel bridges)

STONEY EXPRESS
P.O. Box 526
Tecumseh, MI 49286
517-423-5980
fax: 517-423-5980
e-mail: stoneyex@ini.net
www.stoneyexpress.com
(ceramic structure reproductions)

SUPERSMOKE
Bart's Pneumatics Corp.
1952 Landis Valley Road
Lancaster, PA 17601
717-392-1568
(smoke fluid for toy and model trains)

THE INK WELL
P.O. Box 3053
York, PA 17402
800-946-5935
(miniatures for O gauge layouts)

TM BOOKS & VIDEOS
Box 279
New Buffalo, MI 49117
800-892-2822
fax: 219-879-7909
e-mail: tmbooks@aol.com
www.tmbooks-video.com
(publisher of toy train videos and price guides)

TOWN & COUNTRY HOBBIES
P.O. Box 584
Totowa, NJ 07512-0548
973-942-5176
fax: 973-790-8151
www.TownCountryHobbies.com
(replacement light bulbs)

TRAINAMERICA STUDIOS
970 Windham Court, Suite #9
Youngstown, OH 44512
330-629-7625
fax: 330-629-6052
www.tastudios.com
(TMCC control system and sound system upgrades and installation)

TRAIN REPAIR PARTS
Div. of Hobby Surplus Sales
287 Main St.
P.O. Box 2170
New Britain, CT 06050
860-223-0600
www.TrainRepairParts.com
(repair parts and manuals for Lionel and Flyer)

T-TRACKER
Dept. 2
3735 N.E. Shaver St.
Portland, OR 97212
(track assembly/tightening device; track accessories)

VALLEY MODEL TRAINS
P.O. Box 1251
Wappingers Falls, NY 12590
914-297-7511
fax: 914-297-3514
e-mail: vmt@isdi.net
www.isdi.net/~vmt/
(Big Buck Buildings in O and HO scales)

WESTERN HOBBYCRAFT
P.O. Box 7449
Mesa, AZ 85216
480-654-9224
fax: 480-654-8692
(O gauge trolleys and rolling stock)

WM. K. WALTHERS, INC.
P.O. Box 3039
Milwaukee, WI 53201-3039
414-527-0770
www.walthers.com
(manufacturer and national distributor for products in all scales)

WOODLAND SCENICS
P.O. Box 98
Linn Creek, MO 65052
573-346-5555
e-mail: webmaster@
  woodlandscenics.com
www.woodlandscenics.com
(various scenery materials for all scales)

major retailers of O scale and O/O27 gauge products

This list of O scale/gauge retailers includes dealers who support the hobby through published (in print and/or on line) advertising of their product lines, and whose advertising indicates that they stock or specialize in O scale/gauge products. This list should not be considered all-inclusive. There may be other retailers in your local area who are not listed here, but who do stock O scale/gauge products—consult your local phone directory Yellow Pages. Support of your local dealer is always encouraged.

For names and addresses of "authorized" sales or service stations, contact the product manufacturer, or check the manufacturer's web site on the Internet.

AL **HOMEWOOD TOY**
& HOBBY
2830 S. 18th St.
Homewood, AL 35209
205-879-3986
e-mail: Tbusenlehn@aol.com

UNCLE AL'S HOBBIES
6017 E. Shirley Lane
Montgomery, AL
36117-1977
334-277-1715
fax: 334-277-1628
e-mail: aluncle@aol.com

AR **DAN COOK'S**
112 N. 6th
Arkadelphia, AR 71923
870-246-9823
www.dancooks.com/trains

ARKANSAS TRAVELER
HOBBIES
1611 Brentwood Dr.
Pine Bluff, AR 71601-6821
870-850-7245

AZ **BURLING'S TON**
OF TRAINS
16939 E. Colony Dr.
Fountain Hills, AZ 85268
480-816-6501

ARIZONA TRAIN DEPOT
755 E. McKellips Rd.
Mesa, AZ 85203-2555
480-833-9486
www.arizonatrain-
depot.com

ESOTERIC AUDIO
4120 N. Marshall Way, #1
Scottsdale, AZ 85251
602-946-8128
fax: 602-946-9923
e-mail: esoteric@dancris.com
www.dancris.com/~esoteric

GERRY'S TRAINS & TOOLS
7337 E. Indian Bend Rd.
Scottsdale, AZ 85250-4513
480-991-2536

ARIZONA TRAINS
2420 North Treat Ave.
Tucson, AZ 85716
520-325-2321
fax: 520-325-2905
e-mail:aztrains@earthlink.net
www.aztrains.com

CA **ARIZONA TRAINS**
& HOBBIES
5584 E. La Palma Ave.
Anaheim, CA 92807
714-779-9893
fax: 714-779-6708
www-aztrainsca.com

TOY TRAIN SHOP
1829 W. Lincoln
Anaheim, CA 92801
714-991-1040
fax: 714-991-3220
www.toytrainshop.com

THE TRAIN SHACK
1030 N. Hollywood Way
Burbank, CA 91505
818-842-3330
www.trainshack.com
www.nrhsa.org

TRACKSIDE TRAINS
1675 Rollins Rd, #B-1
Burlingame, CA
94010-2320
650-692-9724

JUST TRAINS
5650-H Imhoff Dr.
Concord, CA 94520
925-685-6566
fax: 925-685-7997
e-mail: email@
just-trains.com
www.just-trains.com

THE TRAIN CROSSING
1089-C Baker St.
Costa Mesa, CA
92626-4127
714-549-1596

GLENDALE STATION
ANTIQUES
225 E. Main St.
El Cajon, CA 92020-3911
619-590-1460

CLASSIC HOBBIES & TOYS
17632 Chatsworth St.
Granada Hills, CA
91344-5601
818-368-7317

REED'S HOBBY SHOP
8039 La Mesa Blvd.
La Mesa, CA 91941
619-464-1672
www.nrhsa.org

HOBBY WAREHOUSE
4105 E. South St.
Lakewood, CA 90712-1043
562-531-1413

ELECTRIC TRAIN CO.
16206 Hawthorne Blvd.
Lawndale, CA 90260
310-370-3839

ROGER'S RAILROAD JUNCTION
12 West Oak St.
Lodi, CA 95240
209-334-5623
fax: 209-334-1640
e-mail: roger@
railroadjunction.com
www.railroadjunction.com

ALLIED MODEL TRAINS
4411 S. Sepulveda
Los Angeles, CA 90230
310-313-9353
fax: 310-313-9365
e-mail: alliedtrn@aol.com
www.alliedmodeltrains.com

THE LOOSE CABOOSE
4225 Solano Ave.
Napa, CA 94558-1611
707-258-1222

DOLLHOUSES, TRAINS & MORE
14 Commercial Blvd. #111
Novato, CA 94949-6110
415-883-0388

THE ORIGINAL WHISTLE STOP INC.
2490 E. Colorado Blvd.
Pasedena, CA 91107
626-796-7791
www.nrhsa.org

LOCO-BOOSE ELECTRIC TRAIN SHOP
260-D. Main St.
Redwood City, CA
94063-1733
650-368-1254

CLASSIC TRAINS
18927 E. Colima Rd.
Rowland Heights, CA
91748-2942
626-912-0774
fax: 626-912-1033
www.classictrains.com

BRUCE'S TRAIN SHOP
2752 Marconi Ave.
Sacramento, CA
95821-4914
916-485-5288

RON'S WORLD
241 Avenida DelMar
San Clemente, CA 92672
949-361-5596
www.nrhsa.org

THE VILLAGE DEPOT
170 Del Mar
San Clemente, CA 92672
949-366-0930
www.cyber-rail.com

THE TRAIN STOP
211 W. Bonita Ave.
San Dimas, CA 91773
909-599-2602
fax: 909-599-1566
www.trainstop.com

CHAN'S TRAINS & KITS
2450 Van Ness Ave.
& Union St.
San Francisco, CA
94109-1826
415-885-2899

TIN PLATE JUNCTION
342 Scott Street
San Francisco, CA 94117
415-861-2896

TALBOT'S HOBBIES
445 South "B" St.
San Mateo, CA 94401-4118
650-342-0267

THE TRAIN SHOP
1829 Pruneridge Ave.
Santa Clara, CA 95050-6528
408-296-1050

TRUCKS, TRAINS, HOBBIES AND COLLECTABLES
4237 Montgomery Dr.
Santa Rosa, CA 95405-5306
707-537-6586

PACIFIC TRAINS
5939 Pacific Ave.
Stockton, CA 95207
209-473-3410

ALL ABOARD MODEL RR EMPORIUM
3867 Pacific Coast Hwy.
Torrance, CA 90505
310-791-2637
www.nrhsa.org

THE SQUARE ROUNDHOUSE
1468 Lander Ave.
Turlock, CA 95380-6202
209-668-4454

THE WESTERN DEPOT
1650 Sierra Ave #203
Yuba City, CA 95993-8986
530-673-6776
fax: 530-673-5590
e-mail: wdepot@
westerndepot.com
www.westerndepot.com

ARNIE'S TRAINS
6452-B Industry Way
Westminster, CA 92683
714-893-1015
www.nrhsa.org

CO **MOUNTAIN TRAINS
& PLANES**
9316 W. 58th Ave.
Arvada, CO 80002-2002
303-456-1255

**CUSTOM RAILWAY
SUPPLY**
432 W. Fillmore 80907-
6046
Colorado Springs, CO
719-634-4616

SUNBIRD TRAIN MART
3650 Austin Bluffs Pkwy
#130
Colorado Springs, CO 80918
719-528-8811
fax: 719-260-8166
www.sunbirdtrainmart.com

CABOOSE HOBBIES
500 S. Broadway
Denver, CO 80209
303-777-6766
303-777-0028
www.caboosehobbies.com

**HANK'S MODEL TRAINS,
INC.**
728 Main St.
Louisville (Denver), CO
80027-1830
303-666-5468

MIZELL TRAINS
3051 W. 74th Ave.
Westminster, CO 80030
888-717-4196
e-mail: info@
mizelltrains.com
www.MizellTrains.com

CT **BERKSHIRE HILLS
HOBBY SUPPLY**
93 Main St.
Canaan, CT 06018-2463
860-824-0527

RAILWORKS, INC.
5 Padanaram Rd.
Danbury, CT 06811-4835
203-797-8386

**TROLLEYS, TRAINS
& PLANES**
122 Prospect Hill Rd.
East Windsor, CT 06088
860-292-1348

**NEW ENGLAND HOBBY
SUPPLY-TRAIN EXCHANGE**
71 Hillard St.
Manchester, CT 06040
860-646-0610
860-645-0504
www.nehobby.com

NATIONAL HOBBY SUPPLY
247 Naugatuck Ave.
Millford, CT 06460-5540
203-882-8392
www.railsite.com

**SHELTON RAILROAD
SYSTEMS**
15 Elm St.
Shelton CT 06484-3008
203-924-8761
www.clearhght.com/
~adraini

DE **KATHIE'S TRAINS**
296 Robbins Rd.
Frederica, DE 19446-1954
800-400-0478/
302-335-1850

TRAINS N THINGS
23 Penn Mart Center
New Castle, DE 19720-4206
800-510-3613/
302-322-8343

JUSTRAINS
2622 Capitol Trail (Rt. 2)
Newark, DE 19711
302-453-9742
www.justrains.com

FL **TRAINLAND**
451 East Altamonte Drive
Altamonte Springs, FL
32701
407-260-8500
407-260-2380
www.trainlandaltamonte
.com

A HOBBY PLACE, INC.
1425-F Main St.
Dunedin (Clearwater), FL
34698-6247
727-733-5953

THE AMHERST DEPOT
349 W. Dearborn St.
Englewood, FL 34223-3156
941-475-2020
www.amherst-depot.com

THE WIND-UP KEY
5425 Mile Stretch Drive
Holiday, FL 34690
727-943-8216

TRAINMASTER
5001-B NW 34th St.
Gainesville, FL 32605
352-373-4222
fax: 352-373-4468

HOLLYWOOD STATION
1917 Hollywood Blvd.
Hollywood, FL
954-921-2700
e-mail: trainman@
bellsouth.net
www.hollywood-station.com

THE DEPOT HOBBY SHOP
603 Ridge Rd.
Lantana, FL 33462-1523
561-585-1982

READY TO ROLL
831 NW 143rd St.
Miami, FL 33168
305-688-8868
fax: 305-948-0339
e-mail: rtrtrains@aol.com
www.readytorolltrains.com

PDK TRAINS
1009 NE 14th Street
Ocala, FL 34470
352-622-1957
fax: 352-622-5458
pdk@atlantic.net
www.pdktrains.com

TRAINS OF OCALA
1405 SW 6th Ave.
Ocala, FL 34474-3240
352-369-5152

**FRANK'S TRAINS
& HOBBIES, INC.**
110 Pine Ave. S.
Oldsmar, FL 34677-3025
813-855-1041

**COLONIAL PHOTO
& HOBBY INC.**
634 N. Mills St.
Orlando, FL 32803
407-841-1485

H & R TRAINS, INC.
6901 U.S. 19 at Haines Rd.
Pinellas Park, FL 33781-
6247
727-526-4682

ROUNDHOUSE SOUTH
4611 Ridgewood Ave.
Port Orange, FL 32127
904-304-7002/904-304-
7003
fax: 904-304-7004

GULF COAST MODEL RR
3222 Clark Rd.
Sarasota, FL 34231-8302
813-923-9303

HAPPY HOBO TRAINS
4040 W. Waters Ave.
Tampa, FL 33614
813-886-5072

CHESTER HOLLY
3812-20 S. Himes Ave.
Tampa, FL 33611
813-831-7202

GA **GANDY DANCERS**
5438 Peachtree Indust. Blvd.
Atlanta (Chamblee), GA
30341-2232
770-451-7425

TOY TRAINS N THINGS
2055 Beaver Ruin Rd.
Atlanta (Norcross), GA 30071
770-446-7868

BUFORD JUNCTION
359 Shadburn Ave.
Atlanta (Buford), GA 30518
770-945-3222

LEGACY STATION LTD.
251F Hurricane Shoals Rd.
Lawrenceville, GA 30045
770-339-7780
fax: 770-339-4417
e-Mail: trainwrk@
mindspring.com
www.trainworks.com

BULL STREET STATION
151 Bull St.
Savannah, GA 31401-3726
912-236-4344
www.bullst.com

IL **THE HOBBY DEPT**
*(Located in Hannah's
Home Accents)*
455 W. Lake St.
Antioch, IL 60002-1405
888-784-6638
info@hannahs.com

**DENNY'S TRAINS
& THINGS**
906 Bangs St.
Aurora, IL 60505
630-585-6964
dennytrain@aol.com

**BERWYN'S TOY TRAINS
& MODELS**
7025 Ogden Ave.
Berwyn, IL 60402
708-484-4384

HOBBY CITY
6910 Cermak Rd.
Berwyn, IL 60402
708-795-0280

WIMPY'S HOBBY WORLD
263 Convent St. #8
Bourbonnais, IL 60914
815-932-6100

**THE GOLDEN SPIKE
TRAIN SHOP**
6357 W. 79th St.
Burbank, IL 60459-1149
708-598-3114

**SF & C MODEL TRAINS
& HOBBYS**
2329 W. Belmont Ave.
Chicago, IL 60618-6422
773-472-1710

CHICAGOLAND HOBBY
6017 N. Northwest Hwy
Chicago, IL 60631
773-775-4848

AL'S HOBBY SHOP INC
121-123 Addison St.
Elmhurst, IL 60126
630-832-4908

FAIRBURY PAINT STORE
108 E. Locust St.
Fairbury, IL 61739
815-692-3325

CARDIFF BROTHERS TRAINS
(In the Metra Station)
Geneva, IL
630-262-0727

AMERICA'S BEST TRAIN & HOBBY
136 E. Army Trail Rd.
Glendale Heights, IL 60139
630-539-8551

OAKRIDGE HOBBIES
15800 New Ave.
Lemont, IL 6043903680
630-257-0909
www.oakridgehobbies.com

TRAINS & CARS OF YESTERDAY
7923 W. Golf Rd.
Morton Grove, IL
60053-1040
847-470-9500

HILL'S HOBBY & COLLECTORS' SHOP
10 Prairie Ave.
Park Ridge, IL 60068-4042
847-823-4464
www.hillshobby.com

ACE HARDWARE HOME CENTER
659 W. Railroad (Rt. 134)
Round Lake, IL 60073
847-546-4668

NORTH SHORE HOBBY & COLLECTORS GALLERY
4901 Oakton St.
Skokie, IL 60077-2903
847-673-4849

TIMELESS HOBBIES
75 Danada Sq. East
Wheaton, IL 60187-8484
708-690-5542

IN **JIM'S RR CROSSING**
4194 Grant St.
Gary, IN 46408
219-887-0791

GEORGE'S TRAIN SHOP
254 N. Warren Rd.
Huntington, IN 46750-9204
219-468-2186

TRAIN CENTRAL
6742 E. Washington St.
(U.S. 40)
Indianapolis, IN 46219-6737
317-375-0832

TRAIN EXPRESS
4310 W. 96th Street
Indianapolis, IN 46268
317-879-9300
fax: 317-879-9311
www.trainexpress.com

S & S HOBBIES
2213 Westwood Ct.
Marion, IN 46952-3210
765-664-8753
www.sandshobbies.com

GUPTA HOBBY CENTER
1701 W. Jackson St.
Muncie, IN 47303-4963
765-288-6505

Y.O.R.K. TRAINS
8208 Calumet Ave.
Munster, IN 46321-1704
219-838-9999
http://member.aol.com/
  YORKtrains

TRAIN DEPOT
14 S. 9th St.
Terre Haute, In 47807-3710
812-232-5645

VALPARAISO PET & HOBBY SHOP
18 North Washington
Valparasio, IN 46383-4767
219-462-8346

IA **HOBBY HAVEN**
7672 Hickman Rd.
Des Moines, IA 50322
515-276-8785
fax: 515-252-0112
e-mail: hhaven@
hobbyhaven.com

KY **BERKSHIRE TRAINS**
209 Rosemont Gdn
Lexington, KY 40503
606-278-8082
fax: 606-873-6863
e-mail: BB1140@aol.com
www.berkshiretrains.
  qpg.com

LA **UNION AUTO SUPPLY & TOY TRAINS**
1225 Magazine St.
70130-4219
New Orleans, LA
504-581-1471

MA **TRAINS ON TRACKS**
21 Summer St.
Chelmsford, MA 01824
978-256-3465
www.trainsontracks.com

DUXBURY GREEN, INC.
382 Kingsown Way (Rt. 53)
Duxbury, MA 02332-4605
781-585-2164
781-585-0054

THE TOY DOCTOR
17 Meredith Rd.
Forestdale, MA 02644
508-477-1186
e-mail: Toy Doc@aol.com

DR. TINKER'S ANTIQUE TOY TRAINS
1 Belfry Terrace
Lexington, MA 02421-4909
781-862-5798
www.ttrains.com/drtinker

CHARLES RO SUPPLY, CO.
662 Cross St.
P.O. Box 100
Malden, MA 02148
781-321-0090
fax: 781-321-6459
www.charlesro.com

**THIS, THAT & TRAINS
AT MASHPEE**
538 Falmouth Rd.
Mashpee, MA 02649-3304
508-539-9627

MODELER'S JUNCTION
88 Lowell St. (Rt. 113)
Methuen, MA 01844-3616
978-683-0885

ACE HOBBIES
670 Depot St. # 2
North Easton, MA
02356-2742
508-539-9627

NORTH EAST TRAINS
18 M ain St.
Peabody, MA 01960-5552
978-532-1615

**BILL'S FRIENDLY
TRAIN SHOPPE**
414 Center St.
Randolph, MA 02368-5325
781-986-5295

ED'S BOXCAR
611 Center St.
Raynham, MA 02767
508-822-6563

**FLYING YANKEE
HOBBY SHOP**
1416 Centre St.
Roslindale, MA 02131-1412
617-323-9702

THE HOBBY CONNECTION
4 Franklin St.
Stoneham, MA 02180-1862
781-438-1697

MD **MA & PA JUNCTION**
8 Pikehall Pl.
Baltimore, MD 21236
410-256-7992
fax: 603-754-7223
e-Mail: mapajct@
hotmail.com
www.mapajunction.com

M.B. KLEIN, INC.
162 North Gay St.
Baltimore, MD 21202
410-539-6207
fax: 410-685-1357

**TOYS OF CHRISTMAS
PAST**
3608 Falls Rd.
Baltimore, MD 21211-1814
410-889-4940

**FRENCH'S TRAINS
& HOBBIES, INC.**
30-1/2 N. Dundalk Ave.
Baltimore, MD 21222-4221
410-285-5809
**DENNISON'S TRACKSIDE
HOBBIES**
14 S. Main St.
Berlin, MD 21811-1427
800-972-6898

BURRETT HOBBIES
9920 Rhode Island Ave.
College Park, MD
20740-1460
301-982-5032

**TRAINS, PLANES -
AUTOMOBILES**
239 S. Bridge St.
Elkton, MD 21921
410-620-5595
fax: 410-620-5596
e-mail: tpa store@
  yahoo.com

FOREST HILLSTATION
15 E. Jarrettsville Rd.
Forest Hill, MD 21050-1631
410-893-1089

**TRAINS, TOYS
& TREASURES**
1507 W. Patrick St.
Frederick, MD 21702-3732
301-662-5202

ENGINE HOUSE HOBBIES
315-G East Diamond Ave.
Gaithersburg, MD 20877
301-590-0816

HOUSE OF PLASTIC
800 View Street
Hagerstown, MD 21740
301-797-3575
e-mail: modeler101@
  aol.com

THE TRAIN ROOM
360 S. Burhans Blvd. E.
Hagerstown, MD
21740-5339
301-745-6681

LIONEL BUY & SELL
3610 University Blvd.
Kensington, MD
20895-2120
301-949-4000

TRAIN DEPOT
214 S. Main St.
Mt. Airy, MD 21771
301-607-8155

**CATOCTIN MOUNTAIN
TRAINS & HOBBIES**
3 W. Main St.
Thurmont, MD 21788-1825
800-532-6589/
301-694-8331
e-mail: trainspj@aol.com

THE TOY EXCHANGE
11265 Triangle Lane
Wheaton, MD 20902
301-929-0690

ME **SMALL'S TRAIN REPAIR**
273 Tuttle Rd.
Cumberland, ME
04021-9376
207-829-3757

RAINY DAY TRAINS
10 Oak Hill Terrace
Scarborough, ME
04074-8992
207-883-7400/
800-552-9831

TRAINS & MORE!
41 Roosevelt Trail
Casco, ME 04015-4211
207-655-2550

MI **JUNCTION VALLEY
RR HOBBY SHOP**
7065 Dixie Hwy
Bridgeport, MI 48772-9702
517-777-3480

**TEWSLEY'S TRAINS
AND THINGS**
321 Selma St.
Cadillac, MI 49601-1752
231-775-6615

P & D HOBBY SHOP
31902 Groesbeck Hwy
Fraser, MI 48026-3914
810-296-6116

THE TRAIN BARN
10234 East Shore Drive
Kalamazoo, MI 49002-7466
616-327-4016

MERRI-SEVEN TRAINS
19155 Merriman Rd.
Livonia (Detroit), MI
48152-1754
248-477-0550

TOOT'S TRAIN STATION
6 E. 1st St.
Monroe, MI 48161-2227
734-242-0003
www.tootstrains.com

THE TRAIN DOCTOR
1576 River Rd.
Millersburg, MI 49759-9642
517-733-2101

**MICHIGAN MODEL
TRAIN CENTER**
9260 McFregor Rd.
Pinckney, MI 48169-9460
734-426-1651

L&J HOBBIES
8847 Portage Rd.
Portage, MI 49002
616-323-1010
fax: 616-323-0597

TRAIN CENTER HOBBIES
32722 Woodward Ave.
Royal Oak (Detroit), MI
48073-0953
248-549-6500

**BRASSEUR ELECTRIC
TRAINS**
410 Court St.
Saginaw, MI 48602-4209
517-793-4753

**BOB'S HOBBY
& COLLECTOR'S SHOP**
115 N. Main St.
Watervliet, MI 49098-9787
616-463-7452

EUREKA TRAINS
1219 Eureka
Wyandotte, MI 48192-6111
734-284-0521

MN **III RAIL TRAINS**
536 Northdale Blvd.
Coon Rapids, MN 55448
612-767-9545/
888-291-7245

STEVE'S TRAIN CITY
912 Main St.
Hopkins, MN 55343-7516
612-933-0200

PERRY'S HOBBIES
114 Vernon Ave.
P.O. Box 68C
Morgan, MN 56266
507-249-3173

MAINLINE TRAINS
912 Tile Dr.
Red Wing, MN 55066-1974
651-388-3772
(phone and fax)
www.commandtrains.com

MO **MEADOW RIDGE
TRAIN DEPOT**
5824 Meadow Ridge Dr.
Jefferson City, MO
65101-8837
573-395-4910
fax: 573-395-4993

M&W CLASSIC TRAINS
315 N. English St.
Marshall, MO 65340-1762
660-886-7404
e-mail: rwhitlock@dido.com

P.M. TRAINS AND ROCKS
10101 E. 64th St.
Raytown, MO 64133-5123
816-358-6160

KIRKWOOD HOBBIES
127 W. Jefferson
St. Louis, MO 63122-4007
314-821-5596

TRAINS TO GO
115 W. Lockwood
St. Louis, MO 63119-2915
314-961-9150

ELECTRIC TRAIN OUTLET
8961 Page Blvd. Ste. E
St. Louis, MO 63114
314-428-2211

TRAINS LIMITED
8151 Delmar
St. Louis, MO 63139-3729
314-721-2939

MS **THE EMPORIUM**
136 Rue Magnolia
Biloxi, MS 39530-4218
228-432-1326

HOBBYTOWN USA
6380-D Ridgewood Ct.
Jackson, MS 39211-1840
601-957-9900

NC **TRAINS LTD., LLC**
5600 Albemarle Rd.,
Suite 300
Charlotte, NC 28212-2645
704-566-9070

THE HOBBY HOUSE
1211 Asheville Hwy
Hendersonville, NC
28791-3411
828-692-6683

LELAND'S TOY TRAINS
302 S. Center St.
Hildebran, NC 28637
828-397-2457
fax: 828-397-2457
e-mail: trains@twave.net
http://users.twave.net/trains

DRY BRIDGE STATION
236 N. Main St.
Mount Airy, NC 27030
336-786-9811
e-mail: mikek@
   drybridgestation.com
www.drybridgestation.com

HOBBY SHOP
2020 Cameron St.
Raleigh, NC 27605-1311
919-833-1123

THE FREIGHT YARD
1126 S. Pollock St.
Selma, NC 27576-2934
919-965-6101

**LITTLE CHOO CHOO
SHOP**
500 S. Salisbury Ave.
Spencer, NC 28159-2102
800-334-CHOO

TODD'S TRAIN DEPOT
3169 Wendell Blvd.
P.O. Box 849
Wendell, NC 27591
919-365-5006
fax: 919-365-3917

RERUNS TS
4007-D Country Club Rd.
Winston-Salem, NC
27104-3613
336-760-9817

NE **GRAND CENTRAL LTD.**
6901 Seward Ave.
P.O. Box 29109
Lincoln, NE 68529
402-467-3738
fax: 402-467-3795
www.grandcentralltd.com

NH **BRENTWOOD ANTIQUES**
The Castles at Brentwood
Rt. 101
Brentwood, NH 03833
603-679-1500
fax: 603-672-3451
www.TheTrainShop.com

**B & G RAILROAD
& HOBBIES**
244 Sheep Davis Rd.
Concord, NH 03301-8515
603-224-9258

MOUNTAIN TRAINS
25 Lowell St.
Manchester, NH 03101
603-622-8982/
603-641-1113
fax: 603-625-4060
e-mail: mtntrain1@aol.com
www.mountaintrains.com

TREASURED TOYS, INC.
5N Broadway
Salem, NH 03079
603-898-7224
www.treasured-toys.com

NJ **COUNTRY AND STUFF**
127 Main St.
Andover, NJ 07821-4525
973-786-7086

RAILS-N-WINGS
6 Hamilton St.
Bound Brook, NJ
08805-2015
732-764-0079

GENE'S TRAINS
1905 Rt. 88 East
Brick, NJ 08724
732-840-9728
fax: 732-840-3466
www.genestrains.com

**COAST TRAINS
& COLLECTIBLES**
400 Higgins Ave. Suite D
Brielle, NJ 08730-1414
732-528-0226

TONY'S TRAIN TOWN
575 Pompton Ave.
Cedar Grove, NJ
07009-1720
973-857-2337

M & G HOBBIES
Tenby Plaza
2902 Rt. 130 N.
Delran, NJ 08075
856-461-3553
fax: 856-461-3886
e-mail: sales@
   mandghobbies.com
www.mandghobbies.com

ATLANTIC RAILS
1228 Mays Landing Rd.
Folsom (Hammonton),
NJ 08037
609-567-8490

Z & Z HOBBIES
101 Sloan Ave.
Hamilton, NJ 08619-2260
609-586-2282/
800-586-2281
www.z-zhobbies.baweb.com

HAZLET TRAIN STOP
25 Brailley Ln.
Hazlet, NJ 07730
732-264-7429

C. B. TRAIN DEPOT
107 Prospect Place
Hillsdale, NJ 07642-2047
201-666-9598

HOBOKEN TRAIN EXCHANGE
503 Third St.
Hoboken, NJ 07030-1969
201-792-3700
www.hobokentrainexchange
.com

GENE'S GRAND CENTRAL STATION
228 Belleville Tpke.
Kearney, NJ 07032-3203
800-955-3992

ALL ABOARD TRAIN SHOPPE
P.O. Box 451
Lincroft, NJ 07738
732-842-4744
www.trainshoppe.com

STANDARD HOBBY SUPPLY
P.O. Box 801
Mahwah, NJ 07430
201-825-2211
www.standardhobby.com

STAFFORD TRAINS
747 Rt. 9
Manahawkin, NJ 08050
609-597-3626

J & B TRAINS INC.
108 E. Main St.
Maple Shade, NJ 08052
609-414-0092

LARRY'S MODEL TRAINS
211 Greenwood Ave.
Midland Park, NJ 07432
201-444-0052
fax: 201-444-9078

MILLBURN TRAIN & HOBBY CENTER
156 Main St.
Millburn, NJ 07041-1114
973-379-4242

TOY TRAIN EMPORIUM
Emporium Bldg.,
208 Creek Rd.
Mount Laurel, NJ 08054-2090
609-273-0606

THE TRAIN STATION
12 Romaine Road
P.O. Box 381
Mountain Lakes, NJ 07046
973-263-1979
fax: 973-402-6192
www.train-station.com

AM HOBBIES
110 N. Foxford Lane
Mullica Hill, NJ 08062
609-478-6029

WHISTLE STOP STATION
14 N. Main St.
Mullica Hill, NJ 08062-9407
609-478-6029

TOY TRAINS OF YESTERYEAR
1 Longview Court
Old Tappan, NJ 07675
201-768-5931/
201-768-9218
fax: 201-768-1505

TRAIN COLLECTOR'S WAREHOUSE, INC.
1521 Route 46 East
Parsippany, NJ 07054
973-334-3399

RAILROAD SHOP
250 Vail Ave.
Piscataway, NJ 08854
732-968-5696

RAILS TO COTTAGES
44 W. Main St.
Rockaway, NJ 07866
973-627-6416

CHOO CHOO EDDIE'S
38 Ames Ave.
Rutherford, NJ 07070-1702
201-438-4588

WALKER'S HARDWARE
294 Union Blvd.
Totowa, NJ 07512-2552
973-942-2694

TRAINS & THINGS
242 Scotch Rd.
Trenton, NJ 08628-2513
609-883-8790

ANTIQUE TRAINS
Greentree & 1 Lantern Ln.
Turnersville, NJ 08012-2119
609-589-6224

TRAINS 'N THINGS
936 E. Weymouth Rd.
Vineland, NJ 08360-1874
856-697-8844
www.trainsnthings.com

LASKEY'S TRAINS
5A Star Plaza
Washington, NJ 07882
908-835-0799

NM **TRAINS WEST, INC.**
6001 San Mateo N.E. B-3
Albuquerque, NM 87109
505-881-2322

NV **THE TRAIN ENGINEER**
2550 Chandler #53
Las Vegas, NV 89117
702-597-1754
e-mail: JOTraineng@aol.com

TRAIN EXCHANGE
6008 Boulder Hwy
Las Vegas, NV 89122
702-456-8766

RENO RAILS
1229 E. 4th St.
Reno, NV 89512-3602
775-337-6669

NY **GARDNER,
"THE TRAIN DOCTOR"**
8967 Ridge Rd.
Alton (Rochester), NY
14652
315-483-6577

RLR RAILROAD
15 Jackson St.
Batavia, NY 14020-3201
716-344-8874
www.rlrrailroad.com

YARDMASTER HOBBIES
1115 Smithtown Ave.
Bohemia, NY 11716-2197
516-244-8393

**PUTNAM TRAIN
STATION LTD. INC.**
175 E. Main St.
Brewster, NY 10509-1537
914-279-0200

**GOLDEN SPIKE
INTERNATIONAL**
1700 Grand Concourse
Bronx, NY 10457
718-294-1614
fax: 718-294-5319
www.goldentrains.com

PEARL PHARMACY
717 Burke Ave.
Bronx, NY 10467
718-882-4524

TRAINWORLD
751 McDonald Ave.
Brooklyn, NY 11218
718-436-7072
fax: 718-972-8514
www.trainworldny.com

K-VAL HOBBIES
277 Hinman Ave.
Buffalo, NY 14216
716-875-2837
www.kvalhobbies.com

**NIAGARA HOBBY
& CRAFT MART**
3366 Union Rd.
Buffalo, NY 14225-5110
716-681-1666

**KURT'S TRAINS
& HOBBIES**
3133 Main St.
Caledonia, NY 14423-1219
716-538-2960
kth@eznet.net

**NASSAU HOBBY
CENTER INC.**
13 W. Merrick Rd.
Freeport, NY 11520
516-378-9594

ARTCRAFT TRAINS
5914 Camp Rd.
Hamburg (Buffalo), NY
14075-4424
716-649-3079

LANTZ TRAIN SHOP
8 Hanover Square
Horseheads, NY 14845-2457
607-738-3100

**HURLEY COUNTRY
STORE INC.**
2 Wamsley Place
Hurley, NY 12443-5935
914-338-4843

**BOOKBINDER'S
"TRAINS UNLIMITED"**
84-20 Midland Parkway
Jamaica, NY 11432
718-657-2224
fax: 718-657-2264
www.netpage1.com/
   bookbinderstrains

DOLLHOUSE JUNCTION
679 Hawkins Ave.
Lake Ronkonkoma, NY
11779-2208
516-467-1222

CHOO CHOO CHARLIE'S
109 S. Main St.
Liberty, NY 12754-1812
914-292-4826

TRAINLAND
293 Sunrise Hwy.
Lynbrook, Long Island,
NY 11563
718-436-7072
fax: 718-972-8514
www.trainworldny.com

RUDY'S HOBBY & ART
3516 30th Ave.
Long Island City, NY
11103-4623
718-545-8280

THE BLUE CABOOSE
722 Bullville Rd.
Montgomery, NY 12549
914-361-2414
fax: 914-361-2414
www.bluecaboose.net

CLASSIC TOYS
218 Sullivan St.
New York, NY 10012
212-674-4434

THIRD STREET STATION
7820 Porter Rd. (Rt. 182 E.)
Niagara Falls, NY
14304-1606
716-297-7103

GENCO AND DAUGHTERS
16 E. Central Ave.
Pearl River, NY 10965-2304
914-620-7604
www.gencotrains.com

**DUTCHESS TRAIN
& HOBBY**
23 H Vassar Rd.
Poughkeepsie, NY
12603-5201
914-463-3417

DESPATCH JUNCTION
2222 Lyell Ave.
Rochester, NY 14606
716-426-6685

TRENT'S TRAINS
69 Harney Rd.
Scarsdale, NY 10583
914-722-2559
fax: 914-722-2563

**MOHAWK VALLEY
RAILROAD CO.**
2937 Hamburg St.
Schenectady, NY
12303-4326
518-372-9124

ISLAND TRAINS
4041 Hylan Blvd.
Staten Island, NY 10308
718-317-0762/
718-317-0008
e-mail: itrains@home.com
www.islandtrains.com

**SCAG'S ELECTRIC TRAIN
SHOP**
114 Victory Blvd.
Staten Island, NY
10301-2946
718-727-7373
fax: 718-727-5183

RED PUMP NURSERY INC.
398 Washington St.
Tappan, NY 10983-2614
914-359-4976

KROSS HARDWARE, INC.
989 Little East Neck Rd.
West Babylon,
NY 11704-2401
516-669-3069

LBC MODEL TRAINS
121 S. Long
Williamsville (Buffalo),
NY 14221-6625
716-631-3081
fax: 716-631-1250

**WESTCHESTER
CENTRAL TRAINS**
217 E. Post Rd.
White Plains,
NY 10601-4902
914-421-1262

COLLECTOR'S STATION
600 N. Broadway
White Plains, NY 10603
914-684-6951

OH **E&S TRAINS
AND HOBBIES**
980 Kenmore Blvd.
Akron, OH 44314-2150
330-745-0785

GLEN'S TRAIN SHOP
587 Grant St.
Akron, OH 44311-1531
330-253-6527
fax: 330-253-6567

TK HOBBY SHOP
312 Main St.
Bridgeport, OH 43912
740-633-6607
fax: 740-633-5127
www.tkhobbies.com

TRAIN AMERICA
4199 Boardman-Canfield Rd.
Canfield, OH 44406
330-533-7181
fax: 330-533-7208
e-mail: TrainAm@aol.com
www.TrainAmerica.com

GOLF MANOR HOBBIES
2235 Losantiville Ave.
Cincinnati, OH 45237-4222
513-351-3849

**TRADING POST TRAIN
SHOP**
4394 Pearl Rd.
Cleveland, OH 44109-4208
216-661-7300

**WARREN'S MODEL
TRAINS**
20520 Lorain Rd.
Cleveland, OH 44216-3424
440-331-2900
fax: 440-331-2559
e-mail: trains@
wmtlionelparts.com
www.wmtlionelparts.com

TIN PLATE STATION
6342-B Far Hills Ave.
Dayton, OH 45459-2724
937-428-9667

**HUDSON TOY, TRAIN
& HOBBY**
144 N. Main St.
Hudson, OH 44236-2827
330-653-2997

CORNER STORE
1249 Colorado Ave.
Lorain, OH 44052-3313
440-288-2351
TRAIN-O-RAMA
6732 E. Harbor Rd.
Marblehead, OH 43440
419-734-5856
e-mail:
TrainORama@aol.com

HARMAR STATION
220 Gilman St.
Marietta, OH 45750-2837
614-374-9995
www.eekman.com/
hamarstation/

G & M TRAIN & HOBBY
301 S. 4th St.
Martins Ferry, OH
43935-1313
740-633-6055

DAVIS ELECTRONICS
217 Main St.
Milford, OH 45150
513-831-6425
fax: 513-831-4256

TRAINS-N-THINGS
6593 Whipple Ave. NW
North Canton, OH
44720-7339
330-499-1666

CROUSE TRUE VALUE
11788 Market Street
North Lima, OH 44452
330-549-2143
e-mail:
NorthLima@webtv.net

STOCK YARD EXPRESS
49293 Plate Rd.
Oberlin, OH 44074-9619
440-774-2131
fax: 440-774-7575

HELEN'S HOBBY SHOP
4273 Harper St.
Perry, OH 44081-9744
440-259-4267

RICK'S TOY TRAINS
4807 Lewis Ave.
Toledo, OH 43612-2822
419-478-0171

OK **S & S HOBBIES**
108 S. Main
Broken Arrow, OK
74012-4139
918-251-0330

J & J TRAINS, LTD.
125 Hal Muldrow Dr.
Norman (Oklahoma City),
OK 73069-5222
405-573-9633

ACTION HOBBIES
4955 S. Memorial Dr.
Tulsa, OK 74145
918-663-8998

TRAIN & TOY HOUSE
3302 S. Peoria 74105-2029
Tulsa, OK
918-742-6378

OR **OLD TOY TRAIN TRADING CO.**
665 Virginia St.
P.O. Box 1112
North Bend, OR 97459
541-756-4594
fax: 541-756-4594

WHISTLE STOP TRAINS
11724 SE Division St.
Portland, OR 97266-1033
503-761-1822

ALL ABOARD HOBBIES
2421 W. Harvard Ave.
Roseburg, OR 97470
541-672-0280
fax: 541-672-2091
e-mail: info@
allaboardhobbies.com
www.allaboardhobbies.com

PA **AMERICAN HOBBY CENTER**
932 Brodhead Rd.
Aliquippa, PA 15001-2721
724-378-3930

ON THE RIGHT TRACK
1822 Union Ave.
Altoona, PA 16601-2026
814-942-4345

WYOMING VALLEY HOBBY
Irenes Collectables
34 South Main St.
Ashley, PA 18706
717-822-4418
e-mail: IrenesCol@aol.com
http://hometown.aol.
  com/irenescol/

MAINLINE HOBBY SUPPLY
15066 Buchanan Trail East
Blue Ridge Summit,
PA 17214
717-794-2860
e-mail:
mainline@innernet.net
www.innernet.net/
  mainline/index/htm

NICHOLAS SMITH TRAINS
2343 W. Chester Pike
Broomall, PA 19008
610-353-8585

WAGNER & SONS, INC.
28 E. Willow St.
Carlisle, PA 17013-3929
717-258-0839

PITTSBURGH RECEIVER & GAUGE
148 W. Pike St.
Canonsburg, PA 15317
724-746-6871
home.earthlink.net/~prandg

ROMAINA'S TRAINS & TOYS
200 Main St.
Catawissa, PA 17820-1314
570-356-7712

THE OLD TRAIN SHOP
724 Pine Street
Denver, PA 17517
717-336-2225

BARRY'S TRAIN SHOP
2 W. High St.
Elizabethtown, PA
17022-2017
717-367-4745

CHARLES SIEGEL'S TRAIN CITY
3133 Zuck Rd.
Erie, PA 16506
814-833-8313
fax: 814-838-3237
www.traincity.com

LOCO LOUIE'S
2365 MacDade Blvd.
Holmes, PA 19043-1301
610-583-7711

JIM'S TRAIN SHOP
25 Pine St.
Homer City, PA 15748
412-479-2026

IMPERIAL TRAIN COMPANY
450 Penn Lincoln Dr.
Imperial, PA 15126-9781
724-695-7552
fax: 724-695-7552

HENNING SCALE MODELS, INC.
126-128 South Line St.
Landsdale, PA 19446
215-362-2442

CONESTOGA HOBBIES
321 E. Main St.
Leola, PA 17540-1927
717-656-0666

ELLIE'S LOKIE SHOP
135 W. Mahanoy Ave.
Mahanoy City, PA 17948
717-773-2174
fax: 570-773-3811
e-mail: ellies@ptd.net
www.ellies-lokie.com

ENGLISH'S MODEL RR SUPPLY
21 Howard St.
Montoursville, PA 17754
570-368-2516

THE UNDERGROUND RAILROAD SHOPPE
1906 Wilmington Rd.
New Castle, PA 16105
724-652-4912

B&E JUNCTION
2 Center Square
New Oxford, PA 17350
717-624-4372/
717-757-3494

TOY TRAIN STATION
21 East Street Rd.
Feasterville (Philadelphia),
PA 19053-6047
215-322-5182

S & H HARDWARE
6700 Castor Ave.
Philadelphia, PA 19149
215-745-9375

GREAT TRADITIONS TOY TRAINS
11706 Bustleton Ave.
Philadelphia, PA 19116-2516
215-698-1993

IRON HORSE HOBBY SHOP
1950 Painters Run Rd.
Pittsburgh, PA 15241-3014
888-628-TOOT
ironhorse@sgi.net

JOSEPH A. GRZYBOSKI, JR.
P.O. Box 3475
Scranton, PA 18505
570-347-3314/
570-347-3315
e-mail: grzybosk@epix.net

SCRANTON HOBBY CENTER
517 Lackawanna Ave.
Scranton, PA 18503
570-342-2949
fax: 570-343-3775

EASTERN DEPOT
509 Canton St.
Troy, PA 16947
570-297-1975
fax: 570-297-1976
eastern@epix.net

J & J'S RAILROAD CROSSINGS
104 Church St.
Turtle Creek, PA 15145-1902
412-824-6009

FAIRCHANCE PHARMACY
90 Church St.
Uniontown (Fairchance),
PA 15436-1196
888-454-6635
www.hhs.net/fairchance

DR. K'S TRAIN & HOBBY SHOP
State Hwy 45
P.O. Box 25
Vicksburg, PA 17883
570-966-9577
e-mail: ejnk@hotmail.com

THE TRAIN SHOPPE
334 N. Pennsylvania Ave.
Wilkes-Barre, PA 18702-4415
717-824-7688

RI **APPONAUG COLOR SHOP**
1364 Greenwich Ave.
Apponaug (Warwick),
RI 02886
401-737-5506

LITTLE RHODY'S TRAINS
48 N. Olney St.
Johnston, RI 02919-5145
401-331-2592

SC **RAIL & SPIKE TRAINS & HOBBIES**
1943 E. Main St.
Easley, SC 29640-3843
864-850-0237

SVC TRAINS
2417 Highmarket St.
Georgetown, SC 29440
843-546-6511/
843-546-7611 (days)
fax: 843-527-6715
e-mail: svcgt2@aol.com
www.svctrains.com

TN **MARY ANN STONE ANTIQUES**
610 State. St.
Bristol, TN 37620-2246
423-968-5181
www.mastone.com

JACK'S TRAINS & HOBBYS
2420 Susannah St.
Johnson City, TN 37601-1748
423-282-9108

**MODEL RAILROAD
& HOBBY**
1266 Sycamore View
Memphis, TN 38134-7648
901-384-6500

TX **HOBBY MAKER**
1424-F Airport Fwy
Bedford (Fort Worth),
TX 76022-6779
817-267-0991

**COLLECTIBLE TRAINS
& TOYS**
109 Medallion Center
Dallas, TX 75214
214-373-9469/
800-462-4902
e-mail: ctt@airmail.net
www.trainsandtoys.com

**BOBBYE HALL'S
HOBBY HOUSE**
4822 Bryan St.
Dallas, TX 75204-6899
214-821-2550
214-824-2101

WOODIE'S TRAIN SHOP
4010 Polk Ave.
El Paso, TX 79930
915-566-0235

**TRAINS & PLANES
HOBBIES**
9737 Westheimer
Houston, TX 77042-3960
713-977-1420

TRAIN SOURCE: TEXAS
3264 South Loop W.
Houston, TX 77025-5201
800-338-5768/
713-662-0809

MIKE'S HOBBY SHOP
212 Main St.
Humble, TX 77338-4515
281-446-7550

**LONE STAR TRAINS
& COLLECTIBLES**
4133 Naco-Perrin
San Antonio, TX 78217
210-655-4665

UT **BOOMER TRAINS LLC**
6229 S. Highland Dr.
Salt Lake City, UT
84121-2125
801-272-1711

VT **BILL PARKER'S
TRAIN SHOP**
12 Juniper Hill Rd.
Springfield, VT 05156-9153
802-886-8151

VA **BRIDGE LINE HOBBIES**
HC 3 Box 107-B
Aroda, VA 22709
540-948-6344
fax: 540-948-3305
e-mail: sales@
bridgelinehobbies.com
www.bridgelinehobbies.com

THE TREASURE TROVE
Rt. 250
P.O. Box 416
Fishersville, VA 22939
540-949-5378

BOBBY'S TOY TRAINS
32 Broad Street Rd.
Manakin Sabot, VA
23103-2213
804-784-4473

KMA JUNCTION
9786 Center St.
Manassas, VA 20110-4128
703-257-9860

TRAIN DEPOT
7214 New Market Ct.
Manassas, VA 20109-2431
703-335-2216

CHESTERFIELD HOBBIES
13154 Midlothian Trnpk.
Midlothian (Richmond),
VA 23113-4245
804-379-9091

DAVIS TV, INC.
3594 Griffin St.
Portsmouth, VA 23707-4023
757-397-1983
www.davishobby.com

KEN'S TRAINS
2328 Orange Ave. NE
Roanoke, VA 24012-8311
540-343-1057

RAIL YARD HOBBY SHOP
6711B Williamson Rd.
Roanoke, VA 24019-4261
540-362-1714

GRANDAD'S HOBBY SHOP
5260-A Port Royal Rd.
Springfield, VA 22151-2113
703-426-0700

**STAUNTON TRAINS
& HOBBIES**
123 W. Beverley St.
Staunton, VA 24401-4204
540-885-6750

T S G HOBBIES
251 W. Lee Hwy
Warrenton, VA 20186
88-TRAINS-88

NORGE STATION
7405 Richmond Rd.
Williamsburg, VA
23188-7224
757-564-7623

WA **EASTSIDE TRAINS**
217 Central Way
Kirkland, WA 98003-6105
425-828-4098

TOY TRAIN HEAVEN
6302 NW 166th Circle
Ridgefield, WA 98642
360-576-1602
fax: 360-576-1632
e-mail: trainheavb@aol.com
www.trainexchange.
 com/tth.htm

**THE ELECTRIC
TRAIN SHOP**
4511 California Ave. SW
Seattle, WA 98116-4110
206-938-2400
Eltraino@aol.com

WI **SOMMERFELD'S TRAINS
& HOBBIES**
12620 W. Hampton Ave.
Butler, WI 53007
414-783-7797
fax: 414-783-9815

CHARLIE'S TRAINS
P.O. Box 158
Hubertus, WI 53003
414-628-1544
fax: 414-628-2651

BARRETT'S HOBBY HUT
2683 E. Main St.
East Troy, WI 53120-1343
414-642-4246
fax: 414-642-4246
Trains@pitnet.net

**HOBBY CRAFT
OF MADISON**
6632 Odana Rd.
Madison, WI 53719-1012
800-HBY-CRFT

TERMINAL HOBBY SHOP
5619 W. Florist Ave.
Milwaukee, WI 53218
414-461-1050/
800-487-2467

LOYAL TOY & HOBBY
2310 Calumet Dr.
New Holstein, WI
53061-9539
920-898-4248

WV **BRADY HARDWARE**
642 Main St.
Barboursville, WV 25504
304-736-1521

PATRICK'S TRAINS
142 29th Street
Wheeling, WV 26003
304-232-0714
www.patstrains.com

associations and clubs for O scale/gauge hobbyists

HIRAILERS UNLIMITED
10433 Shadyside Lane
Cincinnati, OH 45249-3649
513-683-5740
fax: 513-683-6023

IVES TRAIN SOCIETY
c/o Jo Ann Miller
6714 Madison Road
P.O. Box 59
Thompson, OH 44086
216-357-1544
fax: 216-357-1544
www.ivesboy.com

**K-LINE COLLECTOR'S CLUB
(KCC)**
*(sponsored by K-Line Electric
Trains)*
P.O. Box 2831
Chapel Hill, NC 27515
800-866-9986
fax: 919-929-4050
Collector's Club:
   kcc@k-linetrains.com
www.k-linetrains.com

**LIONEL COLLECTORS CLUB OF
AMERICA (LCCA)**
P.O. Box 479
La Salle, IL 61301
www.lionelcollectors.org

**LIONEL RAILROADERS CLUB
(LRRC)**
(sponsored by Lionel LLC)
50625 Richard W. Blvd.
Chesterfield, MI 48051-2493
810-940-4100
e-mail: talktous@lionel.com
www.lionel.com

**LIONEL OPERATING TRAIN
SOCIETY (LOTS)**
6364 West Fork Road
Cincinnati, OH 45247-5704
www.lots-trains.org

**MARX TRAINS ADVANTAGE
COLLECTOR'S CLUB**
(sponsored by Marx Trains)
209 East Butterfield Rd., #228
Elmhurst, IL 60126
630-941-3843
fax: 630-941-3829
e-mail: marxusa@aol.com
www.marxtrains.com

**M.T.H. RAILROADERS CLUB
(MTHRRC)**
*(sponsored by M.T.H.
Electric Trains)*
7020 Columbia Gateway Drive
Columbia, MD 21046
410-381-2580
fax: 410-381-6122
subscribe on line:
   www.mth-railking.com.
e-mail: club@mth-railking.com

**NATIONAL MODEL RAILROAD
ASSOCIATION (NMRA)**
4121 Cromwell Rd.
Chattanooga, TN 37421
423-892-2846
fax: 423-899-4869
www.nmra.org

**TOY TRAIN OPERATING
SOCIETY (TTOS)**
25 W. Walnut St., Suite 308
Pasadena, CA 91103
626-578-0673
www.ttos.org

**TRAIN COLLECTORS
ASSOCIATION (TCA)**
National Business Office
P.O. Box 248
Dept. 10
Strasburg, PA 17579
www.traincollectors.org

magazines, periodicals, price guides, videos

**CLASSIC TOY TRAINS
MAGAZINE**
Kalmbach Publishing Co.
21027 Crossroads Circle
P.O. Box 1612
Waukesha, WI 53187-1612
800-446-5489
www.classtrain.com

**NARROW GAUGE AND SHORT
LINE GAZETTE MAGAZINE**
4966 El Camino Real, #101
Los Altos, CA 94022
650-941-3823
fax: 650-941-3845
e-mail:
gazette@worldnet.att.net
www.ngslgazette.com

**O GAUGE RAILROADING
MAGAZINE**
P.O. Box 239
Nazareth, PA 18064-0239
610-759-0406
fax: 610-759-0223
e-mail: OGaugeRwy@aol.com
http://members.aol.com/
  OGaugeRwy/ogr.html

THE HIRAILERS BUZZ
Journal of HiRailers Unlimited
and Independent HiRailers
10433 Shadyside Lane
Cincinnati, OH 45249-3649
513-683-5740
fax: 513-683-6023
e-mail: Fequalls@aol.com

TCA QUARTERLY
*(Official quarterly journal, plus
extra issue in April, of the Train
Collectors Association.
Subscription included with
membership.)*
300 Paradise Lane
Ronks, PA 17572-9537
717-687-8623
fax: 717-687-0742
www.traincollectors.org

TTOS BULLETIN
*(Official bi-monthly journal of the
Toy Train Operating Society.
Subscription included
with membership.)*
25 W. Walnut St., Suite 308
Pasadena, CA 91103
626-578-0673
fax: 626-578-0750
e-mail: ttos@ttos.org
www.ttos.org

TROLLEY TALK MAGAZINE
1913 Roanoke Ave.
Louisville, KY 40205-1415

**ANTIQUE TRADER BOOKS/
KRAUSE PUBLICATIONS**
700 E. State St.
Iola, WI 54990
888-457-2873
www.krause.com/Books
*(Publisher of toy and model train
price guides and reference books.
Call for catalog.)*

TM BOOKS & VIDEOS
Box 279
New Buffalo, MI 49117
800-892-2822
fax: 219-879-7909
e-mail: tmbooks@aol.com
www.tmbooks-video.com
*(Toy train videos, value guides,
and reference books. Call for
catalog.)*

GREENBERG BOOKS
Kalmbach Publishing Co.
21027 Crossroads Circle
P.O. Box 1612
Waukesha, WI 53187-1612
800-446-5489
www.books.kalmbach.com
*(Greenberg line of toy train price
guides and reference books. Call
for catalog.)*

web sites of interest to O scale/gauge collectors and operators

www.trainfinder.com
(On-line directory to toy and model train web sites)

www.trainmarket.com
(Site for buying/selling Marx and other classic toy trains.)

http://thortrains.hypermart. net
All-Gauge Model Railroading Home Page
(Emphasis on O/O27 trains, with a variety of topics.)

wwwO.delphi.com/railroad
Delphi Railroading Forum
(Site for general railroad/railfan/model railroad topics.)

www.tmbooks-video.com
Toy Train Revue On-Line
(News and information from the world of toy trains.)

www.napanet.net/~jlbaker/index.htm
The O Gauge Toy Train Page
(On-line link to a large number of O gauge web sites.)

www.railserve.com
RailServe Home Page
(On-line directory to rail-related content on the Internet.)

www.coilcouplers.com
("Clyde Coil's" site for comprehensive information about products and new developments in Lionel's electronic control and sound systems for O gauge trains)

www.traincom.com
(Site provides hardware and software products for O gauge railroading)

www.onelist.com/subscribe.cgi/MarxTrain
(on-line mailing list devoted to Marx and Joy Line trains)

http://web.mit.edu/ldsteve/Public/NAHShome.htm
(North American Hornby Society—Hornby O gauge and Dublo trains)

http://davesrailpix.railfan.net/models/htm
(everything for the traction and trolley enthusiast, including models; 14,000-plus photos)

www.ehobbies.com
(model railroad discussion groups and general interest train topics)

www.eppraisals.com
(On-line appraisal services, including toy and model trains.)

www.modelshopper.com
(on-line model locator)

www.hobbyretailer.com
(on-line hobby dealer locator)

www.amazon.com
(Internet book and auction site)

www.boxlot.com
(Internet auction site)

www.collect.com
(Internet auction site)

www.ebay.com
(Internet auction site)

www.train-station.com
(Internet auction site)

Big, bold, and colorful Standard Gauge electric trains on the layout of toy train enthusiast Dr. Peter Riddle. This photo is from his popular book, *America's Standard Gauge Electric Trains*, one of a number of books he has authored on the subject of model railroading with toy trains.

Photo courtesy of Peter Riddle

STANDARD (WIDE) GAUGE ELECTRIC TRAINS

If you're a nostalgia buff, Standard Gauge model railroading is for you! These are the big, boisterous, colorful, all-metal trains that your grandfather, great grandfather, and even great-great grandfather may have run around the Christmas tree in the early years of the twentieth century. Indeed, most scale model railroaders today can trace their roots in the hobby back to a toy train circling the family Christmas tree at some point in their childhood. And, when it comes to toy trains, Standard Gauge ranks, de facto, as the king of them all!

Standard Gauge and Wide Gauge trains run on three-rail track measuring 2-1/8 inches between the outside running rails. Even though Standard/Wide Gauge locomotives and cars are themselves roughly equivalent in size to many Large Scale trains (see the Large Scale section of this book), this unique 2-1/8 inch track gauge, combined with the three-rail track configuration, distinguishes Standard Gauge from the Large Scale classification, which is based on a 45mm (approximately 1-3/4 inches) two rail track gauge. So, one might logically ask, how and why did this "Standard" thing come about? Good question!

In 1906, just six years after he had begun the manufacturing of "miniature electric cars" in New York City for use as merchant display window attractions, Joshua Lionel Cowen, founding father of Lionel Electric Trains, proclaimed his still-maturing line of electric toy trains as "Standard of the World." The basis for this official proclamation from the seldom-modest entrepreneur was, quite simply, that Joshua Cowen said that it was so; therefore it was!

Nevertheless, there was some ingenious logic and solid business savvy woven into Cowen's bravado. He was, in fact, attempting to create a "standard" size of electric train or, more precisely, a standardized track system for electric trains, which he hoped would stifle competition from other toy train makers, both at home and abroad.

Cowen settled on a track system that measured a distinctive 2-1/8 inches between the running rails, assuring that similarly-sized locomotives and cars offered by his competitors would not be compatible unless they could be reworked to conform to Lionel's self-proclaimed "standard." The track system itself, and the trains that operated upon this track, were thereafter known as "Standard Gauge," a term that has endured to the present day.

Lionel's foremost domestic competitors of the time—most notably Ives and American Flyer—deferred to Lionel's "standard," in fact if not in name, and began manufacturing what they called "Wide Gauge" trains some years later (in 1921 and 1925, respectively), which were made to operate on Lionel's unique three-rail Standard Gauge track system. In effect, these competitors validated Cowen's "Standard" merely by accepting it.

Standard Gauge electric trains were designed to be admired as well as played with. Although they almost never faithfully duplicated the exact appearance or detail of actual locomotives and rolling stock seen on the nation's railways, they compensated in other ways. They were constructed of heavy tinplated metal, adorned with gleaming enamel paint in bright colors, and outfitted with bright nickel or brass trim. Furthermore, they were powered by rugged and reliable motors that were easy to service and repair. Everything about these toys exemplified quality on a grand and colorful scale. It's an awe-inspiring sight to view an eight-foot-long Standard Gauge train streaking toward its imaginary destination amidst equally massive and colorful tinplate buildings, bridges, and signal lights. And, it's a sight that continues to appeal to youngsters and oldsters alike, even to this day.

Standard Gauge effectively dominated the electric toy train landscape in America through World War I and into the years beyond the Great Depression. However, in the period leading up to U.S. involvement in the Second World War, Standard Gauge increasingly lost ground to the smaller and more affordable O Gauge electric trains. By war's end, Standard Gauge had virtually disappeared—destined to be relegated to the rank of museum artifact, save for the products offered by a few small but determined manufacturers who struggled persistently to keep the tradition alive.

But the closing years of the twentieth century saw something of a resurgence of interest in Standard Gauge electric trains. In part, this likely related to nostalgia, and a desire to maintain some link with the treasured artifacts of our nation's past. The so-called Baby Boomer generation and their immediate predecessors were particularly influential in this regard. In 1988, Lionel Trains, Inc., owners of the trademark at the time, reintroduced models of several of Lionel's most desirable Standard Gauge trains and accessories from the 1920s and 1930s. Appropriately labeled as "Lionel Classics," these striking and somewhat costly reproductions nudged their way into train collectors' hearts and pocketbooks.

Today, these colorful, rugged, and boisterous toys are no longer being produced by Lionel, but they are still being offered by a firm that, by most accounts, ranks as Lionel's most formidable competitor in the contemporary toy train marketplace: M.T.H. Electric Trains, with headquarters in Columbia, Maryland. Mike Wolf, the energetic young founder of M.T.H., has openly professed a personal fondness for Standard Gauge, even though he was born long after the original Standard Gauge was in its heyday. The appeal of Standard Gauge tends to transcend the generations.

Depending on condition, many of the original Standard Gauge trains produced by Lionel, Ives, American Flyer, and others, are today quite literally worth their weight in gold. Somewhat ironically perhaps, M.T.H. Electric Trains is offering a gold-plated Standard Gauge set in its "Tinplate Traditions" product line for the year 2000.

Standard Gauge is almost certain to live on well into the twenty-first century and beyond, perpetuated by a small but dedicated following of toy train collectors and operators who happily devote their leisure hours to bringing history to life.

STANDARD/WIDE GAUGE (2-1/8" TRACK GAUGE) RESOURCES

manufacturers of Standard Gauge locomotives, rolling stock, and accessories

---

M.T.H. ELECTRIC TRAINS
7020 Columbia Gateway Drive
Columbia, MD 21046-1532
888-640-3700
www.mth-railking.com
(reproduction Lionel, American Flyer, and Ives Standard Gauge and O gauge tinplate trains, accessories, and track components)

JOSEPH L. MANIA (JLM TRAINS)
17 Douglas Road
Freehold, NJ 07728
732-303-8299
fax: 732-303-8299
www.jlmtrains.com
(reproduction Standard/Wide Gauge and 2-7/8 inch gauge trains)

THE RICH-ART COMPANY
1714 Del Rios Highway
Escondido, CA 92029
c/o Art's Reproductions
334 Nutwood
Orange, CA 92869-4814
714-771-5347
www.trainguy.com/richart2.html
(reproduction and original Standard Gauge locomotives and rolling stock)

after-market manufacturers and suppliers
of Standard/Wide Gauge products

ANTIQUE TRAINS
1 Lantern Drive
Turnersville, NJ 08012
(Standard Gauge train track)

BENNETT DRY TRANSFERS
Janice L. Bennett
P.O. Box 178
Closter, NJ 07624
(reproduction lettering for Lionel, Ives, and American Flyer trains)

CHARLES C. WOOD
P.O. Box 179
Hartford, OH 44424
330-772-5177
e-mail: chas 327@aol.com
(train enamel for pre- and post-war collectible toy trains)

CLARKE SPARES & RESTORATIONS
(Tintown)
90 West Swamp Rd.
Doylestown, PA 18901
215-348-0595
fax: 215-348-4160
(Standard Gauge structures)

EBR PRODUCTS
204-6 Lane Ave.
Gloucester City, NJ 08030
(Standard Gauge train track)

GARGRAVES TRACKAGE CORP.
8967 Ridge Road
North Rose, NY 14516-9793
315-483-6577
fax: 315-483-2425
www.GarGraves.com
(flexible track and other track products for Standard Gauge)

GEORGE TEBOLT TRAIN PARTS
Box 149
Spencertown, NY 12165
518-392-2660
www.georgetebolt.com
(Standard Gauge replacement parts)

GLENN SNYDER DISPLAY SYSTEMS
260 Oak Street
Buffalo, NY 14203
716-852-4676/716-648-5817
fax: 716-852-4677
e-Mail: glenn@gsds.com
www.gsds.com
(wall-mounted train display shelves for Standard Gauge)

IRON HORSE REPRODUCTIONS, INC.
P.O. Box 13269
Pittsburgh, PA 15243
888-628-8668
e-mail: ironhorse@sgi.net
www.sgi.net/ironhorse
(original and reproduction toy
train catalogs)

**JOSEPH L. MANIA
(JLM TRAINS)**
17 Douglas Road
Freehold, NJ 07728
www.jlmtrains.com
(restoration and repair of
Standard/Wide Gauge and
2-7/8 inch gauge trains)

KRAEMER REPRODUCTIONS
E.C. Kraemer
105 Hollywood Ave.
Fairfield, NJ 07006
(decal reproductions)

M. LASTER
P.O. Box 51253
Philadelphia, PA 19152
888-469-0404 (orders only)
(tinplate tools, including wheel
pullers, track pliers, etc.)

MOONDOG EXPRESS
P.O. Box 1707
Lompoc, CA 93438
(roadway materials for
Standard Gauge)

PIONEER VALLEY MODELS
P.O. Box 4928
Holyoke, MA 01041
(scenic backdrops/cardstock
structures for all scales)

PRIDE LINES
651 W. Hoffman Ave.,
Lindenhurst, NY 11757
516-225-0033
fax: 516-225-0099
e-mail: palo@mindspring.com
(reproduction and original design
stations and other tinplate
accessories)

RAIL RAX
786 Seely Ave.
Aromas, CA 95004
831-726-3706
(wall-mounted display shelves
for Standard Gauge trains)

ROBERT E. TAYLOR
5559 Kane Creek Road
Central Point, OR 97502
(reproduction Ives and American
Flyer Standard Gauge tenders
and parts)

RON MORRIS
2723 Beacon Drive
Sinking Spring, PA 19608
(reproduction prewar Lionel
scenic plots)

RR-TRACK
R&S Enterprises
P.O. Box 643
Jonestown, PA 17038
717-865-3444
www.rrtrack.com/rrtrack
(Sectional track layout planning
software)

RYDIN INDUSTRIES
26 W Warrenville Road
Warrenville, IL 60555
(Standard Gauge track and
switches)

SCENIC EXPRESS
1001 Lowrey Ave.
Jeannette, PA 15644-2671
(various landscaping materials
for all scales)

SIEVERS BENCHWORK
Jackson Harbor Rd.
Washington Island, WI 54246
(ready-to-assemble custom
benchwork in all scales)

SMITH METAL WORKS
100 Colburn St.
Newark, NJ 14513
(Standard Gauge yard and shop
structures)

T-REPRODUCTIONS
227 West Main Street
P.O. Box 5369
Johnson City, TN 37604
423-926-4287
(formerly offered reproductions
of Standard Gauge accessories;
currently manufactures reproductions of the larger scale Buddy-L
trains)

TM BOOKS & VIDEOS
Box 279
New Buffalo, MI 49117
800-892-2822
fax: 219-879-7909
e-mail: tmbooks@aol.com
www.tmbooks-video.com
(toy train videos, value guides
and reference books)

TOWN & COUNTRY HOBBIES
P.O. Box 584
Totowa, NJ 07512-0584
973-942-5176
fax: 973-790-8151
www.TownCountryHobbies.com
(replacement light bulbs for electric toy trains of all scales and
gauges)

TRAIN REPAIR PARTS
Div. of Hobby Surplus Sales
287 Main St.
P.O. Box 2170
New Britain, CT 06050
860-223-0600
www.TrainRepairParts.com
(repair parts and manuals for
Lionel and Flyer prewar Standard
Gauge)

major retailers of collectible and/or current production Standard Gauge trains

The following dealers have been identified, through print or on-line advertising, as retailers who regularly stock Standard/Wide Gauge electric train items, either original (vintage) or reproduction (current manufacture). Not all dealers will have all items in stock, so it is a good idea to review their print ads in *Classic Toy Trains* Magazine, or visit their web site, if one is listed, to determine availability. Also, since many of the currently manufactured Standard Gauge items are produced in limited quantities, you may consider placing an advance order with your selected dealer to assure that the item you want will be held for you when it's released.

This list is not all-inclusive, and there may be dealers in your local area who carry, or will order, Standard/Wide Gauge items for you. For example, most authorized M.T.H. Electric Trains dealers can easily order items from the M.T.H. "Tinplate Traditions" line, assuming that factory stocks have not been depleted. A current list of those dealers can be found on the M.T.H. web site, and printed authorized dealer lists are customarily packed inside every new M.T.H. train set box.

As is the case with other model railroad products, you are encouraged to contact, and support, your local dealer first. These folks depend on your business to stay in business!

AL **UNCLE AL'S HOBBIES**
6017 E. Shirley Lane
Montgomery, AL 36117-1977
334-277-1715
fax: 334-277-1628
e-mail: aluncle@aol.com

AR **DAN COOK'S TRAINS**
112 N. 6th St.
Arkadelphia, AR 71923
870-246-9823
e-mail:
kennyb@dancooks.com
www.dancooks.com

MICKEY'S MODEL WORKS
611 Court Street, Suite 4
Conway, AR 72032
501-450-9423
fax: 501-327-6634
e-mail: mickeymw@
  cyberback.com

AZ **ARIZONA TRAIN DEPOT**
755 E. McKellips Rd.
Mesa, AZ 35203
480-833-9486
www.arizonatraindepot.com

CA **THE TRAIN SHACK**
1030 N. Hollywood Way
Burbank, CA 91505
800-572-9929
fax: 818-842-4562
e-mail: info@TrainShack.com
www.trainshack.com

CLASSIC HOBBIES & TOYS
17632 Chatsworth St.
Granada Hills, CA
91344-5601
818-368-7317

DOLLHOUSES, TRAINS & MORE
14 Commercial Blvd. #111
Novato, CA 94949-6110
415-883-0388

THE ORIGINAL WHISTLE STOP INC.
2490 E. Colorado Blvd.
Pasadena, CA 91107
626-796-7791
fax: 626-796-7566
www.thewhistlestop.com

BRUCE'S TRAIN SHOP
2752 Marconi Ave.
Sacramento, CA
95821-4914
916-485-5288

THE VILLAGE DEPOT
170 Del Mar
San Clemente, CA 92672
949-366-0930
fax: 949-361-9814
e-mail: tom@cyber-rail.com

CHAN'S TRAINS & KITS
2450 Van Ness Ave.
& Union St.
San Francisco, CA
94109-1826
415-885-2899

PACIFIC TRAINS
5939 Pacific Ave.
Stockton, CA 95207
209-473-3410

THE WESTERN DEPOT
1650 Sierra Ave #203
Yuba City, CA 95993-8986
530-673-6776

CT **NEW ENGLAND HOBBY SUPPLY-TRAIN EXCHANGE**
71 Hillard St.
Manchester, CT 06040
860-646-0610
fax: 860-645-0504
www.nehobby.com

DE **JUSTRAINS OF DELAWARE**
2622 Capitol Trail (Rt. 2)
Newark, DE 19711
302-453-9742
fax: 302-368-6447
e-mail: kmtrains@
concentric.net
www.justrains.com

FL **TRAINMASTER**
5001-B NW 34th St.
Gainesville, FL 32605
352-373-4222

HOLLYWOOD STATION
1917 Hollywood Blvd.
Hollywood, FL
954-921-2700
e-mail: trainman@
bellsouth.net
www.hollywood-station.com

READY TO ROLL
831 NW 143rd St.
Miami, FL 33168
305-688-8868
fax: 305-948-0339
e-mail: rtrtrains@aol.com
www.readytorolltrains.com

H & R TRAINS, INC.
6901 U.S. 19 at Haines Rd.
Pinellas Park, FL
727-526-4682
fax: 727-526-3439
e-mail:
hrtrains@hrtrains.com
www.hrtrains.com

GA **LEGACY STATION LTD.**
251F Hurricane Shoals Rd.
Lawrenceville, GA 30045
770-339-7780
fax: 770-339-4417
www.trainworks.com

IL **DENNY'S TRAINS
& THINGS**
906 Bangs St.
Aurora, IL 60505-5332
630-585-6964
dennytrain@aol.com

**BERWYN'S TOY TRAINS
& MODELS**
7025 Ogden Ave.
Berwyn, IL 60402
708-484-4384

**SF&C MODEL TRAINS
& HOBBYS**
2329 W. Belmont Ave.
Chicago, IL 60618-6422
773-472-1710

**AMERICA'S BEST TRAIN
& HOBBY**
136 E. Army Trail Rd.
Glendale Heights, IL 60139
630-539-8551

**HILL'S HOBBY
& COLLECTORS' SHOP**
10 Prarie Ave.
Park Ridge, IL 60068
847-823-4464
fax: 847-823-0624
www.hillshobby.com

IN **GEORGE'S TRAIN SHOP**
254 N. Warren Rd.
Huntington, IN 46750
219-468-2186
fax: 219-468-2186
e-mail: leslie@
georgestrainshop.com

KY **HOBBY STATION
(TNC ENTERPRISES)**
Houchens E-Town Plaxa
300 Sycamore St., Suite 27
Elizabethtown, KY 42701
502-737-2000
fax: 270-737-3453
e-mail: tnchobby@aol.com

MA **TRAINS ON TRACKS**
21 Summer St.
Chelmsford, MA 01824
978-256-3465
fax: 978-256-3465
e-mail:
ray@trainsontracks.com
www.trainsontracks.com

TOY DOCTOR
17 Meredith Rd.
Forestdale, MA 02644
508-477-1186
fax: 508-477-1186
e-mail: TDoct@aol.com

CHARLES RO SUPPLY CO.
662 Cross St.
P.O. Box 100
Malden, MA 02148
781-321-0090
fax: 781-321-6459
www.charlesro.com

MO **HALL'S STATION**
Ste. 320 Crown
Center Shops
Kansas City, MO
888-425-5722
www.crowncenter.com

NE **GRAND CENTRAL LTD.**
6901 Seward Ave.
P.O. Box 29109
Lincoln, NE 68529
402-467-3738
fax: 402-467-3795
www.grandcentralltd.com

NC **HOBBY HOUSE**
1211 Asheville Hwy.
Hendersonville, NC 28791
828-692-6683
e-mail:
hobbyhse@bellsouth.net

DRY BRIDGE STATION
236 N. Main St.
Mount Airy, NC 27030
336-786-9811
fax: 336-786-9043
e-mail: mikek@
  drybridgestation.com

**THE TRAIN LOFT
(FORMERLY RERUNS TS)**
4007-B Country Club Rd.
Winston-Salem, NC 27104
336-760-9817
e-mail: Jkonc52032@aol.com

NH **BRENTWOOD ANTIQUES**
The Castles at Brentwood
101 Route 27
Brentwood, NH 03833
603-679-1500
fax: 603-672-3451
www.TheTrainShop.com

MOUNTAIN TRAINS
25 Lowell Street
Manchester, NH 03101
603-622-8982/
603-641-1113
fax: 603-625-4060
e-mail: mthtrains@
  metro2000.net
www.mountaintrains.com

NJ **LARRY'S MODEL TRAINS**
211 Greenwood Ave.
Midland Park, NJ 07432
201-444-0052
fax: 201-444-9078

**TRAIN COLLECTOR'S
WAREHOUSE, INC.**
1521 Route 46 East
Parsippany, NJ 07054
973-334-3399

NY **K-VAL HOBBIES**
277 Hinman Ave.
Buffalo, NY 14216
716-875-2837
e-mail:
mquill1224@aol.com
www.kvalhobbies.com

**BOOKBINDER'S
"TRAINS UNLIMITED"**
P.O. Box 660086
Flushing, NY 11366-0086
800-955-8729
fax: 718-657-2264
www.netpage1.com/
  bookbinderstrains

CHOO CHOO CHARLIE'S
199 S. Main St.
Liberty, NY 12754
914-292-4826
fax: 914-292-4826
e-mail: cdx7037@catskill.net

ISLAND TRAINS
4041 Hylan Blvd.
Staten Island, NY 10308
718-317-0762/
718-317-0008
e-mail: itrains@home.com
www.islandtrains.com

OH **GLEN'S TRAIN SHOP**
587 Grant St.
Akron, OH 44311-1531
330-253-6527
fax: 330-253-6567

TRAIN AMERICA
4199 Boardman-
Canfield Rd.
Canfield, OH 44406
330-533-7181
e-mail: trainam@aol.com
www.TrainAmerica.com

WARREN'S MODEL TRAINS
20520 Lorain Rd.
Cleveland, OH 44126
440-331-2900
440-331-2559
e-mail: trains@
  wmtlionelparts.com
www.wmtlionelparts.com

HOUSE OF TRAINS- OHIO
417 E. 200 St.
Euclid, OH 44119
216-383-9494
fax: 216-383-0966

HARMAR STATION
220 Gilman St.
Marietta, OH 45750-2837
614-374-9995

DAVIS ELECTRONICS
217 Main St.
Milford, OH 45150
513-831-6425
fax: 513-831-4256

OR **OLD TOY TRAIN
TRADING CO.**
665 Virginia St.
P.O. Box 1112
North Bend, OR 97459
541-756-4594
fax: 541-756-4594

THE HOBBYSMITH
4148 NE Hancock St.
Portland, OR 97212
360-696-3530
fax: 360-693-3923
e-mail:
pacmopow@pcez.com

ALL ABOARD HOBBIES
2421 W. Harvard Ave.
Roseburg, OR 97470-2500
541-672-0280
www.allaboardhobbies.com

PA **NICHOLAS SMITH TRAINS**
2343 W. Chester Pike
Broomall, PA 19008
610-353-8585

**JERRY QUINN
CLASSIC TRAINS**
1329 Blackhorse Hill Rd.
Coatsville, PA 19320
610-383-1931
e-mail: JQTrainToy@aol.com

NIEDZALKOSKIS TRAINS
214 South 4th St.
Jeannette, PA 15644
724-523-8035
fax: 724-527-3899
e-mail:
info@needztrains.com

HENNING SCALE MODELS, INC.
128 South Line St.
Lansdale, PA 19446
215-362-2442
fax: 215-412-7712
e-mail:
hhenning@adelphia.net

B&E JUNCTION
2 Center Square
New Oxford, PA 17350
717-624-4372

JOSEPH A. GRZYBOSKI, JR.
P.O. Box 3475
Scranton, PA 18505
570-347-3315
fax: 570-342-3314
e-mail: grzybosk@epix.net
www.grzyboskitrains.com
www.specialtytrains.com

SCRANTON HOBBY CENTER
517 Lackawanna Ave.
Scranton, PA 18503
570-342-2949
fax: 570-343-3775

EASTERN DEPOT
509 Canton St.
Troy, PA 16947
570-297-1975
fax: 570-297-1976
e-mail: eastern@epix.net

SC **SVC TRAINS**
2417 Highmarket St.
Georgetown, SC 29440
843-546-6511/
843-546-7611 (days)
fax: 843-527-6715
e-mail: svcgt2@aol.com
www.svctrains.com

TN **MARY ANN STONE ANTIQUES**
610 W. State. St.
Bristol, TN 37620
888-817-3382
fax: 888-817-4321
e-mail: railnerd@aol.com
www.mastone.com

MODEL RAILROAD & HOBBY
1266 Sycamore View
Memphis, TN 38134
901-384-6500
fax: 901-384-9050
e-mail: mrhs99@earthlink.net

TX **COLLECTIBLE TRAINS & TOYS**
109 Medallion Center
Dallas, TX 75214
214-373-9469/
800-462-4902
fax: 214-373-1622
e-mail: ctt@airmail.net
www.trainsandtoys.com

VA **CHESTERFIELD HOBBIES**
13154 Midlothian Trnpk.
Midlothian (Richmond),
VA 23113
804-379-9091
fax: 804-379-6591
e-mail: chstobb@erols.com

NORGE STATION
7405 Richmond Rd.
Williamsburg, VA 23188
757-564-7623

WI **SOMMERFELD'S TRAINS & HOBBIES**
12620 W. Hampton Ave.
Butler, WI 53007
414-783-7797
fax: 414-783-9815
e-mail: questions@
   sommerfelds.com
www.sommerfelds.com

OWEN UPP RAILROADER'S SUPPLY
11300 W. Greenfield Ave.
West Allis, WI 53214
414-771-2353

associations and clubs for Standard/Wide Gauge hobbyists

TOY TRAIN OPERATING
SOCIETY (TTOS)
25 W. Walnut St., Suite 308
Pasadena, CA 91103
626-578-0673
fax: 626-578-0750
e-mail: ttos@ttos.org
www.ttos.org

TRAIN COLLECTORS
ASSOCIATION (TCA)
National Business Office
P.O. Box 248
Dept. 10
Strasburg, PA 17579
www.traincollectors.org

IVES TRAIN SOCIETY
c/o Jo Ann Miller
6714 Madison Road
P.O. Box 59
Thompson, OH 44086
216-357-1544
fax: 216-357-1544
www.ivesboy.com

LIONEL COLLECTORS CLUB OF
AMERICA (LCCA)
P.O. Box 479
La Salle, IL 61301
www.lionelcollectors.org

STANDARD GAUGE
ENTHUSIASTS OF AMERICA
(SGEA)
c/o Allan Miller
1240-G Ivystone Way
Chesapeake, VA 23320
e-mail: TinpaterAl@aol.com

LIONEL OPERATING TRAIN
SOCIETY (LOTS)
6364 West Fork Road
Cincinnati, OH 45247-5704
www.lots-trains.org

M.T.H. RAILROADERS CLUB
(MTHRRC)
(sponsored by M.T.H. Electric Trains)
7020 Columbia Gateway Drive
Columbia, MD 21046
410-381-2580
fax: 410-381-6122
e-Mail: club@mth-railking.com
subscribe on line:
www.mth-railking.com.

NATIONAL MODEL RAILROAD
ASSOCIATION (NMRA)
4121 Cromwell Rd.
Chattanooga, TN 37421
423-892-2846
fax: 423-899-4869
www.nmra.org

magazines, periodicals, guides, and videos
of interest to Standard Gauge hobbyists

CLASSIC TOY TRAINS MAGAZINE
Kalmbach Publishing Co.
21027 Crossroads Circle
P.O. Box 1612
Waukesha, WI 53187-1612
800-446-5489
www.classtrain.com

TCA QUARTERLY
*(Official quarterly journal, plus
extra issue in April, of the Train
Collectors Association.
Subscription included with
membership.)*
300 Paradise Lane
Ronks, PA 17572-9537
717-687-8623
fax: 717-687-0742
www.traincollectors.org

**LIONEL TRAINS: STANDARD OF
THE WORLD, 1900-1943**
*(Published by the Train
Collectors Association)*
Train Collectors Association
P.O. Box 248
Strasburg, PA 17579
717-687-8623

TTOS BULLETIN
*(Official bi-monthly journal of
the Toy Train Operating Society.
Subscription included with
membership.)*
25 W. Walnut St., Suite 308
Pasadena, CA 91103
626-578-0673
fax: 626-578-0750
e-mail: ttos@ttos.org
www.ttos.org

**ANTIQUE TRADER BOOKS/
KRAUSE PUBLICATIONS**
700 E. State St.
Iola, WI 54990
888-457-2873
www.krause.com/Books
*(Publisher: America's Standard
Gauge Electric Trains book, and
O'Briens Collecting Toy Trains:
Identification and Value Guide
book. Call for catalog)*

TM BOOKS & VIDEOS
Box 279
New Buffalo, MI 49117
800-892-2822
fax: 219-879-7909
e-mail: tmbooks@aol.com
www.tmbooks-video.com
*(Toy train videos, value guides,
and reference books. Call for
catalog.)*

GREENBERG BOOKS
Kalmbach Publishing Co.
21027 Crossroads Circle
P.O. Box 1612
Waukesha, WI 53187-1612
800-446-5489
www.books.kalmbach.com
*(Greenberg line of toy train price
guides and reference books. Call
for catalog.)*

web sites of interest to Standard/Wide Gauge hobbyists

www.IvesTrains.com
(images of early toy trains made by all of the major manufacturers, including Standard and Wide Gauges)

www.jlmtrains.com
(Joseph Mania's home page. Lists products and services, and includes links to other sites of interest to Standard and Wide Gauge enthusiasts)

http://members.aol.com/ivesboy
(Ives Train Society web site—for all Ives enthusiasts, including fans of Ives Wide Gauge trains)

www.geocities.com/motorcity/strip/7141
(subscribe to Standard Gauge mailing list)

www.trainfinder.com
(on-line directory to model train related web sites)

www.trainmarket.com
(site for buying/selling a variety of classic toy trains.)

http://thortrains.hypermart.net
All-Gauge Model Railroading Home Page
(Covers a variety of toy train topics.)

www.tmbooks-video.com
Toy Train Revue On-Line
(news and information from the world of toy trains.)

www.railserve.com
RailServe Home Page
(on-line directory to rail-related content on the Internet.)

www.ehobbies.com
(model railroad discussion groups and general interest train topics)

www.eppraisals.com
(on-line appraisal services, including toy and model trains.)

www.amazon.com
(Internet auction site)

www.boxlot.com
(Internet auction site)

www.collect.com
(Internet auction site)

www.ebay.com
(Internet auction site)

www.train-station.com
(Internet auction site)

Another load of refreshing Coca-Cola moves from the bottling plant to distribution points along the scenic Bikini & Flamingo garden railroad, located in Illinois. The B&F is the handiwork of Valerie Myers, a Large Scale model railroader who enjoys gardening as well as model railroading, and she has managed to successfully combine both interests in a fanciful and colorful outdoor railroad empire. Myers custom-paints many of her locomotives and railroad cars in pastel colors, and says that the B&F represents "a fantasy railroad, where color, creativity, and the fun of just running trains is more important than duplicating the concept or a specific era of a real railroad."

Photo courtesy of Valerie Myers

LARGE SCALE
MODEL RAILROADING

Scales ranging from 1:13.7 to 1:32—
operating on #1 gauge (45mm) track

Large Scale trains are, as the name implies, large in virtually every respect. They are physically big trains—two or more times the size of their O scale counterparts—and they run on hefty and very rugged track. which, for optimum operation and appearance, often requires large curves. The majority of these trains and their related components are durable enough to be operated anywhere—inside the home, if space permits, or outdoors, in nearly all kinds of weather conditions.

Indeed, this "weatherproofed" feature of Large Scale equipment is largely responsible for inspiring a whole new breed of outdoor-oriented hobbyists known as "garden railroaders." Garden railroading, which has truly evolved into a family-oriented affair, offers a variety of fun-filled activities that appeal to both males and females, and to youngsters, oldsters, and everyone in between.

The terms "scale" and "gauge" are perhaps the only real sources of consternation, debate, and confusion in Large Scale model railroading. Basically, the problem stems from operating trains of many different scales on the same gauge of track. Although the track gauge generally stays the same in most Large Scale model railroading—that is, #1 gauge track, which measures 45mm between the rails—the scale of the trains themselves, and even the scale of the track (not its gauge) does lead to some confusion.

Some hobbyists tend to place the blame on the variety of scales that are offered by the manufacturers—ranging from large 1:13.7 models to 1:32 models under the blanket designation "Large Scale." More properly, the blame should be shifted to the track gauge instead, and the major manufacturers' somewhat understandable reluctance to deviate from what has become the de facto standard—meaning a gauge of 45mm.

When Large Scale railroading first gained some following in the United States in the 1970s, that acceptance was largely the result of LGB's introduction of their renowned line of Large Scale trains into this country. These trains, most of which were designed to represent European-style narrow gauge equipment, operated on 45mm gauge track, which usually came packaged with every starter set. As the popularity of the LGB line grew, people naturally built and/or expanded their outdoor rail lines using the readily available LGB track. It wasn't long before the vast majority of garden railroads throughout the nation were strongly rooted to this 45mm track gauge. So, when competing manufacturers decided to build models representing the other types of real-life railroading more commonly seen in this country, they elected to stick with the already-in-place 45mm track gauge. After all, how many enthusiasts could be expected to tear up and replace an entire garden railway full of permanently implanted track?

But, producing models to scales that permitted all to conveniently operate on 45mm gauge track meant that the different models themselves, when compared model-beside-model, seemingly reversed their scale proportions to the real thing. In other words, a correctly scaled 1:20.3 model of a diminutive prototype narrow gauge locomotive was often physically larger than a 1:32 scale model of a giant modern-day standard gauge road diesel. Operating separately, and with each toting correctly-scaled passenger or freight cars, they looked just fine. Placed side-by-side, however, these disparate types of trains looked kind of "funny!" Whereas real-life railroads have nearly always matched their locomotives and rolling stock to the track gauge being employed—small locomotives and cars operating on narrow gauge track, and large locomotives and cars operating on standard gauge track—the model makers made everything to operate on the same 45mm gauge track. So, what was, and still basically is, both cost effective and convenient for the manufacturers has led to considerable confusion within the Large Scale modeling community.

The simple solution, of course, is to just pick one scale (genre, if you will) of locomotives, cars, and accompanying accessories to operate on your own Large Scale railroad, and then religiously stick with that scale. For example, if U.S. narrow gauge prototype railroading appeals to you, stay with models of narrow gauge types of equipment made to 1:20.3 scale: Bachmann's Spectrum line, certain LGB items, and models offered by Accucraft, Hartford Products, and Trail Creek Models, among others. This will keep everything looking just right, since these models conform to the same 1:20.3 scale.

On the other hand, if modern-day railroading behemoths appeal to you, stick with the 1:32 scale models of contemporary standard gauge locomotives, rolling stock, and accessories offered by USA Trains, Märklin, Row & Co., and several others. Regardless of whether you choose steam or diesel, old-time or modern day, these 1:32 scale products will look fine running together.

And, finally, if you're not a nit-picker and simply like to purchase and operate whatever appeals to you, by all means do so! Just enjoy yourself and have fun! After all, that's what this hobby is all about. They're your trains, so do whatever you like!

Save for live steam operations (see that section of this book for more information), garden railroading with Large Scale trains is about as close as you can get in the hobby to experiencing all of the things—good and bad—that real-life railroads face on a day-to-day basis. Your family, friends, and neighbors won't give a hoot about scale and gauge inconsistencies. They'll simply thrill at seeing your handiwork in action. And therein lies the true pleasure!

LARGE SCALE RESOURCES

(Includes the following scales: 1:13.7, 1:16, 1:20.3, 1:22.5, 1:24, 1:29, and 1:32—all operating on 45 mm #1 gauge track)

manufacturers of Large Scale locomotives/rolling stock/accessories)

ACCUCRAFT TRAINS1785
Timothy Drive, Suite #3
San Leandro, CA 94577-2313
510-483-6900
fax: 510-483-9100
www.accucraft.com
(1:20.3 scale electric and live steam locomotives)

ARISTO-CRAFT TRAINS
Polk's Model Craft Hobbies
346 Bergen Ave.
Jersey City, NJ 07304
201-332-8100
fax: 800-310-0521
e-mail: aristo@cnct.com
www.aristocraft.com/aristo
(1:24 scale and 1:29 scale locomotives; rolling stock; track control units; and accessories)

BACHMANN INDUSTRIES, INC.
1400 East Erie Ave.
Philadelphia, PA 19124
213-533-1600
fax: 215-744-4699
e-mail: Bachtrains@aol.com
www.bachmanntrains.com
(Gn3 locomotives and rolling stock)

BERLYN LOCOMOTIVE WORKS
P.O. Box 9766
Denver, CO 80209
303-465-2287
fax: 303-465-2287
(1:20.3 scale brass-construction locomotives)

HARTLAND LOCOMOTIVE WORKS
P.O. Box 1743
3022 North State Road 39
LaPorte, IN 46350
800-362-8411
e-mail: trains@h-l-w.com
www.h-l-w.com
(1:24 scale locomotives and rolling stock)

LGB OF AMERICA
6444 Nancy Ridge Dr.
San Diego, CA 92121
800-669-0607
www.lgb.com
(1:22.5 Gn3 scale locomotives and rolling stock; track; control units. and accessories)

LIONEL LLC
50625 Richard W. Blvd.
Chesterfield, MI 48051-2493
810-940-4100
e-mail: talktous@lionel.com
www.lionel.com
(1:32 scale locomotives and rolling stock)

MÄRKLIN, INC.
16988 W. Victor Rd.
P.O. Box 510559
New Berlin, WI 53151-0559
800-825-0888
www.marklin.com
(1:32 scale, and MAXI line of Large Scale locomotives, rolling stock, track, and accessories)

**MODEL DIE CASTING, INC.
(ROUNDHOUSE)**
5070 Sigstrom Drive
Carson City, NV 89706
775-884-4388
www.mdcroundhouse.com
(Large Scale industrial switcher locomotives and Roundhouse rolling stock)

ROBERTS' LINES
P.O. Box 96
East Rochester, NY 14445-0096
fax: 315-986-8529
(custom-built metal Large Scale train kits)

ROW & CO.
2341 Fern St.
Eureka, CA 95503
707-442-1681
fax: 707-442-1681
e-mail: gaugeone@rowco.com
www.rowco.com
(museum quality 1:32 scale brass-construction locomotives and rolling stock models)

ST. CHARLES STATION
Rt. 1,Box 225B
Guthrie, MN 56461-9751
218-224-2598
fax: 218-224-2950
(1:32 scale custom-made brass diesel locomotives)

TRAIL CREEK MODELS
18746 McFarland Ave.
Saratoga, CA 95070
408-871-0318
www.steamup.com/trailcreek
(1:20.3 track and battery-powered brass-construction industrial-type diesel locomotives, and wood-and-metal scale model rolling stock)

USA TRAINS
P.O. Box 100
Malden, MA 02148
781-322-6084
www.usatrains.com
(1:29 scale locomotives; various Large Scale rolling stock items; LGB-compatible track components)

ABOVE ALL RAILWAYS
7861 Alabama Ave., #5
Canoga Park, CA 91304
818-348-3684
fax: 818-348-6426
www.aboveallrailways.com
(overhead track systems for Large
Scale trains)

APPALACHIAN GARDENS
P.O. Box 82
Waynesboro, PA 17268
717-762-4312
fax: 717-762-7532
(scale-size plants for garden
railroads)

AZTEC MFG. COMPANY
2701 Conestoga Dr., #113
Carson City, NV 89706
775-883-3327
fax: 775-883-3357
e-mail: aztecmfg@usa.net
www.aztectrains.com
(track cleaning cars in all scales)

BARRY'S BIG TRAINS
P.O. Box 93934
Las Vegas, NV 89139-3934
702-260-9111
fax: 702-260-9111
(drive units for repowering
Bachmann 4-6-0 locomotives)

THE BATTERY BACKSHOP
18030 SW Lower Boones Ferry
Road, #2
Tigard, OR 97224
503-624-7491
e-mail: backshop@pacifier.com
(battery powered radio control
units)

BIG TRAIN BACKSHOP
P.O. Box 991
San Luis Obispo, CA 93406
805-541-0546
fax: 805-541-0546
(cast plastic structures for 1:20
and 1:24 scale trains)

BRIDGEMASTERS
1077 Promenade Ave.
Placentia, CA 92870
714-985-9007
fax: 714-985-1976
www.bridge-masters.com
(bridges, trestles, and other
accessories for Large Scale trains)

BRIDGEWERKS
27068 La Paz Rd.
Laguna Hills, CA 92656
949-831-9351
fax: 949-362-9751
www.bridgewerks.com
(electrical control systems for
Large Scale railroads)

**CALIFORNIA & OGREGON
COAST RY (C&OC)/
LLAGAS CREEK**
P.O. Box 57
Rogue River, OR 97537
541-582-4104
fax: 800-866-8635
dmanley@cdsnet.net
(1:20.3 scale switchstand kits;
Llagas Creek track components)

CARGO-TO-GO
P.O. Box 100
So. Weymouth, MA 02190
fax: 781-331-9350
e-mail: barobr@mediaone.net
www.cargo-to-go.com
(cargo loads for Large Scale
trains)

CLASSIC CASE COMPANY
P.O. Box 395
Rolling Prairie, IN 46371
800-897-3374
e-mail: Classic@ccase.com
www.ccase.com
(display cases for Large Scale
models)

DALLEE ELECTRONICS, INC.
246 W. Main St.
Leola, PA 17540
717-661-7041
www.dallee.com
(electronic components for Large
Scale trains)

DEL-AIRE PRODUCTS
321 N. 40th St.
Allentown, PA 18104
610-391-0412
(air-powered turnout control
systems)

**DOUGLAS BROOKS
CREATIVE MODELS**
307 MacKay Ave.
Ventura, CA 93004
http://swiftsite.com/
dbcreativemodels
(model palm trees—all scales)

EAGLEWINGS IRON CRAFT
1522 E. Victory, Suite 1
Phoenix, AZ 85040
(overhead train systems for
Large Scale trains)

EAST CARY CAR CO.
3828 St. Joseph Ct.
Lake Station, IN 46405
(loads, wheelsets, and accessories
for Large Scale rolling stock)

ELDORADO RAILWAYS
28 Encantado Loop
Santa Fe, NM 87505
817-548-5656
(assembled trestle bents and
bridges for Large Scale railroads)

**FALL CREEK RAILROAD
STRUCTURES**
P.O. Box 191636
Sacramento, CA 95819
916-383-6001
e-mail: fcwrr@aol.com
(Large Scale engine display and
test stand; 1:20.3 turntable)

FALL RIVER PRODUCTIONS
4916 Duffer Pl.
Albuquerque, NM 87114
505-792-9279
e-mail: jdclark1@uswest.net
(custom laser-cutting services)

G ACTION MODELS
11920 SW 35 Terrace
Miami, FL 33175
305-221-4872
www.anglefire.com/biz/gaction
*(custom-built operating lift
bridge; passenger cars; other
rolling stock)*

GARDEN TEXTURE
P.O. Box 690444
Charlotte, NC 28227
704-847-7169
fax: 704-814-6993
http://home.earthlink.net/
~gardentextur
*(plans and kits for custom-built
Large Scale buildings and bridges)*

GARY RAYMOND
P.O. Box 1722-G
Thousand Oaks, CA 91358
805-492-5858
*(metal wheelsets for Large Scale
rolling stock in various scales)*

GLENN SNYDER
DISPLAY SYSTEMS
260 Oak Street
Buffalo, NY 14203
716-852-4676/716-648-5817
fax: 716-852-4677
e-mail: glenn@gsds.com
www.gsds.com
*(wall-mounted train display
shelves)*

G.P. RAMSDEN
1602 South 4th Street
Wilmington, NC 28401
910-762-2916
*(coal, log, and oil loads for
Bachmann's Shay and Climax
locomotives)*

HARTFORD PRODUCTS, INC.
18 Ranch Road
Cedar Crest, NM 87008
505-286-2200
fax: 505-286-2141
e-mail: HartfordPr@aol.com
www.hartfordpr.com
*(custom 1:20.3 scale, #1 gauge
rolling stock kits and parts)*

HILLCRAFT MODEL BUILDERS
4195 Chino Hills Parkway, #225
Chino Hills, CA 91709
909-393-0645
www.hillcraftgmodels.com
*(handcrafted Large Scale wood
structures)*

HILLMAN'S RAILCLAMPS
P.O. Box 1253
Lodi, CA 95241
209-389-1868
fax: 209-369-1868
e-mail: hillman-rc@softcom.net
www.hillmansrailclamps.com
*(rail clamping devices for Large
Scale track)*

HOBBY INNOVATIONS
1789 Campbell Rd.
Mountain City, TN 37683
423-727-8000
*(Vinylbed roadbed for indoor/
outdoor use)*

INNOVATIVE TRAIN
TECHNOLOGY
P.O. Box 5042
West Hills, CA 91308
818-992-6124
www.ittcsoundeffects.com
*(digital sound modules for
enhancement of Large Scale
scenes)*

ISABEL CENTRAL ENTERPRISES
P.O. Box 771407
Wichita, KS 67277-1407
*(handmade 1:25 scale wood
structures; roadbed)*

ISTRA METALCRAFT
6089 Lee Ann Lane
Naples, FL 34109
941-597-6445
*(rail bending device for Large
Scale track rails; other accessories)*

JUST PLAIN FOLK
111 West Broad Street
Palmyra, NJ 08065
856-786-0080
fax: 856-786-1481
e-mail: trackntrains@erols.com
www.trackntrains.com
(figures for Large Scale railroads)

KADEE QUALITY
PRODUCTS CO.
673 Avenue C
White City, OR 97503
541-826-3883
fax: 541-826-4013
www.kadee.com
*(couplers for Large Scale locomo-
tives and rolling stock)*

KEITHCO, INC.
P.O. Box 1806
Lake Oswego, OR 97035
503-635-7604
fax: 503-699-0434
www.locolinc.com
*(sound systems for Large Scale
locomotives)*

LARGE SCALE SOUND WORKS
P.O. Box 153
Kingston, NJ 08528-0153
609-924-5089
*(sound system plans and kits for
Large Scale trains)*

LITTLE RAILWAYS
1621 Cherry St.
Williamsport, PA 17701
*(1:20 scale narrow gauge rolling
stock)*

LOCO-BOOSE HOBBIES
P.O. Box 6905
Huntsville, AL 35824
256-828-7500
e-mail: Lbh@bellsouth.net
www.locoboose.com
*(suspended railway systems for
home or business)*

LONE STAR BRIDGE
& ABUTMENT
1218 A-8 Colorado Lane
Arlington, TX 76015
817-548-5656
(custom designed wood bridges)

LOY'S TOYS
P.O. Box 88
Wesley, AR 72773
501-456-2888
e-mail:
LoysToys@compuserve.com
www.loystoys.com
*(installation of Digitrax Digital
Command Control components)*

MEG'S DIRTY TOYS
4 Chickadee Lane
Laguna Beach, CA 92656
(operating western lanterns for Large Scale use)

MICRO ENGINEERING COMPANY, INC.
1120 Eagle Road
Fenton, MO 63026
(G gauge turnout kits)

MICRO FASTENERS
110 Hillcrest Road
Flemington, NJ 08822
800-892-6917
e-mail: microf@blast.net
http://microfasteners.com
(scale screws and other fastening devices for Large Scale equipment)

MODEL RECTIFIER CORPORATION (MRC)
80 Newfield Ave.
Edison, NJ 08837
732-225-6360
www.modelrec.com
(Power packs for Large Scale)

NORTHEAST NARROW GAUGE
P.O. Box 191
Wiscasset, ME 04578
207-882-7154
fax: 207-882-9884
www.nemodel.com
(wood and metal bridge kits)

NORTHWEST SHORT LINE
Box 423
Seattle, WA 98111-0423
206-932-1087
fax: 206-935-7106
e-mail: info@nwsl.com
www.nwsl.com
(wheelsets and other items for Large Scale locomotives and rolling stock)

NORTHWEST REMOTE CONTROL SYSTEMS
8026 NE 124th Street
Kirkland, WA 98034
e-mail: trainsnwrcs@halcyon.com
(remote control systems and parts)

OLD PULLMAN MODEL RAILROADS, INC.
P.O. Box 690128
Vero Beach, FL 32969-0128
(Large Scale Standards Gauge—for checking track gauge/wheel spacing)

OLDE MOUNTAIN MINIATURES
366 Starksville Rd.
Fort Plain, NY 13339
(custom built structures, bridges, and trestles)

OVERHEAD RAILWAYS
25672 -A Taladro Circle
Mission Viejo, CA 92691
800-297-6410
www.overheadrailways.com
(track cleaning car and on-board camera mount for #1 gauge track)

OZARK MINIATURES
P.O. Box 107
DeSoto, MO 63020
fax: 636-586-2480
(white metal castings for Large Scale detailing)

PACIFIC COAST GARDEN RAILWAY SUPPLY
12081 Pradera Rd.
Camarillo, CA 93012
805-491-2025
(structures for Large Scale layouts)

THE PARKER CO.
P.O. Box 1546
Camarillo, CA 93011
fax: 805-987-6432
e-mail: coparker@msn.com
www.coparker.com
(wide-radius turnouts compatible with most Large Scale track)

PARKER'S NURSERY
17 N. Fretz
Edmond, OK 73003
877-839-3367
www.parkersrailroad.com
(Redwood Western Building Kits for Gn3 scale)

PHOENIX SOUND SYSTEMS
3502 West Liberty Road
Ann Arbor, MI 48103-9013
800-651-2444
fax: 734-662-0809
www.phoenixsound.com
(sound systems for Large Scale steam and diesel locomotives, and for railcars)

PINE VALLEY SCENIC RAILWAY PRODUCTIONS
336 Wendell Terrace
Syracuse, NY 13203
315-479-9515
e-mail: ThomRe1App@aol.com
(custom-crafted 1:24 scale Large Scale structures)

PML, INC. PRODUCTS
201 West Beach Ave.
Inglewood, CA 90302
310-671-4345
fax: 310-671-0858
(track connecting devices and switching magnets)

PRECISION PRODUCTS
763 Cayuga St., Unit #2
Lewistown, NY 14092
716-754-2997
www.appliedimaginationinc.com
(various structure-building materials)

RAILBED SYSTEMS
1147 W. Lowell Ave.
Havelhill, MA 01832
978-372-6503
fax: 978-372-6503
www.railbed.com
(#1 gauge track support bed)

RAILDREAMS, INC.
P.O. Box 125
Lake Linden, MI 49945
906-296-0462
fax: 906-296-0862
e-mail: raildrms@up.net
www.raildreams.com
(custom designed and constructed garden railways)

RALPH WILLIAMS LANDSCAPE DESIGN
P.O. Box K
Harvard, MA 01451
978-456-8455
fax: 978-456-8455
(lighting systems for garden railways; on-track speed measuring device for Large Scale)

R&G RAILROAD CO.
15314 Black Shadow Drive
Moreno Valley, CA 92551
909-242-4258
fax: 909-247-8395
www.randgrailroad.com
(overhead/around-the-wall track mounting system for Large Scale trains)

R&S ENTERPRISES
P.O. Box 643
Jonestown, PA 17038
717-865-3444
www.rrtrack.com/rrtrack
*(sectional track layout software—
all scales)*

RITE-O-WAY
Rail Plaque
1022 Wesley
Oak Park, IL 60304
708-386-4350
(roadbed for LGB track)

**RYAN EQUIPMENT
COMPANY, INC.**
749 Creel Drive
Wood Dale, IL 60191
630-595-5711
fax: 630-595-5794
*(D&RGW 1:24 scale freight
car trucks)*

SAN-VAL TRAINS
7444 Valjean Ave.
Van Nuys, CA 91406
800-423-3281
*(Large Scale wheels, track locking
devices, track cleaners, and
smoke fluid)*

**SANTA CLARITA
RAILROAD CO.**
15151 Lotusgarden Drive
Canyon Country, CA 91351
fax: 661-252-3461
e-mail: gregtomey@marfred.com
*(locomotive cradles and track
leveling devices)*

SHILOH SIGNALS
145 East Blvd.
Gloversville, NY 12078
518-773-3078
*(trackside signals for Large
Scale trains)*

**SHORTLINE CAR AND
FOUNDRY**
14918 Lake Forest
Dallas, TX 75240
972-233-6108
fax: 972-233-3172
www.largescale.com/shortline/
  index.htm
*(metal detail castings for Large
Scale trains)*

SIERRA VALLEY ENTERPRISES
2755 Saratoga Ave.
Merced, CA 95340
*(custom built 1:20.3 scale
rolling stock)*

SLM
P.O. Box 28047
Baltimore, MD 21239
http://slm_models.tripod.com
(Large Scale model figures)

SODDERS ENTERPRISES
609 Edgelawn St.
Parkersburg, WV 26101
http://home.wirefire.com/tes
*(scale corrugated metal roofing,
siding, fencing materials)*

SOUNDTRAXX
463 Turner Drive, Suite 104A
Durango, CO 81301
970-259-0690
fax: 970-259-0691
*(digital sound systems for Large
Scale steam locomotives)*

SPLIT JAW RAIL CLAMPS
12705 SE Schiller
Portland, OR 97236
e-mail: Splitjaw@railclamp.com
www.railclamp.com
*(rail clamping devices for Large
Scale track)*

STAINLESS UNLIMITED
P.O. Box 224
Augusta, MO 63332
314-228-4767/314-742-5880
www.stainlessunlimited.com
(stainless steel bridges)

STICKS & STONES
P.O. Box 211
Elbridge, NY 13060
315-689-3402
*(silicon rubber molds for Large
Scale structures)*

STONEWORKS
16935 Main St.
P.O. Box 186
Galesville, WI 54630
608-582-2082
fax: 888-511-4258
www.RRStoneworks.com
*(stone structures and parts for
Large Scale)*

SUNSET VALLEY RAILROAD
13428 209th SE
Issaquah, WA 98027
425-255-2453
fax: 425-255-2453
www.largescale.com/svrr
(track components and tools)

T-TRACKER
3735 N.E. Shaver Street
Portland, OR 97212
*(track assembly devices and other
trackside accessories)*

THE TENDER CASE
812 Aloha Street
Camarillo, CA 93010-2302
800-851-5994
(display cases for Large Scale)

TOMAR INDUSTRIES
9520 E. Napier Ave.
Benton Harbor, MI 49022
616-944-5129
fax: 616-944-5129
*(marker lights for Large Scale
rolling stock)*

VCS REALROAD
8866 Summerhill Point
Alpine, CA 91901-2779
619-445-5145
fax: 619-445-5305
e-mail: realroad@flash.net
*(various Large Scale accessories,
including automatic station stop
devices, etc.)*

VENANGO VALLEY MODELS
Box 2847
Las Vegas, NM 87701
www.kaysingstudios.pair.com
*(Large Scale cast Hydrostone
structure kits and accessories)*

WOODLAND SCENICS
P.O. Box 98
Linn Creek, MO 65052
573-346-5555
e-mail: webmaster@woodland-
scenics.com
www.woodlandscenics.com
*(variety of scenery materials for
all scales)*

retailers specializing in Large Scale products

This list of Large Scale product retailers includes dealers who support the hobby through published (in print and/or on line) advertising of their product lines, and whose advertising indicates that they stock or specialize in Large Scale products. This list should not be considered all-inclusive. There may be other retailers in your local area who are not listed here, but who do stock a variety of Large Scale products—consult your local phone directory Yellow Pages. Support of your local dealer is always encouraged.

For names and addresses of "authorized" sales or service stations, contact the product manufacturer, or check the manufacturer's web site on the Internet.

AZ **ARIZONA TRAIN DEPOT**
755 E. McKellips Rd.
Mesa, AZ
480-833-9486
e-mail: aztraindepot@
  webtv.net
www.arizonatraindepot.com

CA **ARIZONA TRAINS
& HOBBIES**
5584 E. La Palma Ave.
Anaheim, CA 92807
714-779-9893
fax: 714-779-6708
www.aztrainsca.com

THE TRAIN SHACK, INC.
1030 N. Hollywood Way
Burbank CA
818-842-3330
www.trainshack.com

**AMERICAN GARDEN
RAILWAYS**
12 Pheasant Run Court
Chico, CA
530-891-1197

VALLEY TRAIN STATION
3811-B Schaefer Ave.
Chino, CA 91710
909-902-5351
fax: 909-902-5352

JUST TRAINS
5650-H Imhoff Dr.
Concord, CA
925-685-6656
www.just-trains.com

ALLIED MODEL TRAINS
4411 Sepulveda Blvd.
Culver City, CA
310-313-9353
www.alliedmodeltrains.com

**MORGAN'S
BIG TRAINS EMPORIUM**
7390 Center Ave.
Huntington Beach,
CA 92647
714-892-3688
www.nrhsa.org

THE LOOSE CABOOSE
4225 Solano Ave.
Napa Valley, CA
888-99-TRAIN

**THE ORIGINAL
WHISTLE STOP**
2490 E. Colorado Blvd.
Pasadena, CA
626-796-7791
www.thewhistlestop.com

MODELS AND MORE
218 Petaluma Blvd. N.
Petaluma, CA
707-762-2378

LOCO BOOSE
260 Main St., #D
Redwood City, CA
650-368-1254

PACIFIC COAST HOBBIES
6667 Indiana Ave.
Riverside, CA
909-341-0180

RAILROAD HOBBIES
119 Vernon St.
Roseville (Sacramento) CA
916-782-6067

BRUCE'S TRAIN SHOP
2752 Marconi Ave.
Sacramento, CA
916-485-5288

R/C COUNTRY HOBBIES
6011 Folsom Blvd.
Sacramento, CA
916-731-5868

THE TRAIN STOP
211 West Bonita Ave.
San Dimas, CA
909-599-2602
fax: 909-599-1566
www.trainstop.com

THE TRAIN SHOP, LLC
1829 Pruneridge Ave.
Santa Clara, CA
408-296-1050
fax: 408-985-2423

**TRUCKS & TRAINS
HOBBIES & COLLECTIBLES**
4237 Montgomery Drive
Santa Rosa, CA
707-537-6586

UPLAND TRAINS
1808 W. Foothill Blvd.
Upland, CA 91786
909-985-1246

SAN-VAL
7444 Valjean Ave.
Van Nuys, CA 91406
818-786-8274
fax: 818-786-9072

GOLD COAST STATION
4532 Telephone Rd., #113
Ventura, CA
805-339-0379
fax: 805-650-8893
www.goldcoaststation.com

CO MOUNTAIN TRAINS & PLANES
9316 W. 58th Ave.
Arvada, CO
303-456-1255
e-mail: choochoo@
central.com

CABOOSE HOBBIES
500 S. Broadway
Denver, CO 80209-4002
303-777-6766
fax: 303-777-0028
www.caboosehobbies.com

MIZELL TRAINS
3051 W. 74th Ave.
Westminster, CO
303-429-4811
www.cohda.com

CT AL'S TRUCKS & TRACKS
55 S. Park St.
Willimantic, CT
860-456-2602

FL TRAINLAND
Altamonte Mall, Suite 1473
451 Altamonte Drive
Altamonte Springs,
FL 32701
407-260-8500
fax: 407-260-2380
www.trainlandalta
monte.com

WARRICK CUSTOM HOBBIES
1025 S. University Dr.
Ft. Lauderdale, FL
954-370-0708

MICRO MACRO MUNDO, INC.
2604 N.W. 72nd Ave.
Miami, FL 33122
305-594-6950
fax: 305-594-3795
www.rocousa.com

COLONIAL PHOTO & HOBBY
634 N. Mills
Orlando, FL
800-841-1585

H&R TRAINS
6901 U.S. 19 North
Pinellas Park, FL 33781
727-526-4682
e-mail: hrtrains@hrtains.com
www.hrtrains.com

CHESTER HOLLY
3812-20 S. Himes Ave.
Tampa, FL
813-831-7202

GA LEGACY STATION, LTD.
251F Hurricane Shoals Rd.
Lawrenceville, FL
770-339-7780

NATIONAL HOBBY SUPPLY
1975 South Cobb Drive
Marietta, GA 30060
770-333-0190

IL J&A TRAINS
665 Catalpa Lane
Bartlett, IL
630-837-5704

AMERICA'S BEST TRAIN & HOBBY
136 E. Army Trail Rd.
Glendale Heights, IL
630-539-8551

THE RUSTY RAILS
16 W. 280 Hillside Lane
Hinsdale, IL 60521
630-325-5419
fax: 630-325-5419
e-mail: grrbob@aol.com

L&B MODEL TRASINS
10330 South 73 Ave.
Palos Hills, IL
708-599-6250

ST. AUBIN STATION
11100 Rte. 176
Woodstock, IL 60098
815-334-9100
fax: 815-334-0000
www.lgbpola.com

CHICAGOLAND GARDEN R.R. SUPPLY INC.
6759 W. 111 St.
Worth, IL 60482
708-923-6372
fax: 708-923-6375
e-mail: cgrrs@cgrrs.com
www.cgrrs.com

IN WHITING HOBBIES
1206 119th St.
Whiting, IN
219-659-1370

WATTS' TRAIN SHOP
9180 Hunt Club Rd.
Zionsville, IN 46077
800-542-7652
fax: 317-873-6522
www.wattstrainshop.com

IA JULIA'S HOBBIES
202 8th St., SW
Altoona, IA
515-967-4500
fax: 515-967-1900

KS HOBBYTOWN USA
2108 W. 27th St., Suite H
Lawrence, KS
785-865-0883
fax: 785-865-2553
e-mail: htusa@idir.net

ENGINE HOUSE HOBBIES
2718 Boulevard Plx
Wichita, KS
800-586-4443

MA THE FLYING YANKEE HOBBY SHOP
1416 Centre St.
Boston, MA
617-323-9702

TRAINS ON TRACKS
21 Summer Street
Chelmsford, MA 01824
978-256-3465
www.trainsontracks.com

TRAINS & TREES
Weston Nurseries
Rte. 135
Hopkinton, MA
(exit 21A off Rte. 495)
508-497-2550

CHARLES RO SUPPLY, CO.
662 Cross St.
P.O. Box 100
Malden, MA 02148
781-321-0090
fax: 781-321-6459
www.charlesro.com

MD STAR HOBBY
1244 Ritchie Hwy., Suite 16
Arnold, MD 21012
410-544-7547
fax: 410-315-9541
e-mail:
hobby@starhobby.com
www.starhobby.com

BURRETT HOBBIES
9920 Rhode Island Ave.
College Park, MD
301-982-5032

**MI JUNCTION VALLEY
RR HOBBY SHOP**
7065 Dixie Highway
Bridgeport, MI
517-777-3480

J&W MODEL TRAINS, INC.
6450 E. Becht Rd.
Coloma, MI 49038
800-443-0440
www.jwmodeltrains.com

JACKIE'S TRAINS
7710 S. Dixie Hwy.
Erie, MI
313-848-2068

G SCALE TRAINS
41411 Gloca Mora
Harrison Township,
MI 48045-1448
fax: 810-465-2902

TRAIN CENTER HOBBIES
32722 Woodward Ave.
Royal Oak, MI
248-549-6500

NC TOM'S TRAIN STATION
1239 Buck Jones Rd.
Cary, NC
919-388-7246

**LITTLE CHOO CHOO
SHOP, INC.**
500 S. Salisbury Ave.
Spencer, NC
704-637-8717
e-mail: steve@
littlechoochooshop.com

NE HOUSE OF TRAINS
8106 Maple
Omaha, NE 68134
402-934-7245

NJ TONY'S TRAIN TOWN
575 Pompton Ave.
Cedar Grove, NJ
973-857-2337

**GENE'S GRAND
CENTRAL STATION**
228 Belleville Tpke.
Kearny, NJ
800-955-3992

**STANDARD
HOBBY SUPPLY**
P.O. Box 801
Mahwah, NJ 07430
1-800-223-1355 (orders)
fax: 1-201-512-0882
www.standardhobby.com

TRACK N TRAINS, INC.
111 W. Broad St.
Palmyra, NJ
609-786-0080

**SECLUDED ACRES
RAILWAY**
1024 Rt. 47 S. (Delsea Dr.)
Rio Grande, NJ
609-886-8574

SPARTA JUNCTION
180 Demarest Road
Sparta, NJ
973-579-3481
www.sparta-junction.com

TRAINS 'N THINGS
936 E. Weymouth Rd.
Vineland, NJ
856-697-8844
www.trainsnthings.com

NM TRAINS WEST, INC.
6001 San Mateo NE
Albuquerque, NM
505-881-2322
www.trainswest.com

NV J.W. RAILWAYS
3450E S. Procyon
Las Vegas, NV
702-251-5787
www.unlimited.systems.
com/JRRailways

NY RLR RAILROAD
15 Jackson St.
Batavia, NY 14020-3201
716-344-8874
www.rlrrailroad.com

**TRAINWORLD/
TRAINLAND**
751 McDonald Ave.
Brooklyn, NY 11218
718-436-7072
fax: 718-972-8514
www.trainworld.com

**RIDGE ROAD
STATION, INC.**
16131 W. Ridge Road
Buffalo/Rochester, NY
716-638-6000

TRENT'S TRAINS
69 Harney Rd.
Scarsdale, NY
914-722-2559

OH VELK'S FLOWERS & GIFTS
468 Northfield Rd.
Bedford, OH
800-952-0284

**MIAMI VALLEY
TRAIN DEPOT**
257 Wayne Ave.
Dayton, OH
937-224-0695

HARMAR STATION
220 Gilman St.
Marietta, OH
740-374-9995
www.eekman.com/
harmarstation

**DAVIS ELECTRONICS
& TRAINS**
217 Main St.
Milford, OH 45150
513-831-6425
fax: 513-831-4256

G SCALE JUNCTION
7758 Lafayette Road NW
Newark, OH 43055
800-311-9448
fax: 740-967-4453
e-mail: charlesw@wavl.com
www.gscalejunction.com

**CROUSE TRUE
VALUE TRAINS**
11788 Market Street
North Lima, OH 44452
330-549-2144
fax: 330-549-0463
e-mail: sales@
  truevaluetrains.com
www.truevaluetrains.com

OK **WOODWARD'S**
4401 W. Memorial Rd.
Oklahoma City, OK
405-751-4994
e-mail:
woodwards@aol.com

OR **TRAIN & TOY HOUSE**
3302 S. Peoria
Tulsa, OK
918-742-6378

**QUALITY FARM TOYS
& HOBBIES**
701 Main St.
Oregon City, OR
503-650-8023

WHISTLE STOP TRAINS
11724 SE Division St.
Portland, OR
888-700-4449

PA **NICHOLAS SMITH TRAINS**
2343 West Chester Pike
Broomall, PA 19008
610-353-8585
www.nstrains.com

**CRANBERRY
HOBBY DEPOT**
20327 Perry Hwy.
Cranberry Twsp., PA
724-776-3640

TOY TRAIN STATION
21 East Street Rd.
Feasterville (Philadelphia),
PA 19053-6047
215-322-5182

**LIN'S JUNCTION AT
HENNING SCALE MODELS**
128 S. Line St.
Landsdale, PA
215-412-7711

**SCRANTON
HOBBY CENTER**
517 Lackawanna Ave.
Scranton, PA 18503
570-342-2949
fax: 570-343-3775

TN **JACK'S TRAINS & HOBBYS**
2420 Susannah St.
Jonhson City, TN
423-282-9108

**CHRISTMAS PLACE TOYS
& TRAINS**
2470 Parkway
Pigeon Forge, TN
800-445-3396
www.1sttrainstop.com

TX **TRAINSOURCE: TEXAS**
3264 S. Loop West
Houston, TX
713-662-0809

THE TRAIN STORE
2511 University Blvd.
Houston, TX
713-521-4587
www.eTrainSale.com

MIKE'S HOBBY SHOP
212 Main St.
Humble, TX
281-446-7550

UT **ALMOSTA JUNCTION**
1161 South State
Clearfield, UT
801-776-1656

VA **TRAIN DEPOT**
7214 New Market Court
Manassas, VA
703-335-2216

DAVIS HOBBY
3594 Griffin St.
Portsmouth, VA 23707
757-397-1983
e-mail: ralph@
davishobby.com
www.davishobby.com

**GRANDDAD'S
HOBBY SHOP**
5260-A Port Royal Rd.
Springfield, VA
703-426-0700

CIRCUS TRAIN LTD.
240 McLaws Circle
Williamsburg, VA
757-220-9321

WA **PACIFIC RIM HOBBY**
124A W. 1st St.
Port Angeles, WA
360-457-0794
e-mail: prhobby@
  olypen.com
www.olypen.com/prhobby

**SUNSET JUNCTION
MODEL TRAINS**
213 E. Sprague Ave.
Spokane, WA
888-838-2379

PACIFIC RAILWAY HOBBIES
5115 100th St. SW
Tacoma, WA
253-581-4453

WI **SOMMERFELD'S TRAINS
& HOBBIES**
12620 W. Hampton Ave.
Butler, WI 53007
414-783-7797
fax: 414-783-9815

HOBBY DEPOT
1524 E. Sumner St.
Hartford, WI
262-670-6242

associations and clubs for Large Scale model railroaders

**LGB MODEL
RAILROAD CLUB, INC.**
c/o Ralph Wilcox
1854 Erin Drive
Altoona, PA 16602
www.lgbmrrc.com

**MÄRKLIN ENTHUSIASTS
OF AMERICA**
c/o Tim Eckert, Sec.
P.O. Box 21753
Charlotte, NC 28221-0153

**NATIONAL MODEL
RAILROAD ASSOCIATION
(NMRA)**
4121 Cromwell Rd.
Chattanooga, TN 37421
423-892-2846
fax: 423-899-4869
www.nmra.org

**TRAIN COLLECTORS
ASSOCIATION (TCA)**
National Business Office
P.O. Box 248
Dept. 10
Strasburg, PA 17579
www.traincollectors.org

magazines, periodicals, and videos
of interest to Large Scale model railroaders

A.W.N.U.T.S. MAGAZINE
P.O. Box 8523
Red Bluff, CA 96080
800-830-2234
www.awnuts.com

BIG TRAIN OPERATOR
MAGAZINE
*(official publication of the LGB
Model Railroad Club)*
c/o Ralph Wilcox
1854 Erin Drive
Altoona, PA 16602
www.lgbmrrc.com

CLASSIC TOY TRAINS
MAGAZINE
Kalmbach Publishing Co.
21027 Crossroads Circle
P.O. Box 1612
Waukesha, WI 53187-1612
800-446-5489
www.classtrain.com

FINESCALE RAILROADER
MAGAZINE
Westlake Publishing Company
1574 Kerryglen St.
Westlake Village, CA 91361
805-494-4070
www.finescalerr.com
*(entire magazine may be viewed
on line at above web address)*

GARDEN RAILWAYS MAGAZINE
Kalmbach Publishing Co.
21027 Crossroads Circle
P.O. Box 1612
Waukesha, WI 53187-1612
800-533-6644
fax: 414-796-1615
e-mail: customerservice@
  kalmbach.com
www.gardenrailways.com

LGB TELEGRAM
*(official publication of LGB
of America)*
P.O. Box 332
Hershey, PA 17033-0332
717-566-9428
fax: 717-566-9400
e-mail:
LGB Telegram@mindspring.com

MÄRKLIN INSIDER MAGAZINE
*(Official publication of the Marklin
Club)*
Märklin Club North America
P.O. Box 510851
New Berlin, WI 53151-0851
414-784-0717
www.marklin.com

*NARROW GAUGE AND SHORT
LINE GAZETTE* MAGAZINE
4966 El Camino Real, #101
Los Altos, CA 94022
650-941-3823
fax: 650-941-3845
e-mail: gazette@worldnet.att.net
www.ngslgazette.com

STEAM IN THE GARDEN
MAGAZINE
P.O. Box 335
Newark Valley, NY 13811
607-642-8119 (Mon.-Thurs.,
before 9 p.m. EST)
fax: 303-975-6211
e-mail: rbrown5@stny.rr.com
www.steamup.com

**"BUILDING A GARDEN
RAILROAD"**
(video)
Robinsong Productions
910 Paloverde Drive
Loveland, CO 80538

DIGITAL VIDEO IMAGES, INC.
(videos—various Large Scale
topics))
P.O. Box 2584
Littleton, CO 80161-2584
303-220-8998
fax: 303-220-8933
www.sni.net/~tpspeer/

**"GARDEN RAILWAY
DREAMIN'"**
(video series)
Valhalla Video
1100 Irvine Blvd., #325G
Tuslin, CA 92780-3534
888-843-3698
fax: 714-544-3290
www.valhallavideo.com

web sites relevant to Large Scale model railroading

www.largescale.com
(Large Scale On-Line home page.
Membership required to access
some features.)

www.lgbmrrc.com
(Web site for the LGB Model
Railroad Club)

**http://largescale.
modelrailroads.com**
(Large Scale On-Line's online
magazine)

**www.scintilla.utwente.nl/
marklin**
(Marklin Mailing List home page)

www.finescalerr.com
(Finescale Railroader Magazine
on-line; includes full content of
each issue)

www.nmra.org
(National Model Railroad
Association web site)

www.trainfinder.com
(On-line directory to model train
related web sites)

www.railnet.net
(prototype information for modelers in all scales)

www.railserve.com
RailServe Home Page
(On-line directory to rail-related
content on the Internet.)

www.ehobbies.com
(model railroad discussion groups
and general interest train topics)

www.eppraisals.com
(On-line appraisal services;
includes toy/model trains.)

www.amazon.com
(Internet auction site)

www.ebay.com
(Internet auction site)

www.boxlot.com
(Internet auction site)

www.collect.com
(Internet auction site)

www.train-station.com
(Internet auction site)

A Prairie live steam locomotive, modified by its owner, Steve Galovics, and outfitted with various Roundhouse-manufactured components, leads an ore train on its early morning run. Like many live steam enthusiasts, Galovics especially enjoys the mechanical aspects of live steam railroading, and he actively participates in local, regional, and national "steamups" attended by small scale live steam operators from around the nation and the world.

Photo courtesy of Steve Galovics

SMALL SCALE LIVE STEAM
(operating on #1 gauge track)

Small Scale Live Steam" is the term generally applied to steam-powered locomotives operating, most commonly, on #1 gauge (45 mm) track—the same track most often used by modelers in the battery and/or electric powered "Large Scale" category described elsewhere in this book. It's called "Small Scale" Live Steam to distinguish it from the significantly larger-scale live steamers, which range from ride-aboard locomotives all the way up to full-size steam locomotives.

Live steam has the distinction of not only being the earliest form of powered railroad models—after all, that's also how the first self-propelled prototype locomotives operated—but of actually pre-dating the introduction of full-size steam locomotives. The inventors and engineers involved with the early development of steam locomotion actually built working models of their creations first, to test their concepts and theories.

Small scale live steam locomotives are truly marvels of engineering in miniature! They operate just like the full-size prototypes they represent, aside from the fact that most of the models' boilers are fired by butane or alcohol instead of the coal, oil, or wood burned in life-size steamers. Small scale live steamers generally come equipped with all of the necessary accouterments, including water-level sight glass, safety value, reversing lever, throttle, steam-operated whistle, and other features. Many small scale live steamers can be outfitted with on-board radio control devices that allow for hands-off running in a realistic manner. Other live steam operators prefer a more hands-on approach, following along on foot as their train navigates its route.

Live steam in any scale is not for the feint of heart. The fuel-fired locomotives operate just like the real thing, and, like their prototypes, they require considerable operator care and maintenance. Fittings need to be adjusted, tightened, and occasionally replaced; care must be given to assure that there is sufficient water in the boiler at all times; and rods and bearings need to be properly and regularly lubricated. And, after the end of an operating session, the locomotive must be drained, cleaned, lubricated, and made ready for its next run.

Live steam locomotives can also be fairly expensive, with some high-end, full-featured locomotives costing several thousand dollars, and up. Still, a number of manufacturers in England and Japan have begun producing affordable, high-quality small scale live steamers that perform very reliably, and that boast many of the features of their more costly counterparts. As with any other product you buy, it pays to do your homework first, and to shop around a bit.

The British model railroading community deserves special mention in this category because England, in particular, is the scene of a hotbed of activity in small scale live steam operations. In fact, our friends across the pond display an affinity for just about everything related to railroading and model railroading, and this is amply reflected in the level of manufacturing done there, and in the number of hobby-related periodicals published in that nation. For that reason, several of the manufacturers, publications, and organizations listed in this section have overseas contacts and addresses.

The fraternity of live steam operators may be relatively small, even when measured on a worldwide basis, but these hearty souls enjoy exceptionally strong bonds of friendship formed out of a common love of railroading and seeing just how it is that mechanical objects operate. Less concerned with scenic details, structure building, and landscaping than their Large Scale garden railroading brethren, live steam fanatics tend to focus more on the fun of actually running their equipment. They often assemble at events knows as "steamups" to run their trains, compare equipment, evaluate new products, swap stories and information, and just enjoy the camaraderie of their fellow live steam enthusiasts. The largest of these events is held in Diamondhead, Mississippi, in late January of each year.

Regardless of where or how the hobby is being pursued, nothing in model railroading can quite compare to the thrill of seeing a live steam locomotive chuffing along under its own power, and behaving just the way its big sisters did when they plied the rails more than half a century ago.

SMALL SCALE LIVE STEAM RESOURCES

manufacturers/importers/distributors
(small scale live steam locomotives and rolling stock)

ACCUCRAFT TRAINS
1785 Timothy Dr., #3
San Leandro, CA 94577
510-483-6900
fax: 510-483-9100
www.accucraft.com
(Accucraft live steam locomotives)

ARGYLE LOCOMOTIVE WORKS
c/o Sulphur Springs Steam Models
Ltd.
P.O. Box 6165, Dept. RB
Chesterfield, MO 63006
314-527-8326
fax: 314-527-8326
e-mail: sssmodels@aol.com
(Argyle live steam locomotives)

ASTER HOBBY
c/o Hyde-Out Mountain Live Steam
89060 New Rumley Rd.
Jewett, OH 43986
740-946-6611
www.steamup.com/aster
*(Aster live steam locomotives
based on American British,
German, and Japanese prototypes)*

BRANDBRIGHT LTD.
c/o P.O. Box 2560
Dale City, VA 22193
703-491-7989
fax: 703-492-8409
e-mail: diesel@erols.com
*(Brandbright live steam
locomotives)*

CATATONK LOG & LUMBER
P.O. Box 335
Newark Valley, NY 13811
607-642-8119
e-mail: docstream@spectra.net
*(live steam Shay and Heisler
locomotives—U.S. distributor)*

CHERRY SCALE MODELS
The Stables: 25 Church
St. Langham, Oakham
Rutland, LE15 7JE England
01572-757392
fax: 01572-724053
(#1 gauge live steam locomotives)

GARDEN RAILWAY SPECIALISTS
Station Studio, Princess Risborough
Bucks, HP17 9DT England
01844-345158
fax: 01844-274352
*(customized models based on
European-prototype locomotives)*

GEOFFBUILT
Box 277
Salisbury
New Brunswick,EOA 3EO, Canada
506-372-4364
*(custom-built #1 gauge live steam
locomotives)*

LEGEND STEAM LOCOMOTIVES
18746 McFarland Ave.
Saratoga, CA 95130
408-871-0318
www.steamup.com/legend
e-mail: info@steamup.com
*(Legend live steam locomotives
based on American prototypes)*

**LONGHEDGE LOCOMOTIVE
WORKS**
Stansted
Essex, CM24 8ST England
01279-815571
shop: 0374 463974 (weekdays,
business hours)
e-mail:
longhedge@compuserve.com
*(Fine Scale live steam locomotives
for #1 gauge)*

**MAMOD/WILESCO
STEAM LOCOMOTIVES**
c/o Diamond Enterprises & Book
Publishers
Div. Yesteryear Toys & Books, Inc.
P.O. Box 537
Alexandria Bay, NY 13607
800-481-1353 (Mon.-Fri., 8-5 EST)
fax: 800-305-5138
e-mail: info@yesteryeartoys.com
www.mamod.com
*(Mamod and Wilesco live steam
locomotives and steam engines)*

PEARSE LOCOMOTIVES
Woodview, Brockhurst, Church
Stretton
Shropshire, SY6 7QY England
01694-723806
fax: 01694-723806
(Pearse live steam locomotives)

**ROUNDHOUSE ENGINEERING
CO., LTD.**
Unit 6, Churchill Business Park
Churchill Road, Wheatley
Doncaster, DN12TF England
011-44-1302-328035
fax: 011-44-1302-761312
e-mail:
sales@roundhouse-eng.com
www.roundhouse-eng.com
(Roundhouse live steam locomotives)

SHAWE STEAM SERVICES, LTD.
Howgate, Kimpton Road, Welwyn
Hertfordshire, AL6 9NN England
01437-814383
(small scale coal-fired locomotives)

WADA WORKS, CO., LTD.
c/o Potomac Steam Industries
P.O. Box 2560
Dale City, VA 22193
703-491-7989
fax: 703-492-8409
e-mail: diesel@erols.com
(Wada live steam locomotives)

after-market manufacturers/suppliers
of small scale live steam products

BARRETT RAILWAYS
991 6th St.
Hermosa Beach, CA 90254
310-379-4929
(#1 gauge rolling stock)

C&OC RWYS.
P.O. Box 57
Rogue River, OR 97537
1-800-866-8635
fax: 1-800-866-8635
(narrow gauge track)

**FINESCALE LOCOMOTIVE
COMPANY**
c/o IE&W Railway Supply
38200 Charles Town Pike
Purcellville, VA 20132-2927
540-882-3886
fax: 540-882-9670
(#1 gauge rolling stock)

GARY RAYMOND
P.O. Box 1722-G
Thousand Oaks, CA 91358
805-492-5858
*(Gn3 gauge and other large scale
wheelsets for rolling stock)*

HARPER MODEL RAILWAYS
3057 Lander Rd.
Pepper Pike, OH 44124
216-464-8126
*(British prototype rolling stock
kits and parts)*

HARTFORD PRODUCTS
18 Ranch Rd.
Cedar Crest, NM 87008
505-286-2200
fax: 505-586-2141
e-mail: HartfordPr@aol.com
www.abqmall.com/HartfordPr.htm
*(rolling stock—kits and ready-
to-run)*

ISTRA METALCRAFT
6089 Lee Ann Lane
Naples, FL 34109
941-597-6445
(7 a.m.-3:30 p.m., EST)
fax: 941-597-6230
*(locomotive carriers and various
accessories)*

MICRO FASTENERS
110 Hillcrest Rd.
Flemington, NJ 08822
800-892-6917
fax: 908-788-2607
e-mail: info@microfasteners.com
www.microfasteners.com
*(various fasteners for live steam
products)*

NORTHWEST SHORT LINE
P.O. Box 423
Seattle, WA 98111-0423
206-932-1087
fax: 206-935-7106
e-mail: info@nwsl.com
www.nwsl.com
*(wheel sets for large scale
rolling stock)*

OZARK MINIATURES
P.O. Box 107
De Soto, MO 63020
fax: 314-586-2480
*(cast metal parts for large scale
and live steam products)*

THE PARKER CO.
P.O. Box 1546
Camarillo, CA 93011
fax: 805-987-6432
e-mail: coparler@msn.com
www.coparker.com
*(wide radius large scale track
turnouts)*

REMOTE CONTROL SYSTEMS
c/o Sulphur Springs Steam
Models Ltd.
P.O. Box 6165, Dept. RB
Chesterfield, MO 63006
314-527-8326
fax: 314-527-8326
e-mail: rcs@alphalink.com.au
www.alphalink.com.au/~rcs/
*(radio control systems for live
steam)*

SIERRA VALLEY ENTERPRISES
2755 Saratoga Ave.
Merced, CA 95340
*(1:20.3 and 7/8-inch scale rolling
stock and wheel sets)*

STICKS & STONES
P.O. Box 211
Elbridge, NY 13060
315-689-3402
(silicon rubber structure molds)

SUNSET VALLEY RAILROAD
13428 209th SE
Issaquah, WA 98027
425-255-2453
fax: 425-255-2453
www.largescale.com/svrr
(track components and tools)

TRACKSIDE DETAILS
1331 Avalon St.
San Luis Obispo, CA 93405
*(Gn3 gauge and 1/2-inch
scale parts)*

**7/8N2 RAILWAY
EQUIPMENT CO.**
54 Claybrook Rd.
Rocky Mount, VA 24151
e-mail: seven8n2@aol.com
*(7/8-inch scale freight trucks
and parts)*

retailers specializing in small scale live steam products

This list includes hobby dealers who support the live steam hobby through regular advertising in the hobby press, in club periodicals, or on-line via Internet web sites. The listings do not necessarily include all dealers who may be listed as "authorized dealers" or "authorized service facilities" by the major live steam locomotive manufacturers. Such information is best obtained directly from the manufacturer, who may be contacted at the addresses listed above. Many manufacturers also list their authorized dealers and service centers on their Internet web sites.

Due to its relatively small and somewhat specialized following, you'll not find many local hobby shops that stock or service live steam railroad items. If you are interested in learning more about live steam products and operations, your best bet would be to visit the Internet web site, *www.steamup.com* to obtain the most up-to-date information on developments in the hobby. Be advised that live steam motive power is generally not mass-produced. Items are often manufactured only after sufficient orders have been received to warrant the production run. For that reason, a wait of several months to several years to receive a new locomotive is neither uncommon or nor unrealistic.

Be sure to consult the Large Scale listings for additional dealers supplying products that are compatible with small scale live steam products and accessories.

CA **S.T.E.A.M.**
P.O. Box 123
Windsor, CA 95492
707-838-8135
fax: 707-838-8135
e-mail: steam4me@metro.net
www.steam4me.com
(Aster locomotive dealer)

FL **RIO PECOS GARDEN RAILROAD CO.**
27136 Edenbridge Court
Bonita Springs, FL 34135
941-495-0491
fax: 941-495-7264
e-mail:
riopecosatsteamteamcom@
    email.msn.com
www.steamup.com/riopecos
www.steamup.com/os
(Aster, Legend, Roundhouse locomotive dealer)

IL **RUSTY RAILS GARDEN RR SUPPLY CO.**
16 W. 280 Hillside Ln.
Hinsdale, IL 60521
630-325-5419
(Mon.-Fri., 5:30-9:00 p.m.;
    Sat., 10 a.m.-5:30 p.m.;
Sun., noon-5 p.m.)
fax: 630-325-5419
e-mail: grrbob@aol.com
(Accucraft locomotive dealer; other large scale items)

LA **BAYOU LTD. GARDEN RAILWAYS**
P.O. Box 4394
107 Easy Street
Houma, LA 70360
504-857-9464
fax: 504-857-9464
e-mail: bayoultd@earthlink.net
www.bayoultdgr.com
(Roundhouse locomotive dealer)

MO **SULPHUR SPRINGS**
Steam Models Ltd.
P.O. Box 6165
Chesterfield, MO
63006-6165
314-527-8326
fax: 314-527-8326
e-mail: sssmodels@aol.com
(Aster, Legend locomotive dealer)

NJ **NORTH JERSEY**
Gauge One Co.
8 Spring Valley Rd.
Park Ridge, NJ 07656
201-391-1493
(Aster locomotive dealer)

OH **CROSS CREEK**
Engineering
P.O. Box 191
Spencer, OH 44275
800-664-3226
fax: 330-667-2047
e-mail: crosscreektrains
@juno.com
(Aster, Accucraft, Wada locomotive dealer; other live steam products)

OR **C&OC RY**
P.O. Box 57
Rogue River, OR 97537
800-866-8635
or 541-582-4104
fax: 800-866-8635
e-mail: dmanley@cdsnet.net
(various large scale acces sories and parts)

TX **DOUBLEHEADER PRODUCTIONS**
3725 Pageant Place
Dallas, TX 75244
972-247-1208
e-mail: dblhdr@iadfw.net
www.gaugeone.com
(various live steam/large scale industrial locomotives and rolling stock)

VA **POTOMAC STEAM
INDUSTRIES**
5595 Saint Charles Drive
Dale City, VA 22193-3503
703-680-1955
fax: 703-590-9399
e-mail: diesel@erols.com
(Legend locomotive dealer)

WI **WEST LAWN
LOCOMOTIVE WORKS**
P.O. Box 570
Madison, WI 53701
608-231-2521
e-mail: mail@locoworks.com
www.locoworks.com
(Aster locomotive dealer)

magazines, periodicals, and videos

**FINESCALE RAILROADER
MAGAZINE**
1574 Kerryglen St.
Westlake Village, CA 91361
805-379-0904
www.finescalerr.com
*(complete magazine is available
on-line)*
*(Focuses on finescale modeling in all
scales, with some emphasis on large
scale trains and garden railroading,
including some coverage of small
scale live steam.)*

GARDEN RAIL
c/o Catherine Ambler
P.O. Box 9, Skipton
North Yorks, BD23 4UX England
01729-830552
fax: 01729-830552

GARDEN RAILWAYS MAGAZINE
P.O. Box 1612
21027 Crossroads Circle
Waukesha, WI 53187-1612
www.gardenrailways.com
*(Largest circulation U.S. magazine
devoted exclusively to garden railroading, including regular coverage
of small scale live steam.)*

G1MRA JOURNAL
C/O Ms. L. Prior
121 Moorside Rd.
Kinson, Bournemouth
Dorset BH11 8DQ England
*(Quarterly journal of the Gauge One
Model Railway Assn. in England)*

LIVE STEAM MAGAZINE
Village Press, Inc.
2779 Aero Park Drive
Traverse City, MI 49686
231-946-3712
fax: 231-946-9588
www.villagepress.com/livesteam
*(Focus is on large scale live steam of
all types, including large scale live
steam and prototype steam, but
regularly includes some small scale
live steam coverage.)*

**NARROW GAUGE AND SHORT
LINE GAZETTE MAGAZINE**
4966 El Camino Real, #101
Los Altos, CA 94022
650-941-3823
fax: 650-941-3845
e-mail: gazette@worldnet.att.net
www.ngslgazette.com
*(Publishes articles of interest to nar-
row gauge enthusiasts in all scales.)*

**STEAM IN THE GARDEN
MAGAZINE**
P.O. Box 335
Newark Valley, NY 13811
607-642-8119 (Mon.-Thurs., before
9 p.m. EST)
fax: 303-975-6211
e-mail: rbrown5@stny.rr.com
www.steamup.com
*(The premier U.S. publication for the
small scale live steam enthusiast.
Focuses exclusively on small scale
live steam railroading and live steam
boats.)*

A.W. N.U.T.S. MAGAZINE
P.O. Box 8523
Red Bluff, CA 96080
800-830-2234
www.awnuts.com
*(Explores the whimsical, fun-filled
approach to garden railroading. The
magazine's name stands for "Always
Whimsical, Not Usually To Scale.")*

**"AN INTRODUCTION TO SMALL
SCALE LIVE STEAM" (VIDEO)**
Sidestreet Bannerworks
Box 460222
Denver, CO 80246
303-377-7785
fax: 303-377-7785
*(Comprehensive video introduction
to O and #1 gauge steam
locomotives)*

associations and clubs
of interest to small scale live steam hobbyists

ASSOCIATION OF 16MM NARROW GAUGE MODELLERS
E. J. Hodson
Brooklands, Stafford Road,
Penkridge
Stafford ST19 5AX England

NATIONAL MODEL RAILROAD ASSOCIATION (NMRA)
4121 Cromwell Rd.
Chattanooga, TN 37421
423-892-2846
fax: 423-899-4869
www.nmra.org

GAUGE ONE MODEL RAILWAY ASSOCIATION
C/0 Ms. L. Prior
121 Moorside Rd.
Kinson, Bournemouth
Dorset BH11 8DQ England

web sites of interest to live steam enthusiasts

www.steamup.com
(Premier site for the live steam enthusiast. Register for Live Steam Chat, post to message board, read product news and reviews, and locate dealers. The "must-visit" site for all live steam modelers and operators.)

www.diamondhead.org
(Diamondhead, Mississippi, International Small Scale Steamup site)

www.largescale.com
(Large Scale On-Line web site. Arguably the most frequented and popular site for the large scale model railroader, including fans of live steam. There's something for just about every large scale garden railway fan here.)

www.iae.nl/users/summer/16mmngm
(Chat site for 16mm scale enthusiasts)

sslivesteam-on@colegroup.com
(Subscribe to the small-scale live steam group list and participate in discussions relating to small-scale live steam operations.)

www.7eights.com
(Site for live steam and diesel power in 7/8-inch scale.)

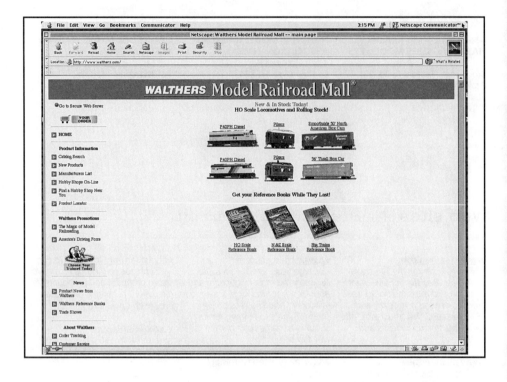

166

MODEL RAILROADING
IN CYBERSPACE

There's no denying that the Internet, and its associated World Wide Web, has dramatically impacted just about every facet of our daily lives. From shopping for groceries or booking vacation reservations to buying a new home, banking, or finding a new job—all of these things, and many more, can be done while sitting at your home computer's keyboard. So, it should come as no real surprise that the hobby of model railroading (and nearly every other hobby, for that matter) has been similarly affected by this speed-of-light electronic exchange of information, and misinformation, in recent years.

In fact, armed with a home computer and a modem connection through your phone line or TV cable service, you have fingertip access to just about everything imaginable relating to the model railroading hobby. You can shop for and purchase the materials you need; download software that will help you to design a track plan on your computer screen; research the history of your favorite prototype railroad; access a manufacturer's current releases to see if that special new locomotive is available; order an item from your favorite dealer; buy/sell/trade train items through Internet "classified listings" or on-line auctions; and even have your collectible items appraised on-line.

If you run into a problem getting your trains to operate properly, you can likely contact the manufacturer's service department via e-mail. Or, if you just want to engage in dialog with your fellow hobbyists around the world, you can participate in real-time "chat" sessions with others in your particular scale, or read messages and post responses via any number of "discussion forums" currently available to the model railroading community.

About all that you can't do on-line is actually construct your miniature rail empire! And that, of course, is probably just as well, because time spent browsing on-line is time spent away from the creative, meaningful, and rewarding hands-on aspects of this leisure pursuit. You'll need to discipline yourself to limit your Internet-related activities, leaving plenty of time to put what you learn on-line into actual practice.

Although an entire book could easily be filled with information about the Internet and its relevance to the hobby of model railroading, only the introductory basics will be covered here. The best way to find out what's "out there" is to go to one of the "key" sites listed below, and start exploring that site and the various links it leads you to. When you do come across a site of particular interest to you, be sure to "bookmark" it, or designate it as a "favorite place," on your web browser. That way, you can easily return directly to that site in the future, without having to enter its URL (web) address.

On-line Information:

If you're in search of a starting point for on-line information about a particular model railroading scale or gauge that interests you, the following web sites, listed by scale, represent some of the recommended "key" sites that provide particularly good links to other topic-related sites.

Z scale:
www.Ztrack.com
www.Z-world.com
www.ete.org
http://members.aol.com/HVMarklin/index.html

N scale:
www.nmra.org (go to Directory of World Wide Rail Sites button)
www.dwmp.com/Nternet
www.Ntrak.mv.com
www.railnet.net
www.mria.org

HO scale:
www.nmra.org (go to Directory of World Wide Rail Sites button)
www.railserve.com
www.trainweb.com
www.mria.org

S scale/gauge:
www.trainweb.org/s-trains
http://home.eznet/~cesmith
http://trainweb.com/crocon/sscale.html

O scale/gauge:
www.trainfinder.com
http://thortrains.hypermart.net
www.homestead.com/ogauge
www.napanet.net/~jlbaker

Std. Gauge:
www.jlmtrains.com

Large Scale:
www.largescale.com

Live Steam:
www.steamup.com
www.largescale.com
www.nmia.com/~vrbass/steam/steamfaq.htm
www.diamondhead.org
www.7eights.com

On-line message boards, discussion forums, and chat rooms:

There are a wide variety of specialized areas on the Internet where model railroaders can meet to share and exchange information, and even "vent some steam" regarding their personal experiences with a particular product, manufacturer, or whatever.

If you've not visited any of these areas before, be advised that some of these sites would, on occasion, likely carry a "PG" or even an "R" rating if the standards that apply to movies were to be applied to Internet dialog (which they aren't). You won't have problems with foul language and such if you visit a moderated group site, wherein a monitor more or less screens the messages before they are posted, but you do need to be a bit wary of the more open public forums, where there is no appointed moderator to keep things orderly and civil. The same advice applies to "chat rooms," where

exchanges and debate can sometimes get a bit heated, or even off-topic. If you're a parent, you will, of course, want to check regularly on sites your son or daughter frequents by himself or herself, or ones that they share with you.

With twenty million-plus members, the most visible of all the on-line "message boards" are likely those on America Online (AOL). On AOL, if you are a member, you'll find message boards devoted to just about every imaginable topic, including model railroading. In fact, the "railroad model/ railfanning" section of AOL's Hobby Central, lists some 50 individual message boards for topics ranging from Z scale to Large Scale, and everything in between. Some of these boards are even devoted to individual manufacturers, such as Lionel, American Flyer, M.T.H. Electric Trains, K-Line, Williams, and others.

On-line buy/sell/trade:

As recently as a half-dozen or so years ago, a model railroader wanting to sell a few items from a personal collection or inventory— hopefully in order to replace them with some new trains—had relatively few choices available for promoting the sale. Short of placing things in the hands of an auctioneer, the usual choices included: local or regional train shows; classified ads in a hobby-related or club publication, or in the local newspaper; or selling/trading the item or items to a dealer (generally for about half of what the dealer will expect to re-sell the item for).

Of those options, perhaps the best, in most cases, would be classified ads in hobby-related or club publications, and/or selling at a train show. Problem is, the train show route involves a whole lot of time, expense, and physical effort, and the printed classifieds route usually incurs a delay of anywhere from a couple of weeks to a couple of months before the ad finally appears.

You can avoid the wait, and some of the aggravation, by selling your items through on-line classifieds on the Internet—some of which are available free of charge. The various buy/sell/trade boards aren't listed in this book because they frequently change, but they are out there, and they do have the potential of reaching far greater numbers of potential buyers than would a local newspaper ad, or exposure at a couple of train shows. If you frequent the various message boards, you'll soon learn where others sharing your particular interest go to sell or buy items. And, you find links on some model railroading sites that will lead you to free classifieds areas.

Be aware that not all classified listings on the Internet are free. Some sites will request a "voluntary contribution," which is just a nice way of saying that they will charge you a fee, and perhaps even send you a billing statement based on the number of ads you have placed with them. If free classified listings are what you are looking for, be sure to check the site owner's policy before you list something for sale. Buyers have it a bit easier, since there is generally no charge for buying an item (it would be nearly impossible to track who the buyer was in any event).

Your conduct in selling through on-line classifieds should pretty much adhere to the same general principles applied to on-line auctions. Be sure to identify the item as completely as possible (most classifieds sites do not display photos) , and describe its condition fully and accurately. If you believe the item falls somewhere in between two accepted grading standards, go with the lower/lesser condition in your ad. State the price that you are asking for the item, and specify whether that price includes shipping and insurance charges. Also state the form(s) of payment that you will accept, and provide an e-mail address or phone number so a prospective buyer can get in touch with you.

After a deal is concluded, either on-line via e-mail or by telephone, the buyer is expected to submit a check or money order for the full cost of the merchandise, including any shipping and insurance charges. When the check clears (a reasonable amount of time should be specified for personal checks), the seller should pack the item securely and ship promptly. It is a very good idea to send the buyer an e-mail on the actual date of shipment, advising him/her that the item has been sent, and providing the tracking number (if shipped via UPS or FedEx). As a common courtesy, the buyer should, in turn, send an e-mail to the seller when the item is received, specifying that everything arrived in proper order.

Although there are no specific "rules" governing the return of items that are received in unsatisfactory condition, or are otherwise perceived to be not-as-advertised in the buyer's estimation, it's really a good idea to establish a return policy before the sale is made. Regardless of what policy or procedure is followed, both buyer and seller need to agree, in advance, that this will be agreeable.

Selling your excess toy or model trains on the Internet can be an easy, fast, and efficient way to dispose of no-longer-needed items, and it's a great way to raise money for the new things you want to purchase. The Internet also provides a great (and huge) marketplace for prospective buyers of trains and accessories. Just be sure to exercise care and common sense in conducting your transactions, especially if you're dealing with someone you don't know. "Buyer beware" has always been good advice—the Internet has elevated it to the status of an absolutely essential guideline.

On-line auctions:

If there's any single hobby-related activity on the Internet that's fraught with confusion, misinformation, misunderstanding, and sometimes even downright deception, it's the area of on-line auctions. Auctions of collectibles on the Internet have multiplied to such an extent in recent years that it's nearly impossible to keep track of all of them. And that, of course is not necessarily good from a either a seller's or a buyer's perspective. Obviously, as the slices of the on-line auction pie become smaller and smaller, this reduces a seller's chances of having any given item exposed to the largest possible audience. Potential buyers, on the other hand, are faced with such a myriad of auction-site choices that they are apt to miss out on that special item of interest unless they're able to spend a whole lot of time on-line every day.

The grandfather of all Internet auction sites was, and still is, eBay. As most folks know by now, eBay was the first major player in the on-line auction arena, and it captured—and continues to hold—the lion's share of the action. That site has also had the benefit of relatively long-term experience, slowly but surely learning from its early mistakes and continually refining its ability to conduct a legitimate on-line auction activity. As a result, the majority to toy and model train sellers and buyers are drawn to e-Bay as their "default" auction—at least until something better comes along.

The truth be told, all auctions—whether conducted at a "real" location or in a virtual, on-line location—can pretty much be likened to a sporting event. In a sense, the buyers and sellers represent opposing teams, each trying—somewhat desperately, at times—to "win" the game they're playing. In live, on-scene auctions, the auctioneer functions as the umpire or referee, assuring that everything is conducted on the up-and-up according to an established set of rules, and that all involved parties play "fair."

On-line auctions, for the most part, still lack the services of that expert referee, and the two "teams"—sellers and buyers—are pretty much left to their own self-policing devices when it comes to fair play. And that is the source of 99% of the problems with Internet auctions!

Listed at the end of this section are some of the more significant Internet auction sites that currently cater to the model railroading/toy trains community. However, before firing up that keyboard and modem, you would be well-advised to read and heed a few tips that will help make your cyberspace auction adventure a bit more pleasant and possibly a lot more safe. You can think of these tips as sort of a "Ten Commandments" for participating in the on-line auction scene, and it would be a good idea to commit them to memory before you actually try your hand at any buying or selling.

The Ten Commandments of On-line Auction Participation

1. Be a student of Internet auctions before becoming a participant.

Actually, it's good practice to become familiar with real-life auctions first, even before you partake of the on-line fare that's available. Auctions, including auctions of collectible items, are held regularly in virtually every community and every state. Plan to attend a few of them, even if you don't offer a single bid or purchase a single item, just to see how an auction is supposed to work. If possible, attend with someone who has a bit of auction-buying experience, because he or she will provide valuable insights that may not be readily apparent to the novice.

Then, venture out into cyberspace and see how those auctions work (there are distinct differences, even among the on-line auction sites themselves), and spend as much time as possible simply as an observer. Seek out the sites that seem to offer the most in terms of items you may be interested in buying or selling. Print out a copy of each site's guidelines and rules, and compare one site with another. Plan to spend several weeks, if possible, just exploring these sights, and seeing how they operate.

After you feel relatively comfortable with the mechanics of on-line auctions, go ahead and select a site that seems most appropriate to your interests. Now it's time to "get your feet wet" by bidding on an item—make it (1) one that does not carry a terribly high value, and (2) one you can easily live without in the event that yours is not the winning bid.

2. Do your homework before engaging in any bidding.

This Commandment is closely related to the previous one. Doing your "homework" simply means researching, to the best of your ability, what an item is really worth in the marketplace. This information will help you to determine what it is worth to you—which is really what matters most, in the long run.

How do you go about determining marketplace values? A good place to start is with one or more of the published price guides devoted to your topic. These books and periodicals are generally excellent resources for providing a "ballpark estimate" of an item's going price at the time of publication. Keep in mind, though, that the value of any particular item is always subject to a number of rather subjective factors, including region of the country, scarcity, and even the motivation of the seller. Nevertheless, if you are seeking to buy a collectible, or planning to sell one, you certainly should go into the market armed with sufficient information about its estimated worth.

3. Take the time to learn the vocabulary and terminology of on-line auctions.

To be a savvy auction participant, you need to become familiar with the language of the auction world. Terms such as "opening bid," "reserve," "minimum bid," and "shill" can be confusing to the uninitiated. A good place to start learning the vocabulary of the auction world is at your local library, where books and magazine articles can be found that describe, in detail, the ups and downs of auctions of all types. Also, take time to print out, and read, the terms-of-use agreements that are part of each on-line auction site. These documents tell you what you can and can't do at a particular site, and they establish the rules of conduct that govern activities on the site.

4. Be aware that on-line auctions nearly always favor the seller.

In a real-life auction, the auctioneer performs the valuable service of working with the seller, and on the seller's behalf, to establish fair value estimates for the items being auctioned. This auctioneer is an experienced expert in the field, and he or she does everything possible to assure that the seller realizes the highest possible price for the items being sold. At the same time, the auctioneer performs with a set of professional guidelines that protect the interest of both the buyers and the sellers, and which help to assure that both parties are satisfied with the auction's conduct and results. For example, an experienced auctioneer will assure that something indicated in "excellent" condition is, indeed, in excellent condition as described by established industry guidelines.

In on-line auctions, the seller pretty much performs as his/her own auctioneer—the on-line site simply moderates or monitors the auction event, and collects its commission if/when the item sells. The seller alone determines the item's condition (whether accurately described or not), and the seller often is able to establish the opening bid, minimum bid, and/or reserve price. In effect, this gives every major advantage to the seller, and gives rise to the BUYER BEWARE slogan that should serve as a constant reminder to every on-line buyer.

5. Feel free to question, and to verify, in writing, the seller's description of an item and its condition.

In the world of collectibles, condition is everything. It is as simple as that! In the world of toy and model trains the most widely accepted condition grading system is the one established by the Train Collectors Association. That grading structure is printed at the end of this section. In describing condition, please note that there is no permitted use of the words "almost," or "nearly," or "plus," or "minus." If an item is described as "mint," it must conform, in all respects, to the TCA definition of mint. There is no such thing a "near mint" condition in the world of collectible toy trains.

If you, as a potential buyer, expect the model train you are bidding on to operate, you must ascertain this information in advance. If the seller's description lists "never run," then that is what you have every right to expect. If it lists "test run only," then you also have every right to ask about how the seller defines "test run" or "minimal running time." Print out, and retain, every response that you get to your e-mail inquiries—that's a real advantage over phone calls when it comes to resolving problems or misunderstandings.

6. Never place your complete trust in a seller's photograph of an item.

Some folks believe that a displayed photograph of an on-line auction item provides a good indication of its actual condition. Not necessarily so! In the first place, the photo you see may not even be the actual item that you are bidding on—perhaps the seller has two such items, one of which is in better condition than the other. Or, the photo may have been electronically retouched—a very easy task to accomplish these days. Also, a photo or two only allows you to see what is pictured in the photograph, from the angle the photo was taken. At a real auction, you generally have the opportunity to view the actual object you will be bidding on. In the world of collectibles, that is a very important plus!

7. Determine a maximum amount that you are willing to pay for a given item, and not to exceed that maximum—even by a few dollars.

You've likely heard the term "auction fever." That's what occurs when two or more bidders get caught-up in a frenzy of bids and counter-bids in an effort to "win" the prized item. It's so easy to tell yourself that bidding "just a few dollars more" won't hurt, but that "few dollars" can quickly add up, whether you're at a live auction of bidding against someone on-line. Only you can determine what an item is really worth to you. Decide, in advance, what your limit is, and then stick firmly to it. With rare exceptions, you'll be able to find that identical item later on at another auction or show, and your disappointment in "losing" this initial opportunity will be short-lived.

8. Do not purchase anything on-line that is not backed by a satisfaction guaranteed/full return policy.

As far as on-line auctions are concerned, the hammer has not fallen until the transaction has been concluded. This means that the final price and shipping arrangements (and costs) have been agreed to; that the seller has received his/her money; and that the buyer has received the agreed-to merchandise in acceptable condition. If any of these pieces are missing, the auction has not been completed. And this is the area where most of the problems with on-line auctions occur.

One way to avoid problems, in advance of any serious bidding on your part, is to ascertain the seller's satisfaction-and-return policy. Avoid ANY auction that does not allow you, as a buyer, to return an item if it is not exactly as described. And, you'll want to determine who is expected to pay the shipping charges for a returned item. Anticipating problems in advance allows you to avoid most of them, and obtaining written verification of all of the agreed-to terms provides you with some legal standing in the event that course of action ultimately becomes necessary.

9. Be very careful about giving out credit card information on-line for any transaction you are involved with.

Let's be clear about one thing: Despite the little notices you see stating that "this is a secure site" when you enter a particular web site, be advised that—today, at least—there is really no such thing as a completely "secure" site anywhere on the Internet. Erstwhile computer hackers delight in demonstrating their prowess at breaking into so-called "secure" web locations. You see and hear news reports all the time discussing the ease with which this can be done—sometimes by what many of us regard as mere youngsters. If you must provide credit card information to complete an on-line transaction, do it by fax or telephone if at all possible (although even calls placed via cordless or cell phones can be rather easily monitored). And, finally, NEVER send cash payments in the mail!

10. Always remember that, if and when you become a seller yourself, these "commandments" will apply to you, as well.

Really, it's just a simple matter of adhering to the Golden Rule: Do unto others as you would have them do unto you. If you always keep this in mind—in on-line dealings, as well as off-line buy/sell/trade transactions—you'll likely be a successful seller who draws favorable feedback from an ever-growing number of satisfied buyers.

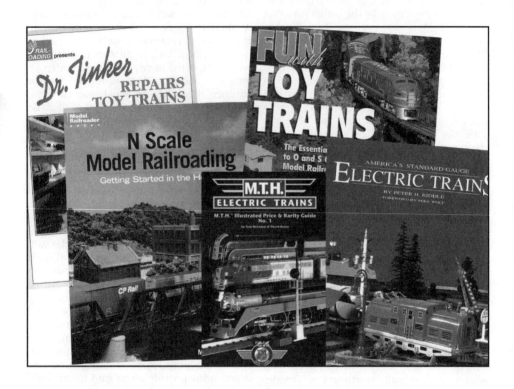

MODEL RAILROAD REFERENCES
Books for the model railroader's library

Following is a list of popular and recommended in-print books for the model railroader's reference library. Books in each section are listed alphabetically, by title. The "all scales" section includes books designed to appeal to any model railroader, regardless of scale preference. Scale-specific books are also listed in the sections that follow. Be aware that some titles may be listed in multiple sections if their content is applicable to those scales.

Over the years, there have been a great many books published on the subject of model railroading and train collecting—certainly enough to fill many shelves in a large library. And, this does not even include the thousands of volumes devoted to prototype railroading. Unfortunately, many of these excellent books are no longer in print, and are no longer available from their publisher. However, you can often find such books at used book stores, at book sales, and even advertised on-line at the various auction sites.

Since the majority of model railroading and toy train books are published by a relatively small number of publishers, the names, addresses, and phone numbers of the publishers listed herein are provided at the end of this section. Contact the publishers directly for a catalog containing detailed descriptions and prices for all of their current offerings.

All Scales

A Treasury of Model RR Photos	Kalmbach Books
America's Driving Force—Modeling Railroads and the Auto Industry	Wm. K. Walthers
Basic Model Railroading: Getting Started in the Hobby	Kalmbach Books
Beginner's Guide to Toy Train Collecting and Operating	Kalmbach Books
Bridge & Trestle Handbook	Carstens Publications
Circus Trains, Trucks & Models	Carstens Publications
Collecting Toy Trains—Identification & Value Guide	Krause Publications
Complete Layout Plans, 3rd ed.	Carstens Publications
Design Handbook for Model Railroaders	Carstens Publications
Electrical Handbook for Model Railroaders, 4th ed.	Carstens Publications
Fun with Toy Trains	Krause Publications
Greenberg's Easy Electronics Projects for Toy Trains	Greenberg/Kalmbach
How to Build Model Railroad Benchwork, 2nd ed.	Kalmbach Books
How to Build Realistic Model Railroad Scenery, 2nd ed.	Kalmbach Books
How to Detail Diesel Locomotives	Kalmbach Books
Layouts of the Masters	Railmodel Journal

Lionel's Model Builder: The Magazine That Shaped the Toy Train Hobby	Greenberg/Kalmbach
Model Operation Handbook	Carstens Publications
Model Railroad Bridges & Trestles	Kalmbach Books
Model Railroading in Small Spaces	Kalmbach Books
Model Railroading with John Allen	Kalmbach Books
Painting and Weathering Railroad Models	Kalmbach Books
Railroading Along the Waterfront	Wm. K. Walthers
Realistic Scenery for Toy Train Layouts	Greenberg/Kalmbach
Scenery Tips & Techniques	Kalmbach Books
Small Railroads You Can Build, 2nd ed.	Kalmbach Books
Tips & Tricks for Toy Train Operators	Greenberg/Kalmbach
The ABC's of Model Railroading	Kalmbach Books
The History, Making & Modeling of Steel	Wm. K. Walthers
Toy Train Collecting and Operating: An Introduction	Greenberg/Kalmbach
Track Design, 3rd ed.	Carstens Publications
Track Planning for Realistic Operation, 3rd ed.	Kalmbach Books
Trackwork Handbook for Model Railroaders, 3rd ed.	Carstens Publications
Traction Planbook, 2nd ed.	Carstens Publications
Trains, Tracks & Tall Timber	Wm. K. Walthers
The V&O Story	Carstens Publications
20 Custom Designed Track Plans	Kalmbach Books
48 Top Notch Track Plans from Model Railroader	Kalmbach Books
150 Years of Train Models	Carstens Publications
222 Tips for Building Model Railroad Structures	Kalmbach Books
303 Tips for Detailing Model Railroad Scenery & Structures	Kalmbach Books

Z scale

Walthers N&Z Model Railroad Reference Book	Wm. K. Walthers Co.

N scale

Basic Model Railroading: Getting Started in the Hobby	Kalmbach Books
Introduction to N Scale Model Railroading	Atlas Model RR Co.

Model Railroading in Small Spaces	Kalmbach Books
Nine N Scale Railroads	Atlas Model RR Co.
Nn3 Manual, 5th ed.	NTRAK, Inc.
N Resources Booklets (#1 through #5)	NTRAK, Inc.
N Scale Modeling	Railmodel Journal
N Scale Model Railroad that Grows	Kalmbach Books
N Scale Model Railroading: Getting Started in the Hobby	Kalmbach Books
N Scale Product Guide	Hundman Publishing
NTRAK Module "How-to" Book	NTRAK, Inc.
NTRAK Manual	NTRAK, Inc.
Small Railroads You Can Build, 2nd ed.	Kalmbach Books
Walthers N&Z Model Railroad Reference Book	Wm. K. Walthers Co.
10 Years of N-Scale, 1989-1999	Hundman Publishing

HO scale

A Realistic HO Layout for Beginners	Kalmbach Books
Basic Model Railroading: Getting Started in the Hobby	Kalmbach Books
Freight Car Models: Techniques, Vol. 1	Railmodel Journal
Freight Car Models: Techniques, Vol. 2	Railmodel Journal
Freight Car Models: Techniques, Vol. 3	Railmodel Journal
HO Lineside Industries You Can Build	Kalmbach Books
HO Model Railroading Handbook, 3rd ed.	Krause Publications
HO Narrow Gauge Railroad You Can Build	Kalmbach Books
HO Railroad from Start to Finish	Kalmbach Books
HO Railroad from Set to Scenery	Kalmbach Books
HO Trackside Structures You Can Build	Kalmbach Books
Model Railroading in Small Spaces	Kalmbach Books
Practical Guide to HO Model Railroading	Kalmbach Books
Small Railroads You Can Build, 2nd ed.	Kalmbach Books
Standard Guide to Athearn Model Trains	Krause Publications
The Brown Book of Brass Locomotives, 3rd ed.	Krause Publications
The Pennsy Middle Division in HO Scale	Kalmbach Books
The Practical Guide to HO Model Railroading	Kalmbach Books

Track Planning for Realistic Operations	Kalmbach Books
Tuning & Upgrading Athearn Locomotives	Railmodel Journal
Walthers HO Model Railroad Reference Book	Wm. K. Walthers Co.
6 HO Railroads You Can Build	Kalmbach Books

S scale/gauge

A.C. Gilbert's Famous American Flyer Trains	Heimburger House
American Flyer Instruction Book	Heimburger House
Building and Operating Model Railroads	Heimburger House
Greenberg's American Flyer Numerical Parts List	Greenberg/Kalmbach
Greenberg's American Flyer S Gauge Operating and Repair Manual, 1945-1965	Greenberg/Kalmbach
Greenberg's Guide to American Flyer S Gauge, Vol. 1, 5th ed.	Greenberg/Kalmbach
Greenberg's Pocket Price Guide, American Flyer S Gauge, 1946-2000	Greenberg/Kalmbach
Service Manual for American Flyer	MDK, Inc.
S Gauge Locomotives & Cars	Heimburger House
Sn3 Modeling	Heimburger House
Souvenir Edition of S Gaugian	Heimburger House
Toy Train Collecting and Operating: An Introduction	Greenberg/Kalmbach
Track Plans for Toy Trains	Kalmbach Books

O scale/gauge

Classic Lionel Display Layouts You Can Build	Kalmbach Books
Collecting Toy Trains, 4th ed.	Krause Publications
Dr. Tinker Repairs Toy Trains (Vols. 1 and 2)	Myron Biggar Group
Greenberg's Guide to American Flyer Prewar O Gauge, 2nd ed.	Greenberg/Kalmbach
Greenberg's Guide to Ives Trains, Vol. II, O Gauge	Greenberg/Kalmbach
Greenberg's Guide to Lionel Trains, 1945-1969, Vol. 1: Motive Power and Rolling Stock (9th ed.)	Greenberg/Kalmbach
Greenberg's Guide to Lionel Trains, 1945-1969, Vol. III: Cataloged Sets (2nd ed.)	Greenberg/Kalmbach
Greenberg's Guide to Lionel Trains, 1945-1969, Vol. IV: Uncatalogued Sets	Greenberg/Kalmbach

Greenberg's Guide to Lionel Trains, 1945-1969, *Vol. V: Rare and Unusual*	Greenberg/Kalmbach
Greenberg's Guide to Lionel Trains, 1945-1969, *Vol. VI: Accessories*	Greenberg/Kalmbach
Greenberg's Guide to Lionel Trains, 1945-1969, *Vol. VII: Selected Variations*	Greenberg/Kalmbach
Greenberg's Guide to Lionel Paper and Collectibles	Greenberg/Kalmbach
Greenberg's Guide to Lionel Trains, 1970-1991, *Vol. II: Promotions, Sets, Boxes, etc.*	Greenberg/Kalmbach
Greenberg's Guide to Lionel Trains, 1970-1997, *Vol. III: Accessories*	Greenberg/Kalmbach
Greenberg's Guide to Lionel HO, Vol. 1, 1957-1966 *(2nd ed.)*	Greenberg/Kalmbach
Greenberg's Guide to Lionel HO, Vol. 2, 1974-1977	Greenberg/Kalmbach
Greenberg's Guide to Marx Instruction Sheets	Greenberg/Kalmbach
Greenberg's Layout Plans for Lionel Trains	Greenberg/Kalmbach
Greenberg's Marx Train Catalogues	Greenberg/Kalmbach
Greenberg's Pocket Price Guide to Lionel Trains, *1900-2000*	Greenberg/Kalmbach
Greenberg's Pocket Price Guide, Marx Trains, 7th ed.	Greenberg/Kalmbach
Greenberg's Roadname Guide to O Gauge Trains	Greenberg/Kalmbach
Greenberg's Wiring Your Lionel Layout (Vols. 1-3)	Greenberg/Kalmbach
How to Build Your First Lionel Layout	Greenberg/Kalmbach
Lionel Train Book	Lionel, LLC
Lionel 1900-2000 Illustrated Price & Rarity Guide *Vol. 1: 1901-1969*	TM Books & Videos
Lionel 1900-2000 Illustrated Price & Rarity Guide *Vol. 2: 1970-2000*	TM Books & Videos
Lionel: A Collector's Guide and History (6 volumes)	TM Books & Videos
Lionel Trains: Standard of the World, 1900-1943, *2nd ed.*	Train Collectors Assn.
M.T.H. Electric Trains: The Official Guide	Kalmbach Books
M.T.H. Illustrated Price & Rarity Guide	TM Books & Videos
Operating O & O-27 Trains	MDK, Inc.
Small Railroads You Can Build, 2nd ed.	Kalmbach Books
The O Gauge Railroading Primer	Myron Biggar Group
The World's Greatest Toy Train Maker	Greenberg/Kalmbach
Toy Train Collecting and Operating: An Introduction	Greenberg/Kalmbach

Toy Train Repair Made Easy	Greenberg/Kalmbach
Toy Trains of Yesteryear	Carstens Publications
Track Plans for Toy Trains	Kalmbach Books
Walthers Big Trains Model Railroad Reference Book	Wm. K. Walthers Co.
3-Rail Illustrated Price Guide	TM Books & Videos
21 O Gauge Layouts for the 21st Century	Atlas O, LLC

Standard gauge

America's Standard Gauge Electric Trains	Krause Publications
Greenberg's Guide to Early American Toy Trains: Carlisle & Finch; Hafner and Dorfan	Greenberg/Kalmbach
Greenberg's Guide to Ives Trains, Vol. I: 1 and Wide Gauges and Accessories	Greenberg/Kalmbach
Greenberg's Guide to Lionel Paper and Collectibles	Greenberg/Kalmbach
Greenberg's Guide to Lionel Prewar Parts and Instruction Sheets	Greenberg/Kalmbach
Greenberg's Guide to Lionel Trains, 1901-1942, Vol. III: Accessories	Greenberg/Kalmbach
Greenberg's Guide to Lionel Trains, 1901-1942, Vol. IV: Prewar Sets	Greenberg/Kalmbach
Greenberg's Repair and Operating Manual: Prewar Lionel Trains	Greenberg/Kalmbach
Lionel: A Collector's Guide and History (6 volumes)	TM Books & Videos
Lionel Trains: Standard of the World, 1900-1943, 2nd ed.	Train Collectors Assn.
Lionel Standard Gauge Era	Carstens Publications
Toy Train Collecting and Operating: An Introduction	Greenberg/Kalmbach
Trains From Grandfather's Attic	Greenberg/Kalmbach

Large scale

Beginner's Guide to Large Scale Model Railroading	Kalmbach Books
Greenberg's Pocket Price Guide: LGB, 1968-1996	Greenberg/Kalmbach
Large-Scale Model Railroading Handbook	Krause Publications
Model Railroading with LGB	Greenberg/Kalmbach
Official Guide to LGB	Kalmbach Books
Walthers Big Trains Model Railroad Reference Book	Wm. K. Walthers Co.

Publishers of books listed

Atlas Model Railroad Co.
603 Sweetland Ave.
Hillside, NJ 07205
information/orders: 908-687-0880
www.atlasrr.com

Atlas O, LLC
603 Sweetland Ave.
Hillside, NJ 07205
information/orders: 908-687-9590
www.atlasO.com

Carstens Publications
108 Phil Harden Rd., Fredon Township
P.O. Box 700
Newton, NJ 07860-0700
information/orders: 800-474-6995
www.rrmodelcraftsman.com

Greenberg/Kalmbach Books
Kalmbach Publishing Co.
21027 Crossroads Circle
P.O. Box 1612
Waukesha, WI 53187-1612
catalog/orders: 800-533-6644
http://books.kalmbach.com

Heimburger House Publishing Co.
7236 W. Madison St.
Forest Park, IL 60130
catalog/orders: 708-366-1973
http://trainweb.com/sgaugian

Hundman Publishing
13110 Beverly Park Road
Mukilteo, WA 98275
catalog/orders: 800-810-7660
www.nscalemagazine.com

Kalmbach Books
Kalmbach Publishing Co.
21027 Crossroads Circle
P.O. Box 1612
Waukesha, WI 53187-1612
catalog/orders: 800-533-6644
http://books.kalmbach.com

Krause Publications
700 E. State St.
Iola, WI 54990-0001
catalog/orders: 800-258-0929
www.krause.com/Books

Lionel, LLC
50625 Richard W. Blvd.
Chesterfield, MI 48051-2493
customer service: 810-940-4100
www.lionel.com

MDK, Inc. (K-Line Electric Trains)
P.O. Box 2831
Chapel Hill, NC 27515
customer service: 800-866-9986
www.k-linetrains.com

Myron Biggar Group
P.O. Box 239
Nazareth, PA 18064-0239
catalog/orders: 610-759-0406
http://members.aol.com/OGauge
Rwy/ogr.html

NTRAK, Inc.
1150 Wine Country Place
Templeton, CA 93465
information/orders: 805-434-5058
www.ntrak.org

Railmodel Journal
2403 Champa St.
Denver, CO 80205
(mail request only)

TM Books & Videos
Box 279
New Buffalo, MI 49117
catalog/orders: 800-892-2822
www.tmbooks-video.com

Train Collectors Association
P.O. Box 248
Strasburg, PA 17579
information/orders: 717-687-8623

Wm. K. Walthers, Inc.
5601 W. Florist Avenue
Milwaukee, WI 53218
www.walthers.com

GLOSSARY OF MODEL RAILROADING AND ELECTRICAL TERMS

I f you're going to "walk the walk" in the world of railroading—whether prototype or model—it helps a bit if you can "talk the talk." The following select list of model railroading and relevant electrical terms (with a few basic prototype railroading terms included) is derived from a more extensive list appearing on the web site for Lionel Trains—www.lionel.com—and is presented here with the permission of Lionel LLC.

AC (Alternating Current): Electric current that repeatedly alternates (Cycles) from positive to negative a specified number of times per second (usually 60 in the U.S.). Toy train transformers typically operate on, and output, AC current to run the trains. See also, DC.

Ampere: Unit of measure for determining the strength of electrical flow in a circuit; abbreviated as Amps. The higher the amperage, the greater the flow, or volume, of current passing through the circuit. Technically, the amount of current produced by the force of one volt acting through one ohm of resistance.

Arc: A spark created by the passage of electric current across a gap; also a curve.

Articulated Locomotive: A steam-powered locomotive with two separate sets of wheels and cylinders—each of which pivots on separate frames. Certain types of electrically-powered locomotives may also be articulated.

Automatic Block Signal: A trackside signal activated by the movement of trains over/past a detecting device.

Automatic Coupler: Couplers that couple and uncouple automatically through the use of uncoupling ramps, and permanent or electro-magnets; permits remote operation of couplers instead of manual coupler operation.

Auxiliary Tender: A second tender attached to the primary tender of a locomotive; permits longer runs by reducing fuel and water stops.

Ballast: Cinders, crushed rock, or gravel placed on the roadbed to hold track ties in place and to promote uniform drainage.

Bascule Bridge: A counter-balanced lift bridge, generally used where relatively low-lying railroad tracks pass over narrow waterway channels which must be used by waterborne traffic.

Belt Line: A connecting rail line between two or more other railroads; so-called because it often encircles a city like a belt.

Big Boy: Common name for the largest steam locomotive: a 4-8-8-4 Union Pacific.

Birney: A short, single-truck (4-wheel) trolley car designed for use in congested urban areas where tight track curves are required.

Blind Drivers: Driving wheels without flanges which permit locomotives to negotiate sharper curves than the wheel arrangement would normally allow; widely used on narrow gauge locomotives.

Block: In prototype railroading, a section of track through which rail traffic is controlled as a unit. In model railroading, commonly the designation for a length of track with an independently controlled power supply, constructed so two or more trains may operate independently on, for example, a simple oval of track.

Block Signals: A signal or series of signals, usually automatic, which control a block.

Bobber: A short, four-wheel caboose.

Boiler: That portion of a steam locomotive, usually round, where the steam is generated.

Bolster: The crosswise member of the frame of a railroad car at the truck (body bolster) or the crosswise piece at the center of a truck (truck bolster).

Box Cab: Electric or diesel locomotive with a cab shaped like a box.

Brakeman: A member of a freight or passenger train crew. His duties are to assist the conductor in any way necessary.

Branch Line: Secondary line of a railroad.

Brownies: In model railroading, demerits given to members of model railroad clubs for various infractions of operating rules; a form of good-natured punishment for making a mistake.

Bumper: A device for stopping railroad cars at the end of a spur track.

Brill: A type of two-truck, eight-wheel trolley car used primarily in urban areas.

Cab Control: A system for switching control of a series of blocks on a model railroad so that two or more throttles are capable of controlling operation in those blocks, depending on which locomotive is to use the blocks at any given time.

Cab-Forward: A type of steam locomotive (most commonly used by the Southern Pacific) built so the cab portion is at the front for added visibility and safety from smoke and fumes in tunnels and snowsheds.

Camelback: A steam locomotive with the cab set astride the boiler. The fireman on this type of locomotive rides under a hood at the rear. Also called a "Mother Hubbard."

Car Barn: Storage house for trolley and interurban cars.

Catenary: A system of overhead wires suspended over the track to provide power for electric-type locomotives.

Circuit Breaker: A device for interrupting an electrical circuit if a short or overload occurs.

Classification Lamps: Lights (or flags) mounted on the front of a locomotive to indicate the status of the train. White lamps (or flags) indicate an "Extra," while green indicates all sections but the final one of multi-section trains.

Clerestory Roof: Raised center portion along the length of a roof of certain passenger cars or trolleys which feature small "clerestory windows" along the sides to allow natural light into the car.

Climax: A type of geared steam locomotive used primarily by logging railroads. The locomotive's twin cylinders drive a crankshaft aligned parallel with the axles; power is transmitted to the trucks through an arrangement of bevel gears and a
driveshaft; rods couple the axles on each truck.

Coil: In model railroading, a tightly wound "spool" of thin wire which is a component of electrical devices such as solenoids and electromagnets.

Cold Joint: In electrical work, a soldered connection in which the materials being joined were insufficiently heated to melt the solder and cause it to flow and bond.

Common Ground: In model railroading, the use of a single wire to complete a circuit for numerous track sections or accessories. Eliminates the need for a large number of "ground" wires, one for each accessory or track.

Commutator: The rotating part of an electric motor which contacts stationary carbon brushes to complete the electrical circuit.

Consist: The full set of cars which make up a train, usually used in reference to a freight train.

Contactor: In model railroading, a switch-like device that fits beneath a section of model train track, and is activated by the weight of a train passing over it.

Continuous Rail: Rails that have been welded together to form a very long single rail, thereby eliminating rail joints which are the weakest part of the track. Also known as Welded Rail or Ribbonrail.

Convertor: Electrical device for changing Direct Current (DC) into Alternating Current (AC).

Coupler: A device at the ends of a car or locomotive used to connect that car to other cars or locomotives.

Covered Wagon: A diesel unit with a full-width (streamlined-appearing) cab, as opposed to a "Hood Unit."

Cowcatcher: Early term for a locomotive's pilot. A pointed device used on the front of a locomotive to shove livestock off the track. Now used to prevent any object from going under the locomotive's wheels.

Crankpin: Pin or screw attached to the driving wheels which holds side rods in place, while still allowing them to turn.

Crossing: An intersection between two tracks on the same level.

Crossing at Grade (also Grade Crossing): An intersection between a road or highway and railroad tracks on the same level.

Crossover: Combination of track and switches which enable trains to cross from one parallel track to another.

Current: The movement or flow of electricity.

Cycles: In electricity, the alternation of the direction of current flow, generally expressed as cycles per second. In the U.S., most household current alternates at 60 cycles per second. Also known as "hertz."

DC (Direct Current): Electric current which flows in only one direction. Model railroad power packs for two-rail trains typically input AC (household) current, and convert (rectify) it for output as low-voltage DC current to run the trains.

DCC (Digital Command Control): A system of operating model trains via "coded" electronic signals transmitted through the track.

Depot: A station for passengers and freight; term usually applied to a rather small facility in a town or village.

Derail: A device placed over the rail to prevent a car from rolling out of a siding (for example) and onto the main line.

Doodlebug: A rail motor car.

Draft Gear: Mechanism that connects the coupler to the frame of the car. In model railroading, the coupler mounting box is often so-named.

Drawbar: The bar that connects (couples) a steam engine to its tender.

Driving Gear: The arrangement of rods and cranks that are used to transfer piston energy to the driving wheels.

Driving Wheels: The powered wheels of a locomotive.

Dual Gauge: A mixed track gauge, often seen at interchange points between standard gauge and narrow gauge railroads.

Dynamic Brake: (1) A system on a diesel locomotive which converts its traction motors into electric generators— the resulting resistance provides a braking action to help slow a train, especially when going down a grade. (2) The protrusion on some engines which is often called the dynamic brake is really only a cooling mechanism for the heat produced by the excess energy being generated.

E-Unit: An electrically-activated mechanical reversing device on some model locomotives, especially those made prior to 1990. Most recent model locomotives are equipped with solid-state electronic reversing units.

Eccentric Crank: A large, forged casting attached to the main drive wheels of a steam engine which allows a rod to rotate in an elliptical path, thereby opening and closing the cylinder slide valves.

Electromagnet: A device made of a core of iron or steel wrapped in a wire coil, which attracts other ferrous metals when
current is passed through the wire.

Engine: Common term applied to mean "locomotive," but properly relates only to the cylinders and their drivers.

ETD: End-of-train device. A box-like apparatus equipped with a flashing warning beacon, and often train status detectors, which is mounted on the end of the last car in a freight train. On most contemporary railroads, an ETD replaces the caboose.

Facing Switch: A turnout (switch) situated with the points facing traffic.

Feeder: In model railroading, a power connection from the transformer or power pack to the track, and then on to another
portion of the trackwork. Also a short branch road feeding traffic to a main line.

Fixed Voltage Post: In model railroading, a terminal post on a transformer or power pack which is permanently configured to provide a set amount of voltage at all times. Generally used to power accessories and lamps.

Flange: A protruding lip on a grinder or wheel; the inside edge of a railroad car wheel which guides the wheel and keeps the wheelset on the track.

Flexible Track or Flex-Track: In model railroading, long (about 3 feet) straight sections of track manufactured so one or more of the rails slide somewhat freely through the spikes or tieplates, thereby allowing the track section to be curved into a customized configuration.

Frog: The portion of a turnout which is grooved for the wheel flanges; so-named for its resemblance to a frog.

G Scale: Model railroading in a scale of 1:22.5; often erroneously applied to other scales in large scale model railroading such as 1:20.3, 1:24, 1:29, and 1:32—all of which also operate on #1 gauge (45mm track). See also "Large Scale."

Gas-electric: Self-propelled car powered by a gasoline engine driving a generator which supplies electric current to motors on the axles; commonly used for branchline passenger service in the 1920s and 1930s.

Gauge (track): The distance measured between the inside edges of the running rails.

Gauge (wire): In electricity, a measure of the thickness of electrical wire, generally expressed as a number. The higher the number, the thinner the wire; e.g., 18 gauge is finer than 14 gauge.

Geep: Slang for a series of Electro-Motive Division (General Motors) road switchers designated as GP-7, GP-9, etc. (GP stands for General Purpose).

Grab Irons: Handholds on the sides, ends, or roofs of railroad cars.

Grade: The degree of inclined elevation of the track's surface over a given distance, usually expressed as a percentage.

Ground: One of the two poles of a battery, transformer, or power pack which, in conjunction with the "hot" wire from the other pole, completes an electrical circuit.

Heisler: Type of geared steam locomotive used by logging railroads. It has two cylinders arranged in a "V" connected to a driveshaft which, in turn, is connected to the trucks. See also, "Climax" and "Shay."

Helper: The second or added locomotive on a double-header; or a locomotive cut-in to the consist or pushing on the end to assist the train up a grade.

Hertz: See "Cycles."

Hi-Rail or Hi-Railer: Term commonly applied to toy train operators who prefer prototypical operations and a realistic operating environment on their model railroad—often including scale-proportioned and detailed locomotives, rolling stock and accessories—even though the track itself may have three rails or an unrealistically high profile.

HO Scale: Model railroad scale in the proportion of 1:87. Pronounced as "aich-oh." Roughly half the size of O Scale, or Half-O. The most popular model railroading scale in use today.

Hood Unit: A road switcher, so-called because of the construction of the locomotive, with the machinery covered by a hood rather than a full-width cab.

Hot Wire: A wire connected to one of the two primary poles of a battery, transformer, or power pack which provides power to an electrical device (in conjunction with the Ground). A model train transformer or power pack may have several "Hot" poles—each providing a different voltage.

Induction: In electricity, the process of creating an electrical field or electrical current in a body that is in proximity to, but not connected with, the generating force; the principal behind voltage reduction in a model train transformer.

Insulating Track Pin/Insulated Rail Joiner: In model railroading, a small track-connecting pin or fishplate-shaped joiner made of a non-conductive material which substitutes for the metal pin(s) or joiner normally used to connect two track sections. Prevents the flow of electricity from one section to the next section.

Insulated Track Section: In model railroading, a modified section of toy train track in which one of the outside running rails is insulated from the metal track ties by fiber strips or some other non-conductive material, and which is further insulated from adjacent rails by insulating track pins; commonly used to operate accessories.

Interurban: A streetcar/trolley-style car used for passenger service (sometimes including light freight and mail service, and often in multiple units) between cities and towns, as opposed to local streetcar service. The term applied to such transportation systems and service in general.

Journal: The load-bearing part of a railroad car axle. The weight of the axle is carried by the journal bearing, enclosed in the journal box.

Kingpin: The pivot on which a truck swivels (also known as a Center Pin).

Kit-bash: A term used to denote the making of a model railroad structure, car, etc., from parts of two or more ready-to-assemble kits.

Knuckle Coupler: Couplers on the ends of railroad cars and locomotives (standard in the U.S.) which, when viewed from above, resemble two hands with the fingers bent to grip one another.

Large Scale: Term commonly used to designate all model railroading scales in the nominal proportions of 1:20.3, 1.22.5, 1:24, 1:29, and 1:32 which operate on #1 Gauge (45mm) track. Also, the trade name applied to a line of such model train products produced by Lionel Trains. See also, "G Scale."

Layout: In model railroading, the term applied to an arrangement of tracks on a table or platform; also commonly applied to the complete assembly of tracks, accessories, and scenery. See also, "Pike."

Lichen: A moss-like plant which, when dried, preserved with glycerin, and dyed, is commonly used as a scenic decoration to simulate foliage, brush and undergrowth on model railroad layouts.

Lockon: A device used to connect wiring to tracks, especially on a three-rail model railroad. Allows the operator to directly connect wires from the transformer to the outside (ground) rail and inside (power) rail.

LRV (Light Rail Vehicle): Term used to categorically identify railway equipment and systems such as trolleys and rapid transit cars—either electrically-powered or self-propelled.

Mallet: An articulated steam locomotive named for the designer. The term is generally applied to any articulated steam locomotive.

Modular Layout/Modular Railroading: A type of model railroad layout in which the layout itself is comprised of portable modules constructed to specifications that permit each module to be joined to others, thereby creating a large layout limited only by space and number of modules available.

MU (Multiple Unit): Cars or locomotives which contain their own power, but which can be controlled from the foremost car or locomotive; commonly used on commuter trains and diesel locomotives.

N Scale: Model railroad scale in the proportion of 1:160. The second most popular (after HO Scale) of the model railroad scales in use today.

Narrow Gauge: Term designating railroad track having a rail spacing (gauge) of less than the North American standard of 4 feet, 8-1/2 inches—typically mining, industrial, and scenic railways which most commonly have rail spacing of either 3 feet or 2 feet. In model railroading, narrow gauge is designated by the modeling scale, followed by an "n" (narrow gauge), and then the modeled track gauge—for example, On3 or HOn2.

O Scale/O Gauge: Model railroad scale in the proportion of 1:48 (nominally, 1/4 inch = 1 foot); includes O scale, O gauge, O27 gauge, and On3 and On2 scale model trains and equipment. The standard track gauge for O/O27 measures 1-1/4 inches between the running rails.

Ohm: In electricity, the fundamental unit of electrical resistance. It is a measurement which describes the resistance of a circuit to the flow of electricity passing through it. A greater number of Ohms indicates a higher resistance, or impediment, to current flow.

Open-top or Open-Grid Layout: A type of layout design which uses a wooden frame with joists, thereby allowing the roadbed to rise and fall beneath the top level of the frame by means of cross members and strips of wood called stringers.

O27 Gauge: Toy train track which has the same distance between the outside running rails as O Gauge (1-1/4 inches), but is lighter in weight, has a lower profile, and measures only 27 inches over the diameter of a full circle. Also, the term applied to O27 trains, which generally are shorter and/or somewhat smaller than their true O Gauge counterparts—made so to negotiate the smaller-radius curves.

Pantograph: The collapsible, adjustable, "floating" structure which provides electrical contact with overhead wires on an electric locomotive, so-called for its pivoting capability.

Parallel Circuit: In electricity, a single electrical circuit serving several electrical devices (such as lamps), each of which is connected directly to both poles of the power source. All devices in the circuit will receive the full amount of electrical voltage available from the two poles. (See also Series Circuit).

Passing Siding: A siding intended specifically for passing complete trains in the same or opposite direction.

PCC Car: Abbreviation for "President's Conference Committee" streamlined-style streetcars and interurbans produced from the mid-1930s through the mid-1940s.

Phase or Phasing: In model railroading, the connection of two or more toy train transformers in such a way that the continuous movement of alternating current (AC) in all of the transformers from positive to negative is identical. Two transformers that are "Out of Phase" can be corrected by rotating the wall plug of only one of them 180-degrees.

Pickup Roller: A device mounted on the underside of a toy train car or locomotive which contacts the third (center) rail to supply electrical power to the motor(s) or lamp(s).

Pike: A model railroad layout.

Pilot: Correct nomenclature for the guard structure at the front of a steam locomotive; often called a "cowcatcher."

Pilot Truck (also lead or leading truck): The truck located in front of a steam locomotive's drive wheels which, in addition to providing support, helps guide the engine into curves and turnouts.

Polarity: In electricity, the condition of either positive or negative magnetic or electrical attraction which cause current to flow.

Pole: In electricity, each of the two opposing parts of a battery or other power source which exhibit attraction for each other, thus inducing a flow of electric current.

Power Pack: In model railroading, normally a train control device configured to convert household AC current to low-voltage DC current which is used for the operation of most model trains that run on two-rail track.

Primary Coil: The lighter wire winding in the core of a toy train transformer that connects directly to the household electrical supply by means of a wall plug. See also, Secondary.

Prototype: The real, life-size object on which a scale model is based.

Railfan: An individual who enjoys riding, watching, photographing, and reading about trains.

RDC (Rail Diesel Car): A lightweight, self-powered commuter and/or mail-carrying car often operated in multiple units; manufactured by the Budd Company.

Rectifier: In electricity, a device used to transform alternating current (AC) into direct current (DC). May be used with an AC-type transformer to power equipment which requires DC current. See also, Power Pack.

Relay: In electricity, an electrically-powered switch which, in turn, effects a change (activates other switches) in some other electrical circuit or circuits.

Resistor: In electricity, a device which impedes current flow, thereby reducing the voltage passing through a circuit; resistance is measured in ohms.

Rheostat: In electricity, a device for adjusting the amount of resistance in an electrical circuit, thereby varying the amount of voltage produced in that circuit.

Right-of-Way: The track, roadbed, and property alongside which is owned by the railroad.

Roadbed: The surface upon which track is laid. This surface is usually raised above ground level by rocks topped with wooden or concrete ties, upon which the tracks are laid and then ballasted.

Road Engine: Locomotive used regularly for mainline passenger or freight service.

Rolling Stock: Non-powered freight and passenger cars which are pulled by a locomotive.

Roundhouse: A circular (usually) structure meant to house locomotives during servicing. The roundhouse customarily faced a turntable which was used to direct a locomotive onto and off of one of the roundhouse tracks.

S Scale: Model railroad scale in the proportion of 1:64. Popularized by A. C. Gilbert's American Flyer electric trains in the 1940s through the 1960s. Today, American Flyer trains continue to be produced on a limited basis by Lionel, LLC.

Scale: The ratio in size between a model and its prototype, expressed as a fraction or a proportion (for example-- 1/48 or 1:48 for O Scale).

Scenicking: Slang term for the application of scenery materials of various types to a model railroad layout.

Scratch-building: In model railroading, the act of constructing scenery, buildings, rolling stock, or locomotives from raw materials by hand, rather than from a ready-to-assemble kit.

Secondary Coil: In electricity, the heavier wire winding within the core of a transformer that produces reduced voltage and which connects directly (in model railroading) to the track and accessories. See also, Primary.

Sectional Track: In model railroading, pieces of track in any scale or gauge manufactured to specific geometric proportions, which can then be joined together in straight lines, curves, and circles.

Sectional Layout: A type of model railroad layout made up of various smaller sections that are joined together to form the larger layout; designed this way so the layout can be disassembled and/or moved without destroying any major components.

Series Circuit: In electricity, an electrical circuit serving several devices (such as lamps) wherein the current passes from one pole of the power source through each device in succession before reaching the other pole. In this type of circuit, each lamp receives only a portion of the total voltage available at the source. For example, if there are two lamps, each receives half the power; if there are three lamps, each receives one-third the power; etc. See also, Parallel.

Shay: A gear-driven steam locomotive used extensively in logging and mining operations. It has three cylinders mounted vertically on the right side of the boiler driving a crankshaft geared to all axles—sometimes including the tender's axles, when present.

Siding: A section of track accessed off the mainline by means of a turnout. A dead-end siding connected to the mainline by a turnout at one end only is called a "spur." A siding connected by turnouts at both ends is called a "Passing Siding."

Slip Switch: A piece of trackwork that combines a crossing and four turnouts to permit trains to move from one track to the other or to stay on the same track.

Spike: A nail-like device with a large, offset head that is driven into ties to anchor rail in place and to maintain proper track alignment.

Spur: A divergent track (siding) having only one point of entry; a branch line over which irregular service is offered.

Standard Gauge: In model railroading, toy trains larger than O gauge that operate on track measuring 2-1/8 inches between the running rails. Standard Gauge products were introduced by the Lionel Corporation in 1906 and were commonly produced by Lionel and others up until the start of World War II. In prototype railroading in the U.S. (and in some other countries), track measuring 4 feet, 8-1/2 inches between the inside edges of the running rails.

Stub: A short diverging track (siding) ending in a bumper. A stub has a turnout only at one end.

Superelevation: The slight raising of the outer rail on a curve; banking.

Switcher (also Shifter): An engine primarily used to move and position cars on different tracks, such as in a yard.

Tank Engine: Steam locomotive that carries its fuel and water supplies in tanks hung over or placed alongside the boiler, or on a frame extension (bunker) at the rear, instead of in a tender.

Tender: The car immediately behind a steam locomotive which is used to store the water and fuel (wood, coal, or oil) needed for the locomotive's operation.

Third Rail: The center rail on Lionel-type toy train track. On prototype electric, subway, and even some scale model railroads, a third rail for electric current pickup may be located outside one of the running rails.

Throttle: The speed control on a locomotive. In model railroading, a rheostat generally functions as the throttle by controlling the voltage which reaches the track.

Tie: A supporting cross piece—usually of wood or concrete on prototype railroads—that holds the rails of railroad track the proper distance apart (Gauge) and in proper alignment.

Tin-Litho: Tinplate sheets which have been decorated by a printing process known as lithography. A process commonly used in the construction of toy trains in the period before World War II.

Tinplate: Stamped-steel (usually) surfaces which have been coated with a layer of tin to prevent rust and corrosion. Most toy train track is tinplated, and this term has, by extension, commonly been used to refer to all toy trains and their operators ("Tinplaters").

Track Clips: Devices used to attach two ties of adjoining track sections together in a toy train layout. These are used to fasten track sections together in temporary layouts.

Track Pin (also Rail Joiner): In model railroading, a short metal electrically-conductive rod or flat plate-like device that is used to connect adjacent sections of track.

Traction: In the context of rail transportation and associated modeling, a term generally used to connote electric trolley, streetcar, and interurban lines and equipment.

Trailing Switch: A turnout or switch whose points face away from oncoming traffic.

Trailing Truck: A two- or four-wheeled truck located behind a steam locomotive's driver wheels which helps support the rear of the engine.

Train Set (also Trainset): In real railroading, the term applied to a passenger train consist—often including the engine(s)—which customarily is not broken up except for special work on a component. In model railroading, a set of equipment usually consisting, at minimum, of a locomotive, cars, track, and transformer of power pack.

Transfer Table: A laterally-moving geared set of rails used to move a locomotive or cars from one track to another. Typically used in engine service facilities which have a rectangular engine house or shops rather than a roundhouse.

Transformer: A device for changing (transforming) high-voltage Alternating Current (AC) into low-voltage AC.

Transition Curve: A section of track with a gradually diminishing radius between the straight track and the circular portion of the curve.

TT Scale: Model railroad scale in the proportion of 1:120. Early competitor to HO scale and still being manufactured in very limited numbers, but no longer considered a major force in scale model railroading.

Trolley: Name commonly given to a streetcar which receives its power from overhead electric lines. Also, the name of the pole-like device used to collect and transfer electricity from the overhead lines into the streetcar itself.

Trucks: The wheels, axles, and related assemblies on railroad rolling stock.

Turbine Locomotive: One with power supplied by a steam turbine.

Turnout: Generally regarded as the correct nomenclature for a track switch—a device configured with movable rails which allow a train to enter an alternate route.

Turntable: A large, pivoted circular apparatus which rotates in a pit and is used to turn locomotives around, or to position them for movement to a different track.

Uncoupling Track: Special section of track in tinplate railroading used to activate couplers by means of a brief electromagnetic charge sent from the transformer.

Vanderbilt Tender: A steam locomotive tender with a distinctive, rounded, tank-style compartment behind a squared-off front portion.

Variable Voltage Post: In model railroading, the terminal post on a transformer that is connected internally to a rheostat and which provides different amounts of voltage output according to the positioning of a movable control handle.

Volt: A unit of electrical measurement which determines the level of force or pressure behind an electrical current. The greater the voltage, the more powerful the current. Specifically, it is the amount of pressure that will cause one ampere of current to flow through one ohm of resistance.

Watt: The unit of electrical energy expended in powering a device. This term is used to illustrate the top power capacity of an electrical device such as a transformer or light bulb.

Whyte Classification System: The numbering system used to describe various types of steam engines by their wheel arrangement. The system uses three numbers: one for the number of wheels on the pilot; one for the number of drive wheels; and one for the number of wheels on the trailing truck. For example: 2-6-4 indicates two pilot wheels; six drive wheels; and four trailing-truck wheels.

Worm Gear: A gear with slightly slanted teeth which are designed to mesh with a "worm." In model railroading, the worm gear is usually mounted on the driving axle.

Wye (sometimes given as "Y"): A track system comprised of three switches and three long legs of track which enables an entire train to turn around as a unit.

Z Scale: Model railroad scale in the proportion of 1:220. Introduced by the German toy and train manufacturer, Märklin. The smallest commercially-available model railroading scale.

READER NOTES & CORRECTIONS

READER NOTES & CORRECTIONS

READER NOTES & CORRECTIONS